QUEER YOUTH CULTURES

SUNY series, INTERRUPTIONS:
Border Testimony(ies) and Critical Discourse/s

Henry A. Giroux, editor

QUEER YOUTH CULTURES

Edited by
Susan Driver

State University of New York Press

Chapter 1, "What's That Smell? Queer Temporalities and Subcultural Lives," by Judith Halberstam, originally appeared in *International Journal of Cultural Studies* 6, 3 (2003): 313–333, and appears here by permission of Sage Publications Ltd.

Chapter 9, "Brandon Goes to Hollywood: *Boys Don't Cry* and the Transgender Body in Film," by Melissa Rigney, originally appeared in *Film Criticism* 28, 2 (2003–2004).

Published by
State University of New York Press, Albany

For information, contact State University of New York Press, Albany, NY
www.sunypress.edu

Production by Kelli W. LeRoux
Marketing by Anne M. Valentine

Library of Congress Cataloging-in-Publication Data

Queer youth cultures / edited by Susan Driver.
    p. cm. — (Interruptions : border testimony(ies) and critical discourse/s)
  Includes bibliographical references and index.
  ISBN 978-0-7914-7337-5 (hardcover : alk. paper)
  ISBN 978-0-7914-7338-2 (pbk. : alk. paper)
  1. Gay youth. 2. Gay teenagers. 3. Gays in popular culture. 4. Mass media and teenagers. I. Driver, Susan.

HQ76.27.Y68Q44 2008
306.76'60835—dc22
                2007024545
          10 9 8 7 6 5 4 3 2

CONTENTS

INTRODUCING QUEER YOUTH CULTURES

Susan Driver

Over the past decade, queer youth have become innovative participants in do-it-yourself media projects, popular culture narratives, local drag performances, anti-oppression activisms, online communities, and music subcultures. Involving a broad array of media including television, photography, Internet, film and print, as well as utilizing several modes of representation including visual, written/spoken word, and performative embodiments, queer youth cultures defy narrow definitions and open up new ways of understanding and imagining what it means to be a youth today. Queer youth challenge us to rethink the very status of gender, generation, sexuality, and culture, and they push us to become nuanced in the ways we read, watch, and listen to young people telling their own stories and envisioning their futures. As demonstrated throughout this book, contemporary queer youth and their cultural practices are not classifiable as either mainstream or marginal, they are neither inside nor outside dominant cultural institutions; rather, they criss-cross commercial mass media, grassroots subcultural, and activist realms. Configured within multiple spaces of cultural production and consumption, a broad range of queer youth subjects have emerged to expand public spaces, corporeal relations, and textual forms. The emergence of such a rich and diverse proliferation of queer youth activities is practically empowering for young people, providing tools for self-expression and social communication, and also presenting opportunities for adult educators and policymakers to approach youth as smart, imaginative, and desiring cultural producers. Paying attention to queer youth as cultural and political catalysts, the essays throughout this collection attempt to recognize and value the everyday struggles and work undertaken by youth to represent themselves and their communities. At the same time,

1

the goal is not merely to celebrate the living cultures of queer youth but also to question and theorize the very languages and contexts through which they emerge to contest heteronormative expectations and unfold new ways of growing up and becoming queer.

Queer youth cultures call for new ways of researching, theorizing, and writing about youth. Utilizing the term "queer youth" to signify young people who identify in ways that exceed the boundaries of straight gender and/or sexual categories, the point is not to entrench a new label, but to impel contingent and unpredictable ways of naming and interpreting youth. In this sense, "queer youth" encompasses those who name themselves as gay, lesbian, bisexual, transsexual, transgender, intersexual, queer, and/or questioning (GLBTTIQQ) without necessarily being confined to a narrow set of terms. Queer youth are not discursively containable, and they are not reducible to any single dimension of their embodiment, identity, or situation. The complexities of their subjectivities and social lives imbricate class, race, ethnic, geographic, and age relations through which queer youth become meaningful to themselves and others. In this sense, any attempt to understand queer youth must work against totalizing concepts and generalizing depictions, eliciting the partial and layered ways in which queer differences becomes refracted through the dialogical movements of young people.

"Queer youth" is an always, already contradictory and imperfect notion, simultaneously challenging restrictive categorizations while constructing new subjects and sites of regulation and resistance. Reclaiming this phrase as strategically useful in political, research, and policy contexts that work to support and focus attention onto marginalized youth, this approach shifts away from abstract appeals to the problem of queer youth that tend to lose touch with the messy, desiring, and materially located bodies of young people. In this sense, the very process of who, what, and how notions of "queer youth" make sense needs to be scrutinized in highly specific ways, treated as a site of analysis and critical questioning that works against binding young people within new definitional regimes of control. The goal is not to encapsulate queer youth once and for all but rather to initiate provisional and detailed analysis of the ways they precariously make and unmake sense of their lives in relation to the world around them. This approach consciously works against attempts to formulate disciplinary knowledges about who queer youth are and what they want and need, preferring to gather a loose and diverse collection of narratives staying close to the uncertainties and challenges of queer youth cultures. Rather than define queer youth as a fixed demographic or unified concept, the chapters throughout this book work against abstractions by exploring the concrete terms through which the desires, identities, and activities of sexual and gender minority youth are constituted within the mobile life worlds of young people as they interact with popular culture, join subcultures, forge communities, and participate in political movements. Up against pervasive institutional denials, threats of physical violence, pathologizing experts, and educational neglect it is astounding how imaginative, insightful, and playful the cultures of queer youth have become despite the odds. Attending to the specificities of social experience and representation, the goal of this collection is to learn about queer youth by carefully listening to their stories and silences, as well as watching their gestures, images, and protests, while trying to avoid invasive powers of surveillance and knowledge.

CONTROLLING CLASSIFICATIONS
OF SEXUAL MINORITY YOUTH

While there is little doubt that queer youth are fashioning complex representations and collaborative projects, academic disciplines that focus on youth culture rarely seem to notice. Gloria Filax writes that "sexual minority youth are produced through their absence or as a special area of interest, as the abject Other; that is, as a deviant outsider within the realm of youth studies" (59). As queer youth enter the purview of popular and academic texts, the discourses used to describe and interpret this group of minority youth often ends up foreclosing the ambiguous, desiring, relational, and ephemeral dimensions of their experiences. When queer youth are included within educational, psychological, and social science literature, their marginalized social status is often emphasized in ways that construct them as victims. While some accounts do try to affirm the potential for queer youth survival and empowerment (Dobinson 2004; Owens 1998; Gray 1999), queer youth are frequently cast as victims of homophobic violence or heterosexist exclusion in ways that inscribe them within tropes of victimization and risk. The negative effects of subordination become the focal point of research in which queer youth are defined reactively against dominant systems and denied the chance to exceed hegemonic discursive influences. Not only are sexual minority young people repeatedly associated with pathological conditions and oppressive relations, but the subjective

contours of their lives get reiterated in terms of psychic trauma, alienation, and shame. Susan Talburt writes that "queer youth suicide became
a refrain, such that article after article, essay after essay, and report after
report portrayed youth as a risk through statistics on queer youth suicide,
drug and alcohol abuse, sexual transmitted diseases, homelessness, dropping
out, depression, verbal and physical assaults and so on" (28). Commonsense
constructions of queer youth identities fixate on their wounded status,
leaving little space within which to listen for alternative youth voices that
might express complex strengths, pleasures, and curiosities.

Without ignoring the social and psychic vulnerabilities of queer
teens or denying raw facts about suicide and homelessness, it is important to question the ways in which queer youth are perpetually contained within stories of doom and gloom. The continual use of statistics
to frame the experiences of queer youth ends up constructing them as
subjects in crisis needing to be rescued and cared for by others. Characterized in terms of endangerment and victimization, the lives of
queer youth become objectified, precluding nuanced ways of understanding the changing and multilayered contours of their daily lives.
Mary Louise Rasmussen argues that

> Scientific classifications thus perpetuate the infantilization and
> abjection of LGBTI-identified young people, providing a ratio-
> nale for adults to act in their best interests rather than to work
> with them. This process may consequently have the effect of
> reducing young people's agency under cover of providing them
> assistance. The repetition of tropes of adolescence as a stage of
> turmoil and stress also obfuscates peoples' economic, scientific,
> strategic and psychoanalytic investments in the abjection of
> young people who are LGBTI identified. (141–142)

Rasmussen calls attention to the ways queer youth categorizations foreground individualized emotional and social problems that not only
delimit public knowledge and policy but also constitute modes of self-
representations through which youth imagine and speak about their
lives. The very languages that render queer youth intelligible and unified create pathos toward sexual minority youth while at the same time
undermining possibilities for questioning the very terms of normality
that abject queer youth differences in the first place.

Eric Rofes calls attention to the repetitions of what he calls the
"martyr-target-victim" narrative of persecution that influence how queer

youth become socially legitimized. He considers "whether repeated public use of martyr-target-victim images, narratives, visuals and historic incidents works to narrow who and what we think of as GLBT youth." A common outcome of these images are attempts to rectify denigration through uplifting stories of acceptance and inclusion. Queer youth become integrated into normalizing models of respectable sameness in a gesture of liberal unity and equality, often at the expense of coming to terms with heterogeneous desires. Liberal notions of tolerance are upheld as the ultimate goal of youth advocacy, reversing the effects of their "deviant" minority status, while also folding young queers into the values and beliefs of majority culture. Even the most well-meaning attempts to help queer youth often fall prey to patronizing efforts to impose "healthy" normative ideals on youth in order to simplify their complexities for the sake of mainstream recognition. Empowerment becomes a sign of fitting into familiar and nonthreatening models of identity and belonging. Toward this end, progressive media accounts of a transgendered youth leading the student council or a lesbian going to the prom with her girlfriend become evidence of success and signs of positive change and integration. Within such paradigms, queer youth become valued and supported as long as they don't challenge the status quo by looking or acting too queer. What is especially disturbing is an almost complete silence surrounding queer youth sexual pleasures, subcultural counter publics, and political resistance. Normalization works to desexualize and depoliticize youth once again, creating safe, sanitized images that conform with white middle-class standards of visibility and value.

Categorizing queer youth as passive victims or normalized subjects obscures a more fractured and complex dynamic of power and inequality through which youth negotiate their gender and sexuality across racial, national, class, ethnic, age, and ability boundaries of desire and identification. The racialized politics of queer youth are both concealed and constituted in the universalizing and oppositional terms of scientific discourses. Whiteness remains the unmarked center of heteronormative ideologies as well as the unacknowledged frame of evaluation against which youth are defined as different. As such, whether interpretations focus on youth victimization or resilience, the assumed status of acceptance, health, and integration are contained within hegemonic racialized ideologies. This has theoretical implications in terms of what is considered meaningful and valued within the field of GLBTTIQQ studies, and it also influences the empirical scope of what and who count as appropriate research subjects. In this way, languages of risk highlight a narrow range of individual and social conditions, failing to consider how historical experiences such as racial discrimination and marginalization, immigration, poverty, cultural and linguistic alienation, and isolation might destabilize the narrow parameters within which queer youth are studied. Homogenizing notions of youth sexual identities guiding academic texts, popular cultures, and social services become the site of exclusionary ways of seeing and knowing that contribute to the oppression of youth who do not fit in or measure up. The problem, in other words, is not the individual gendered bodies or sexual desires of youth of color but rather the structural norms of white visibility that discount and erase their specificity.

How queer youth are conceptualized powerfully influences which young people are considered worthy of attention and resources and also the ways youth are approached and assisted at institutional and interpersonal levels. Along these lines, the editors of the groundbreaking anthology *Youth and Sexuality* claim that

> The complexity of queer youths' subjectivity, agency, sexuality, and cultural practices is flattened by a dominant framing of them in terms of danger and victimization. If adults tacitly acknowledge queer youths' desire, subjecthood, or creativity they do not frequently actively address these elements of their lives or consider them as something from which adults might learn. Queer youth agency, whether linked to sexual desire or activity, or to projects of crafting the self and relations to others, is relegated to the domain of the unthinkable. (Rasmussen, Talburt, and Rofes, 7)

The means through which queer youth are named and interpreted becomes profoundly important in shaping a social, cultural, and psychic process of recognition and comprehension. What tend to get overlooked in the field of sexual minority youth studies are theories and methods that turn attention away from individual problems and onto hierarchical institutional formations. Such approaches would not necessarily ignore the subjective feelings and voices of queer youth but work to situate them within broader contexts of social, economic, and symbolic power that simultaneously delimit and enable possibilities for personal transformation and collective resistance. Rather than congeal assumptions, such critical approaches trouble adult expectations, unsettle norms, and exceed liberal terms of social inclusion.

This book is propelled forward in an attempt to counter prescriptive and authoritative discourses that claim to know who queer youth are and what they need and want. The challenge becomes generating representational styles and reflexive knowledges that question how the category "queer youth" is being deployed? Asking: Why are queer youth being studied in the first place? For whose benefit and under what precise terms and conditions? Who counts and is visible? What ideas and issues become centered or elided? How do racialized norms shape what constitutes queer identity and practice? What are the languages through which queer youth articulate and shape their identities? Is it possible to decipher these languages ethically and establish a dialogue? Who has a stake in asking these questions? How might these questions be answered without finality or closure? What is lost instituting formal knowledges out of the living and ineffable relations of marginalized youth? Are there aspects of youth experience and culture that remain unrepresentable? At what point should youth be left alone outside the prying gaze of research? Framing research and writing around such questions shifts away from static knowledges onto temporal and culturally shifting subjects that leave room for contestation and doubts, multiple identifications, as well as moments of disidentification. Remaining connected to local communities yet open to globalized networks and movements, the very status of young queer selfhood is shaped in dialogical terms.

QUEERING YOUTH STUDIES

Against this backdrop of popular media, public policies and academic texts that peg queer youth down as being "at risk," invisible, suicidal, unruly, pathological, unstable, deviant, vulnerable, and isolated or else heroic and normatively accomplished, I am interested in reorienting research and writing toward culturally transformative engagements that are temporally and spatially located. Beyond statistics and discouraging narratives, energetic communications are forged by youth who refuse to be simplistically characterized according to their wounds and abjections. Marnina Gonick writes that "they have refused to be rendered invisible or to accept the negative stereotypes thrust upon them. Instead they have worked to produce positive self-identitifications and representations and to create the social conditions that will open up new possibilities for living life as queer people" (137). The point is not to discount feelings of shame and social struggles, but to become attuned to ambivalent and willful responses of young people, recognizing moments where they simultaneously avow what has been hurtful and oppressive and pursue what inspires them to affirm their queerness. Research that forgoes the quest for transparent stories, easy definitions, and coherent identities does not result in confusion but acknowledges that for many marginalized youth, surviving depends on averting either/or logics, embracing the challenges of growing up with contradictions. Queer youth cultures unfurl an assemblage of affects, images, words, relations that challenge the containment of youth demographics and the bounded conceptual mappings of subcultural studies. Research becomes oriented toward ephemeral and nonlinear articulations of youth storytelling, stylizations, protests, and performances. Rather than congeal these mobile physical and verbal actions, the aim is to spur dialogical interpretations with a continual reflexive awareness about the very languages and values used to translate and theorize queer youth identities and differences. Queer youth have the potential of invigorating theory through their culturally expressive assertions of desire in a culture that scorns the queer perversions of young love and lust. It is the subtle ways such affirmations defy punitive logics and moralistic judgments as well as bypassing normalizing expert assessments that queer possibilities arise for thinking about youth.

Cultural studies research into the everyday lives of youth has called attention to a richly textured process of meaning-making through fashion, music, dance, and media participation. Focused on the pragmatic edges of media making and reception, this field of youth study loosens essentializing categorizations by following what and how youth create meanings for themselves. Angela McRobbie focuses on productive communications between youth within alternative subcultural formations:

> To ignore the intense activity of cultural production as well as its strongly aesthetic dimensions (in graphics, fashion, design, retail and music production) is to miss a key part of subcultural life—the creation of a whole new way of life, an alternative to higher education. . . . The point is then that far from being merely the commercial low ebb of the subculture, as far removed from resistance as it is possible to imagine, these activities can be seen as central to it. They are also expressions of change and social transformation. (72)

McRobbie decenters prescriptive and isolating narratives as she traces the vibrant cultural work of young people across overlapping contexts.

Her focus is on the ways youth craft intricate subcultural worlds in which they work, play, learn, and socialize beyond official institutional regimes, analyzing opportunities for innovative and informal pedagogies and circuits of communication. In a similar vein, Paul Willis details the symbolic creativity of young people as they make use of media technologies, experiment with styles, combine textual samples and adorn themselves in ways that defy the strictly commercial intentions of media industries. The ingenuity of youth cultural practices and perspectives have become a key source of analysis in several recent texts focused on how youth make media that are receptive to the ways youth devise alternative cultures in collaborative ways. Mary Celeste Kearney follows the ingenuity of contemporary girl media makers, writing that "many girl media producers rely on the practices of appropriation and detournement to reconfigure commercial cultural artifacts in to personalized creations that speak more directly to their concerns, needs, fantasies and pleasures" (13). Along these lines, what many cultural analysts share is attentiveness to the responsive and living languages through which shared meanings are crafted, negotiated through consumer culture ideologies, yet irreducible to static commodifications. Thinking in-between self and others, subjectivities and signs, institutions and experiences, global media and local participation, empirically grounded and mediated youth research enables nuanced interpretive practices.

Pushing empirical research even further to elaborate emotional contours and embodied signifying relations between youth, scholars have begun to analyze the speech acts and corporeal displays of youth through performative methodologies. Interrogating how youth practically use media languages to constitute and resist cultural identifications, performative analysis traces signs redeployed in the casual conversations of youth. Attention focuses on what youth do and say rather than on defining who youth are, following the ways media fictions are circulated by youth to address shared conditions of experience. Greg Dimitriadis writes that such performative elaborations of youth culture become vital in attending to collisions between the experiential body and media saturated environments, framing research around complex discursive systems as well as nuanced responses in the lives of young people. At the same time it is important to acknowledge that a pervasive lack of attention to the cultural lifeworlds of queer youth have impoverished even the most innovative areas of youth studies. At the level of empirical content as well as methodological design and theoretical analysis, a broad field of youth cultural studies remain heteronormatively configured. While it is productive to draw upon existing textual and ethnographic youth research, theorizing queer experiences also calls for closer attention to complex sexually desiring selves often left out of empirical research on youth.

Framing youth in terms of queer performative cultural and political engagements, this book refocuses attention onto active production and deployment of discourses by youth themselves. Queer theories help to direct attention onto socioculturally mediated citational practices, foregrounding sexuality within youth culture research as a process of open-ended self-representation. The very status of normative sex, sexual, and gender categories become the site of critical inquiry, shifting inter- rogation away from an individualizing preoccupation with the aberrations of young individuals who fall outside dominant classifications. Using queer theories to think through youth cultures enables interpretive work attuned to fractured, unexpected and shifting contours of selves, commu- nities, subcultures, and politics by, for, and about young subjects.

Many theorists have deployed the notion "queer" to signify performative dynamics of doing rather than determinate identities (Butler 1990; Fuss 1991; Johnson 2005; Munoz 1991; Sedgwick 1993). Within this body of writing, emphasis is placed on how identifications are practiced and struggled over within specific times and places. Rather than delimit exactly who is queer or what constitutes their queerness, efforts turn to analyzing the ways heternormative knowledges work to naturalize and dichotomize differences. Gender and sexual subjects are not fixed entities to be pinned down and catalogued but rather they are investigated through constellations of words, actions, and interpreta- tions. Identifications and desires emerge as constitutive activities, which according to Judith Butler have no foundational truth apart from a process of articulation, claiming that "if the 'reality' of gender is con- stituted by the performance itself, then there is no recourse to an essential and unrealized 'sex' or 'gender' which gender performances ostensibly express" (1990, 278). Performative frameworks highlight dynamic and complex articulations, Butler claims that "one is not sim- ply a body, but, in some very key sense, one does one's body and, indeed, one does one's body differently from one's contemporaries and from one's embodied predecessors and successors as well" (272).

In a similar vein, Diana Fuss writes that "sexual identity may be less a function of knowledge than performance, or, in Foucauldian terms, less a matter of final discovery than perpetual invention" (7). Attending to fluid and relational languages, bodies, and pleasures, pos- sibilities for invention are nevertheless configured through the specific powers and constraints of material and symbolic systems. Hegemonic social norms and boundaries are not transcended but are reworked in the flux of daily enactments of speech and embodied practices. Judith Butler insists that performativity involves a "reiteration of a norm or set of norms" (1993, 12–13), a continual process of reworking, disturbing, and transforming the limits of normalizing discourses through psychic and collective engagements. Habitual repetitions both reproduce and alter normative identities and expectations, and it is precisely in the slippages and gaps where queer genders and sexualities emerge. A simultaneity of controlling discourses and destabilizing activities calls attention to the precarious dimensions of queer performativity, in between what we expect and know about youth and what expands our frameworks of intelligibility. Performative ways of thinking about identity decenter liberal norms of rational individualized subjecthood, turning attention onto relations that both invoke and question multiple conjunctions of desire and identification, suggesting so much more than can ever be known in advance or guaranteed in the present.

Such pliable notions of performativity as an embodied signifying activity through which subjects come to transform themselves allow for new ways of understanding youth enculturation. At the same time metatheoretical texts rarely speak to the social and semiotically volatile worlds of youth. When cultural examples are studied by queer theorists, they have tended to focus on the sophisticated maneuverings of adult cultural production and reception, ignoring the unique predicaments of young people. Generational hierarchies are unwittingly constructed, which tend to separate adult and youth cultures and implicitly privilege the former, leaving youth stranded as neither fully belonging within mainstream heterosexist cultural research nor integrated within queer cultural niches. While poststructuralist queer theories inform many facets of this book, tensions arise between abstract conceptualization and the changing lifeworlds of youth. The point is to learn to recognize how youth name and unname who they are or want to become, harnessing queer theories as analytical tools grounded in the practical and situated meanings that are relevant and important to youth.

In many ways, youth as a time of transition and flux, in between childhood and adulthood, renders the status of "queer" highly resonant to young people pressured by normative developmental ideals of self and reproductive narratives of maturation. "Queer" has become part of the vernacular modes of expression and communication of young people today, deployed as a noun, verb, and adjective; youth articulate themselves in polyvalent ways. This demonstrates what Donald Hall calls "the utility of reconciling adjectives with nouns and then energizing them into verbs—of transforming descriptors into identities into actions" (18). Taken up as a noun, youth affirm their gender and sexual differences, on the other hand they use "queer" as an adjective to suggest a rich and layered sense of self, evoking a transitional process, refusing to define themselves once and for all. "Queer" also becomes a way of referring to collective movements that include yet go beyond their individual experiences. As a self-descriptor, "queer" is often used by youth to affirm a specific sense of self and community affiliations rather than to foster indeterminacy or deconstructive detachment. This points to the organic ways youth signify and theorize their genders and sexualities, using "queer" as a heuristic device that helps them navigate adult reasoning and regulations. Sometimes "queer" is deployed as a purposefully vague term, opaque and broad enough for youth to escape capture within minority youth classifications. Youth also devise queer reading strategies, engaging creatively with popular culture texts through imaginative perspectives. At other times "queer" is used to inflect ethnic, racial, and national identifications, consciously marking out multiple locations and challenging any claims to universality. Embracing queer notions as a living language responsive of their ongoing insubordination to heteronormative codes, youth claim the term "queer" to accommodate their shame, fears, doubts, rage, and curiosities. All the while, some youth prefer other terms that address them more directly as transgender, bisexual, gay, or lesbian. Paying attention to how a generation of young people has appropriated or refused "queer" to name their complexities, it becomes important to grapple with its impossibly loose and decentered tendencies. Stretching the parameters of adult-centered queer scholarship, this book reconfigures queer theories of cultural and psychic enactment within the diverse school, family, and peer networks of youth. Paying close attention to the provisional representational practices of youth, recognizing that the notion of "queer" is contested as youth come-of-age in the flux of material histories and social contexts.

Grounding queer speculations in diverse and culturally expansive worlds of youth experiences, I borrow from E. Patrick Johnson's elaborations of "quare" studies as part of an emerging field of black queer theory. Overcoming the abstract and white privileged textual abstractions of performative theories by returning theory to the fleshed out mediations of memories, powers, and corporeal knowledges, Johnson explores new modes of research and representation that criss-cross experiential narratives, material structures, and poststructural analysis. Johnson writes that "quare"

> not only speaks across identities, it articulates identities as well. "Quare" offers a way to critique stable notions of identity and, at the same time, to locate racialized and class knowledges. . . . I want to maintain the inclusivity and playful spirit of "queer" that animates much of queer theory, but I also want to jettison its homogenizing tendencies. (127)

Reading queer subjects through the twists and turns of vernacular languages and embedded social relations—attending to how people speak, act, look, and feel in particular and grounded situations—Johnson bridges ethnography and theory to touch base with critical and creative perspectives of queer people of color. Inscribing his subjectivity into theoretical inquiry transforms the status of authority to focus on an expert perspective that implicates personally recollected struggles and pleasures as inextricable from how he frames the lives of other queers. Moving away from detached universalization, "quare" studies provides a way to grapple with the racialized, class, and national contours of youth, situating sexuality and gender variance within rich and interwoven narratives that defy scientific reification. Theory becomes integrally connected to the experiential relations of queer subjects as they act out their desires within and between communities. Without assuming transparent access to individual experiences, Johnson interweaves them within a reflexive analysis of language and power, as part of a critical process of reading and writing queer lives from multiple perspectives.

This move to enjoin reflexive ethnography and theory becomes crucial in directing queer youth research in ways attuned to the innumerable personalized and collectively shaped expressions of self, refusing to stop the flow of relations and stories for the sake of scientific clarity and control. But while queer pluralities are embraced, it is vital to analyze the hierarchical formations of differences between those subjects who become more visible and recognized as sexual minority youth and those who are erased and marginalized within discursive practices. Questioning the terms of intelligibility and inclusivity of research calls for reflection on the boundaries limiting who, where, what, and how subjects stake out claims to queer youth identifications. Queer youth research positions itself precariously between a critical understanding of the institutional legacies and continuing social circumstances that work to "other" gender and sexual variant young people, and an appreciation of the inventiveness of young people who devise alternative styles and spaces of cultural participation and meaning. This collection tries to examine heterogeneous areas and examples of queer youth culture so as to give readers insight into their singularities and interconnections. While the book endeavors to be inclusive of the rich diversity of queer youth texts and practices, it is important to recognize the impossibility of including all aspects of queer youth culture within a single book. Because of a lack of published accounts, there is pressure to try to represent the images, voices, and experiences of all those youth yet to be studied and validated. This is both the exciting part of gathering essays and a sign of its limitations. Instead of trying to encompass the breadth and depth of queer youth cultures, the book makes an effort to include essays that are innovative in their approaches, providing readers with an open-ended picture of dynamic cultural relations. At stake here is not an attempt to list, rank, and compare youth cultures but rather to provide textual openings into an emergent cultural field in which youth negotiate sexual, racial, class, and gender identities in specific and contextual ways. The very notion of "queer youth" is up for grabs as authors trouble binary assumptions and challenge readers to question and explore the complex desires and identifications of youth in culture today.

This book is divided into three parts to help organize the chapters and guide readers through a new body of empirically specific research and reflexive writing about queer youth. The first part, "Performative Queer Youth Cultures, Embodiments, and Communities," focuses on those grassroots representations and subcultures through which youth fashion independent media and cultural meaning and social belonging. Performativity underscores an expansive range of utterances through which youth signify their desires and identifications by reiterating and transforming discursive conventions. The creative edges of queer drag, music, zines, and video performance are drawn out following the unique ways youth signify themselves in playful and politically insightful ways. Refusing to be passively subjected to mainstream discourses, queer youth engage as cultural producers, defining themselves through the process of creative dialogues. Calling attention to the predicaments of daily discrimination, harassment, and devaluation, these cultural enactments go much further than recounting youth suffering. Through the powerful statements of their songs, the humor of their visual cultures, and the intelligence of their writing, queer youth defy simplistic categories that frame them as isolated individuals at risk of victimization. Activating counter-publics, they share and circulate ideas about themselves in collectively meaningful and pleasurable ways. What stands out in these essays are reciprocal relations between researchers and youth cultures, positioning queer adult writers and youth participants as mutually aligned in an interpretive process attuned to the plural voices and embodied lives of queer youth. Authors refuse detached scientific methods, working from their passionate interests as queer scholars to explore artistic and experiential modes of representation by, for, and about queer youth, fostering intergenerational understandings.

The second part, "Desiring Youth in Un/Popular Cultures," focuses on an expansion of mass media within which sexual minority youth are integrated at the level of explicit content and subtextual inscriptions. Paying close attention to the details of media texts, the chapters in this section analyze the images and narratives through which young same-sex desires and gender variations are conveyed within popular cultures. While the problem of recurrent ideological depictions of gay, lesbian, and transgender youth are highlighted by all the authors in this part, semiotic moments that destabilize heteronormative patterns are also unfolded within these essays, attending to subtle visual signs and storylines through which queer differences emerge. The cultural texts examined throughout this section are produced by adults within commercial media industries, yet it is not merely the preferred meanings of producers that are a site of analysis, but also the divergent ways queer youth imaginatively read and respond to them. Attending to the reception practices of queer youth opens up a dynamic field of meaning-making beyond prescribed dimensions of film, TV, and print media. Queer youth animate popular cultures in ways unanticipated within corporate agendas or academic critiques, spurring interpretive practices out of urgent and volatile desires to see, hear, and feel connected to alternative popular fictions. The very status of what is visible or invisible, which examples are regarded as "positive" or "negative," remains unresolved and open for discussion, staying close to the ways queer youth are framed inside and outside media representations. Popular cultures are interpreted as ambivalent sites for queer youth provoking intense fascination and excitement as well as disturbing awareness of symbolic exclusion and violence. The essays tread carefully to respect this ambivalence without offering the readers easy or comforting answers.

The final part, "Tranforming Political Activism," concentrates attention onto the rich field of queer youth political participation. Examining the political dimensions of cultural representations as well as more direct spheres of activism against corporate and state institutions, authors complicate the terms through which youth resist dominant regimes of power. As Cheryl Dobinson argues

> GLB youth challenge social relations of domination in four key ways—first, in the transformation and re-creation of the activities of dominant culture into newly meaningful ones . . . second, through personalized efforts to educate others, represent GLB lives, or defend queer rights; third in the subversive continuation of activities which have been prohibited by authorities . . . and fourth, through involvement in new cultural practices. (72)

While Dobinson leaves out of consideration the specific status and relations of transgender youth, her list opens up a rich field of politically charged modes of resistance that include more conventional forms of protest along with informal and "unorganized" acts of rebellion. The chapters in this part carry these lines of thinking further, expanding terrains of political consciousness and planning to include intersecting relations between nationality, citizenship, race, ethnicity, class, sexuality, gender, ability, and age. In this sense queer youth politics become articulated criss-crossing multiple identities and social conditions of experience in the process of contesting systemic forces of control and regulation. Queer youth challenge simplistic, liberal political formulas, insisting upon the inseparability of bodily, symbolic, socioeconomic, educational, and governmental dimensions of domination. Adopting responses to diverse forms of power within their lives, queer youth utilize a range of strategic methods of resistance that span local acts including community-based performance and video art, street demonstrations, and grassroots organizing around specific issues to broader anticorporate coalition-building in a spirit of globalizing solidarity. The unique interventions of queer youth in the field of politics work to expand conceptions of young queer people in terms of active resistant subjects, while also transforming the very substance and form of youth politics to foreground gender and sexuality in the dynamic conjunction of multiple relations of power and privilege.

Although I have grouped chapters into distinct parts to help to organize the ideas and subjects of individual authors, there are many interconnections between parts and topics. It is my hope that readers make use of this text as a dynamic and flexible medium that encourages questioning and dynamic ways of thinking within and across specific chapters. This book initiates a dialogue of many voices through which the very richness and variability of queer youth cultures become a starting point for a process of understanding across subjective, social, and political differences.

WORKS CITED

Butler, Judith. *Bodies That Matter: On the Discursive Limits of "Sex."* New York: Routledge, 1993.

————. "Performative Acts and Gender Constitution: An Essay in Phenomenology and Feminist Theory." In *Performing Feminisms: Feminist Critical Theory and Theatre*, ed. Sue-Ellen Case. Baltimore: Johns Hopkins University Press, 1990.

Dimitriadis, Greg. *Performing Identity/Performing Culture: Hip Hop as Text, Pedagogy and Lived Practice.* New York: Peter Lang, 2001.

Dobinson, Cheryl. "Everyday Acts of Survival and Unorganized Resistance." In *I Could Not Speak My Heart: Education and Social Justice for Gay and Lesbian Youth,* ed. James McNinch and Mary Cronin. Canadian Plains Research Center, University of Regina, 2004.

Filax, Gloria. *Queer Youth: In the Province of the "Severely Normal."* Vancouver: UBC Press, 2006.

Fuss, Diana. "Inside/out." In *Inside Out: Lesbian Theories Gay Theories*, ed. Diana Fuss. New York: Routledge, 1991.

Gonick, Marnina. *Between Femininities: Ambivalence, Identity, and the Education of Girls.* New York: State University of New York Press, 2003.

Gray, Mary. *In Your Face: Stories from the Lives of Queer Youth.* Haworth Press, 1999.

Halberstam, Judith. *In a Queer Time and Place.* New York: New York University Press, 2005.

Hall, Donald E. *Queer Theories.* New York: Palgrave, 2003.

Johnson, E. Patrick. " 'Quare' Studies, or (Almost) Everything I Know about Queer Studies I Learned from My Grandmother." In *Black Queer Studies: A Critical Anthology*, ed. E. Patrick Johnson and Mae G. Henderson. Duke University Press, 2005.

Kearney, Mary Celeste. *Girls Make Media.* New York: Routledge, 2006.

McRobbie Angela. "Shut Up and Dance: Youth Culture and Changing Modes of Femininity." In *Feminism and Cultural Studies*, ed. Morag Shiach. Oxford University Press, 1999.

Muñoz, José Esteban. *Disidentifications: Queers of Color and the Performance of Politics.* Minneapolis: University of Minnesota Press, 1999.

Owens, Robert E. *Queer Kids: The Challenges and Promise for Lesbian, Gay, and Bisexual Youth.* Haworth Press, 1998.

Rasmussen, Mary Louise. *Becoming Subjects: Sexualities and Schooling.* Taylor and Francis, 2006.

Rasmussen, Mary Louise, Susan Talburt, and Eric Rofes, Eds. "Introduction." In *Youth and Sexualities.* New York: Palgrave 2004.

Rofes, Eric. *A Radical Rethinking of Sexuality and Schooling: Status Quo or Status Queer.* Lanham, MD: Rowman & Littlefield, 2005.

Sedgwick, Eve. *Tendencies.* Durham, NC: Duke University Press, 1993.

Talburt, Susan. "Intelligibility and Narrating Queer Youth." In *Youth and Sexualities,* ed. Rasmussen et al. New York: Palgrave, 2004.

PART ONE

PERFORMATIVE QUEER YOUTH CULTURES, EMBODIMENTS, AND COMMUNITIES

This part launches *Queer Youth Cultures* into a vibrant field of queer youth grassroots expressions. From the start it is important to call attention to the ways young people make meanings and perform desires across a range of contexts and media. Attempts are made within each chapter to frame queer youth as subjects of desire whose meanings are located in the flux of spoken and written words, mediated signs, and corporeal interactions. Rather than try to capture who queer youth are in a single dramatic instance of queer transgression or compile statistics in a quest for scientific generalization, authors cast their research as a tentative process of interpreting case studies situated within broader common cultures. Queer youth become intelligible through the details of what they say, how they do things, and the ways they respond to the world around them. The point is not to ask "who and what are queer youth?" but rather to consider "how do young people forge personal and collective representations that address their immediate conditions and elaborate enriching visions?" Answering such questions compels researchers to pursue prolific performances of youth generating queer possibilities.

There are fields of youth studies that value the transient ways young people create and transform themselves. Some of the most interesting texts dealing with youth subcultures work in close proximity with youths as they use their bodies and imaginations to devise collaborative actions, pleasures, and cultural values. The social semiotic analysis of punk cultures developed by Dick Hebdige delves into the layered corporeal and verbal inscriptions of youth arising in the gaps and margins of dominant discourses. Theorized as inventive cultural provocateurs with the capacity to destabilize and resignify cultural signs, artifacts, and relations, youth cultures become dynamic realms for understanding resistance and social change. Within cultural studies, youth deploy "resistance through rituals" (Hall and Jefferson 1993), practice strategies such as "bricollage" (Hebdige 1979) and "symbolic creativity" (Willis 1990), highlighting the active process through which youth craft identifications within their situated daily environments by drawing upon and struggling against mainstream commercial cultural elements while recombining and reanimating their significance. Although much early work on subcultures ignored issues of gender and sexual specificity, successive feminist explorations (Jiwani et al. 2006; Kearney 2006; McRobbie 2000; Leblanc 1999; Pough 2004) have helped to analyze the ways gendered ideologies and embodiments work to regulate binary identities centered on hegemonic masculine subjects. At the same time feminist attention to the ways girls forge distinct subcultures, challenging oppressive ideals of femininity and asserting sexual diversity and empowerment, has opened up nuanced ways of attending to nonnormative gender performances across multiple realms of youth culture.

Work on subcultures is both useful and limiting when considering the scattered, and sometimes underground, lifeworlds of queer youth. Assumptions about groups of youth as bounded, unified, and visible entities become questionable when considering intersectional and permeable identifications shaping sexual and gender variant youth affiliations. Tracing the fluidity and fragmentation of youth culture, recent ethnographic research (Bennett and Kahn-Harris 2004; Redhead 1997) follows loose configurations of youth cultures that open up spaces for ambiguous and layered identity formations. What gets highlighted are the localized and practical ways youth make meanings, create texts, and participate in cultural scenes. Researchers follow the productive and nonlinear directions of youth as they make and use media, inhabiting local spaces, as part of a do-it-yourself ethos of creative engagement. Such shifts in the interpretive methodologies and theories of youth studies enable ways of approaching queer youth in the performative flux of what they do as constitutive of who they are or want to become. The essays that follow provide affirmative frameworks through which to learn about the transient cultural praxis of queer youth.

Each chapter in this part focuses on specific contexts that include online chat rooms, high schools, drag troops, poetry events, community video projects, zine networks, and music scenes. Authors emphasize the ways youth fluidly represent themselves, figuring out possibilities for self-stylization and interaction that disrupt restrictive dichotomies. Focused simultaneously on the symbolic contours of queer youth dialogues and their material predicaments, authors detail not only who and how youth forge queer identifications but also where such enactments take place, what conditions enable them, and how they foster recognition and create independent counter-publics against the sway of dominant culture. There is an emphasis across these essays on the pragmatic urgency of queer youth cultural developments that challenge heteronomative categorizations while remaining uneasily implicated within regulative regimes of power and control. Even the most hopeful signs of queer youth resistance are critically understood within broader institutional structures that continue to erase, trivialize, and oppress young people. At the same time, what remains central to all the essays is a refusal to reify youth as silent, passive victims, profiling them as thoughtful, willful, and desiring interlocutors.

Judith Halberstam's chapter, "What's That Smell? Queer Temporalities and Subcultural Lives" opens this part, providing one of the few attempts to explicitly bridge youth cultures and queer theory. The essay realigns genealogical, ethnographic, and archival methods of collaboration between grassroots producers and academic "experts." Writing from within detailed and located realms of subcultural participation, Halberstam is able to trace ephemeral and inventive subcultural practices. Halberstam goes a long way toward thinking in between queer adult and youth relations, promoting methodologies that encourage researchers to reflexively share knowledge with youth rather than treat them as objects of adult research. This is a key ethical principle informing the writing throughout this book, as researchers explore the permeable boundaries between their own status as queer subjects within the inquiry process. Writing about dyke music scenes, drag king performances, and spoken word artists from the standpoint of a subcultural participant, Halberstam theorizes from an avid sense of enjoyment and involvement, complicating the very notion of queer youth culture as a strictly age-based sphere, opening up expansive queer temporal and spatial realms of belonging.

Following in this vein, Angela Wilson explores lesbian punk rock music in her chapter, " 'The Galaxy Is Gay': Examining the Networks of Lesbian Punk Rock Subculture." The content of lyrics and performances by girl bands are examined along with local and online communities, exploring some of the ways punk inspires queer girls who seek to challenge hegemonic gender relations within a broader histori-cal trajectory of lesbian feminism. Sketching out differences, tensions, and connections between contemporary punk bands and music rooted in folk traditions from the 1970s, Wilson opens up passages across generations and music genres. Noting common elements, she also fo-cuses on moments of disagreement and rupture between contemporary queer youth and feminist legacies. Discussing the problem of transgender exclusion at the Michigan Women's Music festival, Wilson analyzes a hot spot of conflict between trans-youth and their allies and lesbian feminist institutions. These conflicts mark out important issues driving a young generation involved in queer music scenes to redefine gender and sexual boundaries. Music subcultures provide a rich terrain through which younger musicians and fans engage in fluid identity formations that combine entertainment, community, and political experiences.

Whereas Halberstam and Wilson sketch out exciting possibilities of engagment within urban music subcultures, many youth struggle to forge personalized identifications in the face of a lack of access to, or feelings of belonging within, queer subcultures. For youth who live at a distance from organized queer cultural and political communities, finding alternative venues and media are vital tools for facilitating per-sonal confidence and collective understandings. For youth experiencing racial oppression, poverty, and/or rural isolation, creative programs fa-cilitating self-representation provide invaluable tools of empowerment.

In her chapter, "Redefining Realities through Self-Representational Performance," Jama Shelton discusses the significance of a nonprofit community video/performance project called *Turned Up Volume*, which she claims inspires marginalized queer youth to articulate and share their stories as part of a layered creative process combining fictions, autobiography, and social dialogues. Shelton argues that providing youth with pliable means of self-representation and artistic expression is especially important for queer teens who lack public visibility and power, and who feel confined by the normalizing languages projected by mass media. Through their experimental visual and poetic repre-sentational practices, queer youth challenge adults to rethink assump-tions and expectations. Shelton writes from the perspective of having been a project organizer working with youth over the course of several years. Basing her analysis on intimate knowledge learned within *Turned Up Volume*, she argues that sustained grassroots education fol-lowing artistic and performative approaches becomes key to outreach-ing to queer youth.

In contrast to Shelton's exploration of an adult-run cultural program, Jackie Regales shows how idiosycratic informal practices of zine-making are utilized by youth. Turning attention onto the independent media networks of transgender youth, Jackie Regales' chapter, "My Identity is Fluid as Fuck," investigates the ways in which personal zines provide productive cultural spaces to explore experiences and share intimate knowledges with the flexibility of anonymous modes of authorship, adaptable lines of circulation, and playful forms of communication. Perzines offer trans youth the potential to use language to affirm themselves, naming and imagining aspects of their lives that defy the conventions of binary sex/gender. Regales explores the importance of creative writing in the lives of trans youth as a basis for self-reflection and as a means for spurring mediated yet affectionate community connections and support.

In relation to the more subversive edges of trangender zine production, "Taking a Seat on the Sofa," focuses how teens construct and regulate "lesbian" identities within online dating communities. This chapter looks at the ways queer girls utilize internet communications as a process of "public pedagogy" in which girls chat about themselves through and against dominant discourses of identity. Within a teen forum on a lesbian dating website, The Pink Sofa, the contradictions between the open-ended styles of digital self-representation and disciplinary tendencies are performed within an interactive message board format. The Pink Sofa teen forum raises important questions about the ways online communities generate lines of conversation in several directions while also containing the scope of queer youth representations. The authors analyze the limits of what can be said, how topics get articulated, and what remains silent in the casual conversational flow of online communications between queer teen girls.

David McInnes and Cristyn Davies's chapter, "Articulating Sissy Boy Queerness Within and Against Discourses of Tolerance and Pride," examines the normalizing power of official educational institutional ideologies in relation to the destabilizing subjectivities of sissy boys. This essay addresses the vilification and erasure of the embodied differences of feminine boys within Australian educational contexts while also theorizing dimensions of psychic shame and melancholy attendant with institutional normalization. Using performative theory and psychoanalysis, this chapter addresses the limitations of discourses of homophobia and "safe space" rhetoric in relation to boys' performances of gender nonconformity. Analyzing the complex ways young queer masculinities are emotionally constituted yet publicly disavowed, McInnes and Davies touch on those vulnerable aspects of psychosexual experience bracketed out of educational discourses. Here performativity configures a painful space between queer desires and institutional denials, while also unfolding singular moments of sissy boy experience represented through testimonials that collide uneasily with official educational knowledges.

This part ends with a photo-essay by Cass Bird, gathering together a stunning array of artistic visual portraits of queer individuals. These photographic representations work to supplement the textual orientation of this book, constructing gripping visual languages through which the styles and bodies of queer subjects evoke passionate and seductively charged feelings. The very status of "youth" remains ambiguous as young adults enact scenes and gestures that resonate with the energetic playfulness and erotic allure of youth. While some photographs center on the consciously staged and distinguished beauty and power of transgender subjects, others evoke everyday spontaneous moments of friendship and the casual informal bonds of communities. Viewing these images gives the impression of physical proximity, a closeness to young queer embodiments that is so rarely accessed within public spaces. These images defy the idealized seductions and simplistic stereotypes that pervade mainstream media, raising difficult questions about the status of queer youth within visual cultures. Offering glimpses of what has systematically been rendered invisible, diverse portrayals of young female masculinity emerge within these photos in vivid and direct ways. Yet what appears is not a reversal of familiar images but a transversal of signs and ways of seeing through which new ideas, hopes, dreams, and sentiments are incited. Cass Bird's photos provide opportunities for readers to think about how gender variant and sexually desiring bodies of youth are so often missing or sanitized within our visual landscapes. The defiant strength and intimacy captured within these portraits raises critical questions about how queer youth look and are looked at by others. Readers are left with provocative traces of desire and fascination that provide a basis for further thinking and feeling without textual resolution or finality.

WORKS CITED

Bennett, Andy, and Keith Kahn-Harris. *After Subculture: Critical Studies in Contemporary Youth Culture*. New York: Palgrave, 2004.
Hall, Stuart, and Tony Jefferson. *Resistance through Rituals*. New York: Routledge, 1993.

Hebdige, Dick. *Subculture: The Meaning of Style*. London: Methuen, 1979.

Jiwani, Yasmin, Candis Steenbergen, and Claudia Mitchell. *Girlhood: Redefining the Limits*. Toronto: Black Rose Books, 2006.

Kearney, Mary Celeste. *Girls Make Media*. New York: Routledge, 2006.

Leblanc, Lauraine. *Pretty in Punk: Girls' Gender Resistance in a Boys' Subculture*. New Brunswick: Rutgers University Press, 1999.

McRobbie, Angela. *Feminism and Youth Culture*, 2nd ed. New York: Routledge, 2000.

Pough, Gwendolyn, D. *Check It While I Wreck It: Black Womanhood, Hip-Hop Culture, and the Public Sphere*. Boston: Northeastern University Press, 2004.

Redhead, Steve, Ed. *Clubcultures Reader: Readings in Popular Cultural Studies*. Blackwell, 1997.

Willis, Paul. *Common Culture*. San Francisco: Westview Press, 1990.

CHAPTER 1

WHAT'S THAT SMELL?

QUEER TEMPORALITIES AND SUBCULTURAL LIVES

Judith Halberstam

This chapter is drawn from a book-length study of the explosion of queer urban subcultures in the last decade. My larger purpose is to examine how many queer communities experience and spend time in ways that are very different from their heterosexual counterparts. Queer uses of time and space develop in opposition to the institutions of family, heterosexuality, and reproduction, and queer subcultures develop as alternatives to kinship-based notions of community. In my work on subcultures I explore the stretched out adolescences of queer culture makers and I posit an "epistemology of youth" that disrupts conventional accounts of subculture, youth culture, adulthood, race, class, and maturity.[1] Queer subcultures produce alternative temporalities by allowing their participants to believe that their futures can be imagined according to logics that lie outside of the conventional forward-moving narratives of birth, marriage, reproduction, and death. It is usual in the study of gender and sexuality to use the term "queer" to refer simply to "sexual minorities." And while "queer" certainly takes on this meaning in my study, it can also be defined here as an outcome of temporality, life scheduling, and eccentric economic practices. When we detach queerness from sexual identity in this way, we come closer to understanding Michel Foucault's comment in an interview that "homosexuality

27

threatens people as a way of life" rather than as a way of having sex (310).

Much of the contemporary theory seeking to disconnect queerness from an essential definition of homosexuality has focused upon queer space and queer sexual practices, but such theories depend, implicitly, upon a rarely articulated notion of queer time.[2] They also concentrate almost exclusively upon the activities of white gay men. This study will include material on and by white gay men, but it will focus on lesbian and transgender subcultures (punk, drag, performance, spoken word) and will pay special attention to racialized constructions of youth, leisure, waste, and maturity. The focus on queer subcultures, and dyke subcultures in particular, allow us to make some potentially new claims about agency, style, liminality, community, and history. A broad-based study of queer subcultures, as I have suggested, can provide material evidence for lives lived "otherwise," outside of the conventional life narratives of family and reproduction, but it can also point to those modes of resistance that survive the encounter between marginal subjects and dominant culture.

An essay by Judith Butler in a volume dedicated to the work of Stuart Hall tackles the question of what kinds of agency can be read into forms of activity that tend to be associated with style. She asks: "[. . .] how do we read the agency of the subject when its demand for cultural and psychic and political survival makes itself known as style?" (36). And, building on the work by Hall and others in the classic volume on subcultures, *Resistance Through Rituals*, Butler puts the concept of "ritual" into motion as a practice that can either reinforce *or* disrupt cultural norms. Liminal subjects, she implies, those who are excluded from "the norms that govern the recognizability of the human," are sacrificed to maintain coherence within the category of the human, and for them, style is both the sign of their exclusion and the mode by which they survive nonetheless. The power of Judith Butler's work, here and elsewhere, lies in her ability to show how much has been excluded, rejected, abjected in the formation of human community and what toll those exclusions take upon particular subjects.

Punk has always been the stylized and ritualized language of the rejected; as Poly Styrene of X-ray Spex sings: "I am a reject and I don't care!" Queer punk has surfaced in recent years as a potent critique of hetero- and homo-normativity, and dyke punk in particular, by bands like Tribe 8 and The Haggard, inspires a reconsideration of the topic of subcultures in relation to queer cultural production and in opposition to notions of gay community. Subcultures provide a vital critique of the seemingly organic nature of "community" and they make visible the forms of unbelonging and disconnection that are necessary to the creation of community. At a time when "gay and lesbian community" is used as a rallying cry for fairly conservative social projects aimed at assimilating gays and lesbians into the mainstream of the life of the nation and family, queer subcultures preserve the critique of heteronormativity that was always implicit in queer life. "Community," generally speaking, is the term used to describe seemingly natural forms of congregation. As Sarah Thornton comments in her introduction to *The Subcultures Reader*: "Community tends to suggest a more permanent population, often aligned to a neighborhood, of which family is the key constituent part. Kinship would seem to be one of the main building blocks of community" (2). Subcultures, however, suggest transient, extrafamilial, and oppositional modes of affiliation. The idea of community, writes Jean-Luc Nancy, emerges out of the Christian ritual of communion and expresses a sense of something that we once had that has now been lost, a connection that was once was organic and life giving that now is moribund and redundant. Nancy calls this the "lost community" and expresses suspicion about this "belated invention." Nancy writes: "What this community has 'lost'—the immanence and the intimacy of a communion—is lost only in the sense that such a 'loss' is constitutive of 'community' itself" (12). The reminder that quests for community are always nostalgic attempts to return to some fantasized moment of union and unity reveals the conservative stakes in community for all kinds of political projects and makes the reconsideration of subcultures all the more urgent.

THE BALLAD OF A LADYMAN

Sleater-Kinney's anthem, "Ballad of a Ladyman," describes the allure of subcultural life for the ladyman, the freak who wants to "rock with the tough girls." They sing: "I could be demure like / girls who are soft for / boys who are fearful of / getting an earful / But I gotta rock!" The band layers Corin Tucker's shrill but tuneful vocals over the discordant and forceful guitar playing of Carrie Brownstein and the hard rhythm of Weiss's percussion. This is a beat that takes no prisoners and makes no concessions to the "boys who are fearful of getting an earful [. . .]." And while Sleater-Kinney are most often folded into histories of the "riot grrrl" phenomenon and girl punk, they must also be placed within a new wave of dyke subcultures. When taken separately, riot dyke bands, drag kings, and queer slam poets all seem to represent a queer edge in a larger cultural phenomenon. When considered together, they add up to a fierce and lively queer subculture that needs to be reckoned with on its own terms. This essay tracks the significant differences between the ladymen who rock and roll and drag up and slam their way toward new queer futures and the punk rockers of an earlier generation of subcultural activity. My tour of dyke subcultures takes in riot dyke punk by bands like Sleater-Kinney, The Butchies, Le Tigre, Tribe 8, The Haggard, and Bitch and Animal; drag kings like Dred, and drag king boy band parody group Backdoor Boys; slam poets like Alix Olson and Staceyann Chin. Queer subcultures are related to old school subcultures like punk, but they also carve out new territory for a consideration of the overlap of gender, generation, class, race, community, and sexuality in relation to minority cultural production.

I have long been interested in and part of various subcultural groups. As a young person I remember well the experience of finding punk rock in the middle of a typically horrible grammar school experience in England in the 1970s. I plunged into punk rock music, clothing, and rebellion precisely because it gave me a language with which to reject not only the high cultural texts in the classroom but also the homophobia and sexism outside it. I tried singing in a punk band called Penny Black and the Stamps for a brief two-week period thinking that my utter lack of musical ability would serve me well finally. But, alas, even punk divas scream in key and my rebel yells were not mellifluous enough to launch my punk singing career. Instead of singing, I collected records, went to shows, dyed my hair, and fashioned outfits from safety pins and bondage pants. And so I learned at an early age that even if you cannot be in the band, participation at multiple levels is what subculture offers. I found myself reminiscing over my punk past when I began researching drag king cultures for a collaborative project with photographer Del LaGrace Volcano. Through my new subcultural involvement I began to see some specific features of queer subculture as opposed to larger historical subcultures like punk rock.

After finishing my drag king book in 1999, I received calls every few months from TV stations wanting me to put them in touch with drag kings for talk shows and news shows. Most of these shows would invite the kings on to parade around with some drag queens in front of a studio audience. At the end of the show, the audience would vote on whether each king or queen was *really* a man or *really* a woman. A

few of the kings managed to circumvent the either/or format and offer
up a more complex gendered self; and so, black drag king Dred took
off her mustache to reveal a "woman's" face but then took off her wig
to reveal a bald pate. The audience was confused and horrified by the
spectacle of indeterminacy. Josh Gamson in *Freaks Talk Back* has written
about the potential for talk shows to allow the "crazies" and "queers"
to talk back, but most of the time when drag kings appeared in mass
public venues, the host did all the talking.[3] Drag kings also made an
appearance in HBO's *Sex and the City* and on MTV's *Real Life*. On
every occasion that drag kings appeared on "straight" TV, they were
deployed as an entertaining backdrop against which heterosexual desire
was showcased and celebrated. As someone who has tirelessly promoted
drag kings, as individual performers and as a subculture, I found the
whole process of watching the mass culture's flirtation with drag kings
depressing and disheartening; but it did clarify for me what my stakes
might be in promoting drag kings: after watching drag kings try to go
prime time, I remain committed to archiving and celebrating and analyzing queer subcultures before they are dismissed by mass culture or
before they simply disappear from lack of exposure or what we might
call "subcultural fatigue," namely the phenomenon of burn out among
subcultural producers.

   As the talk show phenomenon vividly illustrates, mainstream culture
within postmodernism should be defined as the process by which subcultures are *both* recognized and absorbed, mostly for the profit of large
media conglomerates. In other words, when TV stations show an interest in a dyke subculture like drag kings, this is cause for both celebration and concern: on the one hand, the mainstream recognition and
acknowledgment of a subculture has the potential to alter the contours
of dominant culture (think here of the small inroads into popular
notions of sex, gender, and race made by the regular presence of black
drag queen Ru Paul on cable TV); but, on the other hand, most of the
interest directed by mainstream media at subcultures is voyeuristic and
predatory. The subculture might appear on TV eventually as an illustration of the strange and perverse, or else it will be summarily robbed of
its salient features and the subcultural form: drag, for example, will be
lifted without the subcultural producers, drag queens or kings. In an
essay that tracks the results of precisely this process, Marco Becquer and
Jose Gatti examine the contradictory effects of the sudden visibility of
Harlem drag balls and their drag practices. In their analysis of the co-
optation of gay vogueing by Madonna's hit single "Vogue" and by

Jennie Livingston's acclaimed independent film *Paris Is Burning*, Becquer and Gatti show how the counter-hegemonic knowledge articulated in vogueing meets with "the violence of the universal." Becquer and Gatti write of Madonna's video and Livingston's film: "Both partake in the production of newness, a process which purports to keep us up-to-date as it continually adds on novelties to a relational system that absorbs them; both contain vogueing beneath the pluralist umbrella of hipness" (452). And so, while the queens in *Paris Is Burning* expressed a desire for precisely the kind of fame and fortune that did eventually accrue to vogueing, the fame went to director Jennie Livingston and the fortune went to Madonna. The subculture itself, the gay black and Puerto Rican children of the houses of Channel, Extravaganza, and LaBeija, disappeared back into the world of sex work, HIV, and queer glamour, and within five years of the release of *Paris Is Burning*, five of the queens in the film were dead.[4]

The mainstream absorption of vogueing highlights the uneven exchange between dominant culture scavengers and subcultural artists: subcultural artists often seek out mainstream attention for their performances and productions in the hopes of gaining financial assistance for future endeavors. Subcultural activity is, of course, rarely profitable, always costly for the producers and it can be very short lived without the necessary cash infusions (in the words of Sleater-Kinney: "This music gig doesn't pay that good, but the fans are alright [. . .]"). Some subcultural producers turn the subculture itself into a source of revenue and as Angela McRobbie comments: "Subcultures are often ways of creating job opportunities as more traditional careers disappear [. . .]" (1994, 162). So while the subcultural producers hope for cash and a little exposure, the dominant culture scavengers are usually looking for a story and hoping for that brush with the "new" and the "hip" described so well by Becquer and Gatti. In my experiences working with drag kings however, we found that while big media reached their "hipness quota" quickly with the addition of a few well-placed drag kings, in return, they almost never paid for drag king services and when they did pay, it was always a pittance. Obviously the payback for the subcultural participants cannot come in the form of material benefits; what seems more useful then, in this exchange between mainstream attention and subcultural product, would be to use the encounter to force some kind of recognition upon audiences that what is appealing about mainstream culture may very well come from subcultures that they do not even know exist or that they have repudiated.

As George Lipsitz's work has shown in relation to ethnic minority cultures, cultural producers often function as organic intellectuals, in a Gramscian sense; as such, minority artists can produce what Lipsitz terms "a historical bloc" or a coalition of oppositional groups united around counter-hegemonic ideas (357). While in Gramsci's formulation, the organic intellectual undermines the role of the traditional intellectual who serves to legitimize and authorize elite political interests, in subcultures where academics might labor side by side with artists, the "historical bloc" can easily describe an alliance between the minority academic and the minority subcultural producer. Where such alliances exist academics can play a big role in the construction of queer archives, and queer memory, and, furthermore, queer academics can and some should participate in the ongoing project of recoding queer culture and interpreting it and circulating a sense of its multiplicity and sophistication. The more intellectual records we have of queer culture, the more we contribute to the project of claiming for the subculture the radical cultural work that either gets absorbed into or claimed by mainstream media.

SUBCULTURES: THE QUEER DANCE MIX

Subcultures have been an important object of study for sociology and cultural studies since the 1920s. In about the 1980s, however, work on subcultures seemed to fall out of favor as scholars began to doubt the utility of the term and the descriptive potential of the binary opposition between subculture and dominant culture. While early work on subcultures from the Chicago school assumed a relationship between subcultures and deviance or delinquency, later work from the Birmingham University Center for Contemporary Cultural Studies characterized subcultures as class-specific "youth formations."[5] One of the most influential texts on subcultures, *Subcultures: The Meaning of Style*, by Dick Hebdige, reads subcultures in terms of the way they challenged hegemony through style rather than simply through overt ideological articulations. Hebdige characterized the recuperation of subcultural disorder in terms of either an economic conversion of the signs and symbols of the subculture into mass culture commodities or an ideological conversion of the subcultural participant into either complete otherness or complete spectacle. Hebdige's work has been both widely celebrated and widely critiqued in the two decades since its original publication and obviously it cannot be applied in any simple way to contemporary subcultural scenes. And yet, it remains an important text for thinking about how to move beyond the contextualization of subcultures in terms of relations between youth and parent cultures and for its formulations of style and historicity.

Almost all of the early work on subcultures, including Hebdige's, has presumed the dominance of males in subcultural activity and has studied youth groups as the most lively producers of new cultural styles. The subcultures that I want to examine here are neither male nor necessarily young and they are less likely to be co-opted or absorbed back into dominant culture because they were never offered membership in dominant groups in the first place. Queer lesbian subcultures have rarely been discussed in the existing literature, and they offer today a new area of study for queer scholarship as well as exciting opportunities for collaborations between queer cultural producers and queer academics. One of the reasons that theorists tend to look to subcultures for political mobilization has to do with the conflation of subculture and youth culture. Dick Hebdige, in an essay on "Youth, Surveillance, and Display," for example, understands youth subcultures to register a dissatisfaction and alienation from the parent culture, which is both "a declaration of independence [. . .] and a confirmation of the fact of powerlessness" (404). Even though this reading provides us with a better understanding of how political protest might be registered in a youth subculture, it remains trapped in the oedipal framework that pits the subculture against parent culture.

Queer subcultures, unlike the male-dominated youth cultures that Dick Hebdige, Stuart Hall, and other members of the Birmingham school have written about, are not located in any easy relation to so-called parent cultures: much of the Birmingham school work on subcultures indeed (and this is partly why it fell out of favor in the early 1990s) presumed an oedipalized structure within which rebel youths reject the world of their parents and create a netherworld within which to reshape and reform the legacies of an older generation. Economic, political, and social conflicts may be resolved in subcultural arenas, according to these arguments, without really effecting any grand changes at the level of superstructure. Of course such a theory of subcultures has long since been replaced by more nuanced understandings of the relations between class, youth, and mass media, and indeed in an essay on youth cultures, "Different, Youthful, Subjectivities: Towards a Cultural Sociology of Youth," Angela McRobbie comments: "There is certainly no longer a case to be made for the traditional argument that youth culture is produced somehow in conditions of working-class purity, and that such expressions are authentic and in the first instance at least uncontaminated by an avaricious commercial culture" (1994, 179). But, while McRobbie goes on to rethink the relations between white youth and youth of color and the meaning of femininity in postmodern youth cultures, she still presumes a heterosexual framework. Queer subcultures illustrate vividly the limits of subcultural theories that omit consideration of sexuality and sexual styles: queer subcultures, obviously, cannot only be placed in relation to a "parent culture"; they tend to form in relation to place as much as in relation to a genre of cultural expression, and, ultimately, they oppose not only the hegemony of dominant culture but also the mainstreaming of gay and lesbian culture. As Michael du Plessis and Kathleen Chapman report in an article about "Queercore," for example: "queercore and homocore not only signaled their allegiances to post-punk subculture, but also positioned themselves as [. . .] distinct from lesbian and gay" (45). Furthermore, queer subcultures are not simply spin-offs from some distinct youth culture like punk: as we will see in relation to riot dyke, queer music subcultures may be as likely to draw upon women's music from the 1970s and early 1980s as from British punk circa 1977.

We need to alter our understandings of subcultures in several important ways in order to address the specificities of queer subcultures and queer subcultural sites. First, we need to rethink the relation between theorist and subcultural participant, recognizing that for many queers, the boundary between theorist and cultural producer might be slight or at least permeable. Second, most subcultural theories are created to describe and account for male heterosexual adolescent activity and they are adjusted only when female heterosexual adolescent activity comes into focus. New queer subcultural theory will have to account for nonheterosexual, nonexclusively male, nonwhite, and nonadolescent subcultural production in all its specificity. Third, we need to theorize the concept of the archive and consider new models of queer memory and queer history capable of recording and tracing subterranean scenes, fly-by-night clubs, and fleeting trends; we need, in José Muñoz's words, "an archive of the ephemeral" (5–18). Finally, queer subcultures offer us an opportunity to redefine the binary of adolescence and adulthood that structures so many inquiries into subcultures. Precisely because many queers refuse and resist the heteronormative imperative of home and family, they also prolong the periods of their life devoted to subcultural participation. This challenge to the notion of the subculture as a youth formation could on the one hand expand the definition of subculture beyond its most banal significations of youth in crisis and on the other hand challenge our notion of adulthood as reproductive maturity. I want to now consider each one of these features of queer subcultural production in relation to specific lesbian subcultures.

QUEER SPACE/QUEER TIME

"Hot Topic": The Death of the Expert

First then, let us consider the relations between subcultural producers and queer cultural theorists. Queer subcultures encourage blurred boundaries between archivists and producers, which is not to say that this is the only subcultural space within which the theorist and the cultural worker may be the same people.[6] Minority subcultures in general tend to be documented by former or current members of the subculture rather than by "adult" experts. Nonetheless, queer subcultures in particular are often marked by this lack of distinction between the archivist and the cultural worker. A good example of this blurring between producer and analyst would be Dr. Vaginal Creme Davis, a drag queen who enacts, documents, and theorizes an array of drag characters. Another would be Juanita Mohammed, Mother of the House of Mashood, a women's drag house in Manhattan. Mohammed keeps a history of the participation of women of color in the drag cultures even as she recruits new "children" to the House of Mashood. Mohammed also goes one step further and makes herself central to AIDS activism in relation to queers of color.

The queer archivist or theorist and the cultural workers may also coexist in the same friendship networks, and they may function as co-conspirators. A good example of this relation would be academic Tammy Rae Carland who runs an independent record label, Mr. Lady, manages dyke punk band The Butchies, and teaches at the University of North Carolina. Finally, the academic and the cultural producer may see themselves in a complementary relationship. Le Tigre, for example, a riot dyke band, have a song called "Hot Topic" in which they name the women, academics, filmmakers, musicians, and producers who have inspired them and whom they want to inspire. They sing: "Carol Rama and Eleanor Antin / Yoko Ono and Carole Schneeman / You're getting old, that's what they'll say, but / I don't give a damn, I'm listening anyway."

More typically, cultural theorists have looked to groups of which they are not necessarily a part, most often youth subcultures, for an encapsulated expression of the experiences of a subordinated class. The youth subculture then becomes the raw material for a developed theory of cultural resistance or the semiotics of style or some other discourse that now leaves the subculture behind. For a new generation of queer theorists, a generation moving on from the split between densely theoretical queer theory in a psychoanalytic mode on the one hand and strictly ethnographic queer research on the other, new queer cultural studies feeds off of and back into subcultural production. The academic might be the archivist or a coarchivist or she might be a full-fledged participant in the subcultural scene that he or she writes about. But only rarely does the queer theorist stand wholly apart from the subculture examining it with an expert's gaze.

"Wildcat Women": Lesbian Punk and Slam Poetry

Second, queer subcultural theory should begin with those communities that never seem to surface in the commentaries on subcultures in general: namely lesbian subcultures and subcultures of color. Cultural theory has created a hierarchy of subcultures that places English punk near the top and then arranges mods, rockers, metalheads, club kids, DJ cultures, ravers, and rappers in some sort of descending order of importance. At the bottom of the pyramid of subcultures we will find girl fan cultures, house drag cultures, and gay sex cultures. Lesbian subcultures almost never appear at all; and so, even in the documentation on balls and drag cultures, women's involvement and relation to drag has been left out of theoretical accounts and subcultural histories. Recording the presence of lesbian subcultures can make a huge difference to the kinds of subcultural histories that get written: whether it is a history of drag that only focuses on gay men, a history of punk that only focuses on white boys, or a history of girl cultures that only focuses upon heterosexual girls.

To give one example of the difference an awareness of lesbian subcultures can make, we can turn to early work in the 1970s on the participation of girls in punk subcultures. Theorists like Angela McRobbie, Jennie Garber, and others talked about the invisibility of female subcultures and the tendency of girls to participate in co-ed subcultures only as girlfriends or groupies. McRobbie and Garber concluded: "Girls' subcultures may have become invisible because the very term 'subculture' has acquired such strong masculine overtones [. . .]" (1975; 1993, 114). In this essay and even in more recent work on girls and subcultures, there tends to be little recognition that some girls, usually queer girls, may in fact involve themselves in subcultures precisely because of the "strong masculine overtones" associated with the activity. And so, a young queer girl interested in punk will not be put off by the masculinity of the subculture—she may as easily be seduced by it. In another essay written some twelve years later and collected in Angela McRobbie's book *Feminism and Youth Culture*, however, McRobbie articulates precisely the failed promise of subcultural membership for young girls: "Whereas men who 'play around' with femininity are nowadays credited with some degree of power to choose, gender experimentation, sexual ambiguity and homosexuality among girls are viewed differently." McRobbie then concludes: "[. . .] the possibility of escaping oppressive aspects of adolescent heterosexuality in a youth culture [. . .] remains more or less unavailable to girls" (1991; 2000, 36). It is not until the 1990s that girls begin to find in subcultural life an escape hatch from heteronormativity and its regulations.

The work of Angela McRobbie over the years has served as a critique of the masculinism of early pronouncements on subcultures; but more than this, McRobbie has returned insistently to the topic of youth cultures and gender, race, and class. Indeed, McRobbie's opus by now stands as a rich, deep, and important theoretical archive on oppositional forms of culture making. In her collection of essays *Postmodernism and Popular Culture*, McRobbie models a form of intellectual practice that she calls "feminist postmodernism," which allows her to "confront questions which otherwise remain unasked" (1994, 2). In the process of engaging these otherwise unasked questions, she suggests, "we also find our academic practice and our politics undergoing some degree of transformation and change" (2). McRobbie's willingness to track the transformations in her own body of work and to trace changes in her own thinking about key topics provides an excellent model for cultural theory in an ever-evolving and shifting field. In one key chapter titled "Shut Up and Dance," McRobbie returns to the topic of femininity and subcultures and considers her position now as the mother of a daughter who attends raves. Commenting that we need to reorient our analyses of youth culture given "shifts in gender relations in the last decade," McRobbie examines the impact of feminism upon both mass media representations of femininity and gender norms circulated by and among young girls. McRobbie concludes that girls are now operating with more flexible gender norms and that "femininity is no longer the 'other' of feminism" (173).

McRobbie does not go on to study the punk femininities within dyke cultures, but if she did, she would find a fabulous array of feminist and queer femme performances. Guitarists like Leslie Mah of Tribe 8 and vocalists like Kathleen Hanna of Le Tigre and Beth Ditto of The Gossip all articulate the explosive potential of a queer femininity that served as an undercurrent to much of the riot grrrl feminism and that is readable as radical style in queer punk. The recent explosion of dyke punk bands like Bitch and Animal, The Butchies, Le Tigre, The Need, The Haggard, Tribe 8 also challenges the conventional understandings of punk as male-dominated and of queercore as a largely gay male phenomenon. This explosion also makes visible the queerness that energized the riot grrrl movement even as it was assiduously ignored by mainstream media. The hardcore styles of many of these bands reminds us that punk in general, contrary to the usual accounts of the subculture, has always been a place for young girls to remake their genders. In her excellent book on women in punk, *Pretty in Punk: Girls' Gender Resistance in a Boys' Subculture*, Lauraine Leblanc tracks the relationship of girls to punk rock; while some girls involved themselves in the scene through their boyfriends, Leblanc argues that some of the really tough girls involved in punk had to become "virtual boys" in order to earn the respect of their male counterparts. While the subculture remains resolutely heterosexual in form, Leblanc found that punk offered girls "strategies of resistance to gender norms" (13).

Lesbian punks are pretty much absent from Leblanc's otherwise excellent and thorough ethnographic study of punk girls; and this may have had as much to do with when she conducted her research as it has to do with the reluctance of the girls she studied to identify as queer. For as the wave of riot grrrl crested and began to recede in the mid 1990s, many of the most interesting bands left standing were queer, female, and loud. Some of these bands, like Sleater-Kinney, retooled femininity and made punk femininity unreliable as a marker of heterosexuality. Sleater-Kinney modeled new femininities at the level of musical performance as much as at the level of style. For example, the band layers two very distinctive guitars over the drums but they omit the bass. The bass can be read here as a "masculine" instrument in terms of its production of noise in the lower registers but it can also be read as a stereotypically "female" instrument given that many women in rock bands have been relegated to bass player because the "lead" guitar was presumed to be a male role.[7] By using two guitars, Sleater-Kinney both undercut the notion of "lead" and they refuse the conventional arrangement of bass, guitar, and drums. Other bands, like The Haggard, a hardcore band from Portland, Oregon, produce a gender-bending sound by combining drum and guitar noise with a butch voice overlay. The singer, Emily, produces a guttural roar that is neither a male voice nor a female voice, and she spews her lyrics in an indecipherable growl. This butch voice shows no concern for intelligibility or virtuosity, but it produces a raw and original sound while redefining the meaning of voice, singing, and lyric.

Just as the recognition of lesbian involvement in punk subcultures changes the way we understand both the punk phenomenon and the recent riot dyke music trend, so lesbian involvement in slam poetry forces commentators to rethink universalizing narratives about youth cultures. While slam poetry is a nationwide phenomenon, the emergence of highly talented lesbian slam poets has changed the nature of the slam event. Two performers in particular have garnered mainstream and local attention: white lesbian Alix Olson and Jamaican-born Staceyann Chin. Alix Olson was a member of the Nuyorican Slam Team, which won the national championship in 1998. She was also the 1999 OUTWRITE slam champion after a long and thrilling slam off between herself and Staceyann Chin.[8] Slam poetry is a form of competitive poetry in which poets perform three-minute poems for a panel of judges chosen from the audience; the judges rate the poems on a scale of 1 to 10 and the slammers move through preliminary rounds until they face off in the finals. This necessitates each poet often memorizing and performing up to ten poems a night.

As popularized by the film *SLAM*, the slam poetry contest can easily degenerate into a macho contest of speed and fury; but it is also an offshoot of rap in terms of its rhythm and combination of spoken word with a beat. Slams therefore do attract poets of color in large numbers. Slam appeals to queer youth and queer youth of color because of the very obvious connections to rap. In places like Oakland, spoken word groups of color have been at the center of queer youth activity. Recently queer poets of color like Sri Lankan slam poet D'Lo and Jamaican-born Staceyann Chin have made the slam a forum for very different messages about love, race, and poetry. In "Dykepoem" from her collection *Wildcat Woman*, Chin begins with the line "I killed a man today" and tells of a young black girl who fights off a rapist and justifies her sinful act saying: "I going to hell anyway / women who like other women go there, you know." The poem closes with a vision of prison as "a place / with only girl children inside / that place ain't no hell / sounds like heaven to me" (16–17). Chin is a superb performer, and she regularly slams at queer people of color events all over New York City—she is as likely to appear in a nightclub as at a rally, at a conference as on the street. And while many of her poems are tough, sexy, and angry, she also infuses her work with a sense of irony and self-reflexivity. In "Don't Want To Slam," Chin writes: "I've decided / I don't want to be / a poet who just writes / for the slam anymore [. . .]." The slam, she goes on to say, is just a "staged revolution," a spectacle of word pimps selling lines and rhymes for a quick "TEN" from the judges. With breath-taking speed, the poem moves through a pointed critique of slamming and makes a call for poems that tell "true histories of me and you [. . .]." But the last verse shows that the slam *is* true history, *is* revolution, and may just change the world by changing the *word*. By the end of the last line, we believe her:

> I want to write / I left my lover and / now I want her back
> poems / I miss Jamaica / but now I'm never going back poems
> / I know it's not a ten / but it sends shivers down MY back
> poems / poems that talk about life / and love and laughter /
> poems that reveal the flaws / that make strikingly real people
> / real poems / poems that are so honest / they slam.

Chin's and Olson's slam poetry takes lesbian feminism and women of color feminism to a new stage and a new audience and make poetry into the language of riot and change.

Shooting Stars: Queer Archives

Third, the nature of queer subcultural activity requires a nuanced theory of archives and archiving. Work on archives and archiving is well under way and can be found in the work of an eclectic group of queer cultural theorists including Ann Cvetkovich, Lauren Berlant, and José Muñoz.[9] Ideally, an archive of queer subcultures would merge ethnographic interviews with performers and fans with research in the multiple archives that already exist on line and in other unofficial sites. Queer zines, posters, guerilla art, and other temporary artifacts would make up some of the paper archives, and descriptions of shows along with the self-understandings of cultural producers would provide supplementary materials. But the notion of an archive has to extend beyond the image of a place to collect material or hold documents, and it has to become a floating signifier for the kinds of lives implied by the paper remnants of shows, clubs, events, and meetings. The archive is not simply a repository; it is also a theory of cultural relevance, a construction of collective memory and a complex record of queer activity. In order for the archive to function it requires users, interpreters, cultural historians to wade through the material and piece together the jigsaw puzzle of queer history in the making.

While some of the work of queer archiving certainly falls to academics, cultural producers also play a big role in constructing queer genealogies and memories; as seen in Le Tigre's song, the lyrics to "Hot Topic" create an eclectic encyclopedia of queer cultural production through unlikely juxtapositions ("Gayatri Spivak and Angela Davis / Laurie Weeks and Dorothy Allison") and they claim a new poetic logic: "Hot topic is the way that we rhyme / hot topic is the way that we rhyme [. . .]." In other words, the historically situated theorists and film-makers and musicians rhyme with each other's work—the rhyme is located in the function and not in the words. Similarly, while many lesbian punk bands do trace their influences back to male punk or classic rock, as we saw in the last section, contrary to what one may expect, they do not completely distance themselves from or counter-identify with 1970s and 1980s "women's music." In fact, some dykecore bands see themselves as very much a part of a tradition of loud and angry women. On their CD *Are We Not Femme?* for example, North Carolina–based band The Butchies perform a cover of feminist goddess Cris Williamson's classic song "Shooting Star." Williamson's soaring, emotion-laden song becomes a tough, percussive anthem in the capable hands of The Butchies, who add drum rolls and screeching guitars to lift the song out of a woman-loving-woman groove and into a new era. On their liner notes, The Butchies thank Cris Williamson for "being radical and singing songs to girls before too many others were and for writing such a kickass song [. . .]." If we look at the covers from The Butchies' CD and Cris Williamson's CD, it would be hard to detect the connections between the two. The Butchies CD pays obvious homage to punk concept band Devo both in terms of its title (Devo's first album was called *Are We Not Men*) and in terms of its iconography. The connection between The Butchies and Cris Williamson however runs much deeper than their relation to punk bands like Devo. The Butchies appear on the cover wearing short, red pleather miniskirts, which do quote the red plastic flower-pot hats worn by Devo on the cover of *Are We Not Men*. Williamson, on the other hand, appears in dungarees and stands in what looks like the Joshua Tree desert. Her album title, *The Changer and the Changed*, references a modality of mutuality, organic transformation, and reciprocity. The song itself, in her hands, tells of a "wonderful moments on the journey through my desert." She sings of "crossing the desert for you" and seeing a shooting star, which reminds her of her lover. The spectral image of the shooting star figures quite differently in The Butchies' version, where it takes on more of the qualities of a rocket than a galactic wonder. But The Butchies' cover version of Williamson's song has the tone of tribute and not parody, and by making her song relevant for a new generation of listeners, The Butchies refuse the model of generational conflict and build a bridge between their raucous spirit of rebellion and the quieter, acoustic world of women's music from the 1970s and 1980s.

In an excellent essay on riot grrrl, feminism, and lesbian culture, Mary Celeste Kearney also points to the continuity rather than the break between women's music and riot grrrl. But, she comments, links between earlier modes of lesbian feminism and contemporary riot grrrl productions are regularly ignored in favor of a history which makes riot grrrl the female offspring of male dominated punk. Like the new grrrl productions, women's music by Alix Dobkins, Cris Williamson, and others was produced on independent labels (like Olivia Records) and received only scant mainstream attention. The earlier music was made for, by, and about women and while much of it did consist of folk-influenced ballads, there was also a hard and angry subgenre that combined lyrics about man hating with loud guitar playing (Maxine Feldman's music, for example). As Kearney points out, however, the noncommercial practices of 1970s lesbian musicians has made them less easy to identify as major influences upon a new generation of "all-girl community," and so while women's music is erased as a musical influence, so lesbianism is ignored as a social context for riot grrrl. Kearney writes: "In spite of the coterminous emergence in the US of riot grrrl and queercore bands like Tribe 8, Random Violet, The Mudwimmin and Team Dresch, there have been relatively few links made by the mainstream press between lesbian feminism, queercore and riot grrrl" (222).

Other lesbian punk or punk/folk bands see themselves both as heirs to an earlier generation of "pussy power" and as pioneers of new genres. Bitch and Animal, for example, authors of "The Pussy Manifesto," describe their CD *What's That Smell* as "tit rock." In live performances, Bitch plays an electric violin and Animal plays an array of percussion. Their songs, like those of The Butchies, are themselves archival records of lesbian subculture. One song from *What's That Smell* is called "Drag King Bar" and it posits the drag king bar as an alternative to a rather tired mainstream lesbian scene. With Animal picking out a "yee hah" tune on the banjo, Bitch sings about a place where "all the boys were really girls and the fags whip out their pearls." Bitch tells of being picked up by one particularly bold king, and the song ends in a rousing symphony of violin and drums. Bitch and Animal document and celebrate the emergence of a drag king scene in contemporary queer clubs, and they blend country-influenced folk with avant garde percussion to do so. But their cover art and their manifestos hearken back to an era of women-loving-women in their embrace of the female body; at their website, furthermore, fans are encouraged to take up terms like "pussy" and "tits" with pride by brushing off the taint of patriarchal insult. Like the The Butchies' decision to cover a Cris Williamson song, Bitch and Animal's pussy power reaches out to an earlier generation of women musicians refusing once and for all the oedipal imperative to overthrow the old and bring on the new. Recent women's music festivals like Ladyfest are also clear inheritors of a tradition of lesbian feminist music festivals, and they revive an earlier model of feminism for a new generation of grrrls.

"I Want It That Way": A Time for Queers

Finally, queer subcultures afford us a perfect opportunity to depart from a normative model of youth cultures as stages on the way to adulthood; this allows us to map out different forms of adulthood, or the refusal of adulthood and new modes of deliberate deviance. Queers participate in subcultures for far longer than their heterosexual counterparts. At a time when heterosexual men and women are spending their weekends, their extra cash, and all their free time shuttling back and forth between the weddings of friends and family, urban queers tend to spend their leisure time and money on subcultural involvement. This may take the form of intense weekend clubbing, playing in small music bands, going to drag balls, participating in slam poetry events, or seeing performances of one kind or another in cramped and poorly ventilated spaces. Just as homosexuality itself has been theorized by psychoanalysis as a stage of development, a phase, that the adolescent will hopefully pass through quickly and painlessly, so subcultural involvement has been theorized as a life stage rather than a lifelong commitment. For queers the separation between youth and adulthood quite simply does not hold, and queer adolescence can extend far beyond one's twenties. I want to raise here the notion of "queer time," a different mode of temporality that might arise out of an immersion in club cultures or queer sex cultures. While obviously heterosexual people also go to clubs and some involve themselves in sex cultures, queer urbanites, lacking the pacing and schedules that inhere to family life and reproduction, might visit clubs and participate in sex cultures well into their forties or fifties on a regular basis.

At the same time that queers extend participation in subcultural activity long beyond their "youth," some queer subcultures also provide a critical lens through which to revisit seemingly heterosexual youth cultures. In new work on subcultures and gender/sexuality, generally speaking, there is the potential to explore the possibilities and the promise of rebellious youth genders. By focusing on the realization of tomboy desires or youthful femme aspirations in dyke punk bands and forms of queer fandom, we can see that pre-adult, pre-identitarian girl roles offer a set of opportunities for theorizing gender, sexuality, race, and social rebellion precisely because they occupy the space of the "not-yet," the not fully realized. These girl roles are not absolutely predictive of either heterosexual or lesbian adulthoods, rather the desires and the play and the anguish they access allow us to theorize other relations to identity.

Gayle Wald's work on boy bands has also drawn our attention to the homoerotic subtext to much teen culture. Boy bands like The Backstreet Boys, Wald suggests, produce and manage anxieties about gay modes of gender performance. Boy bands perform what Wald calls "a girlish masculinity," and they channel the fantasy of perpetual youth referenced by the moniker "boy"; but they also play out socially acceptable forms of rebellion ("backstreet" for example conjures up images of working-class youth) that can be both expressed and neatly channeled into white, middle-class heteronormativity. The phenomenon of boy bands, for me, raises a number of questions not simply about the performance of masculinity but also about what Wald refers to as the threatening aspect of the "ecstatic responses that they elicit" (1–39). After all, while music critics love to dismiss fandom as a passive "teenybopper" subculture, there is something all too powerful about a nearly hysterical audience of teen girls screaming and crying together; this activity may well have as much to say about the desire between the screamers as it says about their desire for the mythic "boys." Wald argues that the phenomenon of teenybopper fans and young boy bands creates a homophobic fear of both boy fandom and homoerotic dynamics on stage between the boy performers. The policing of male homosexuality, however, she continues: "creates opportunities for girls to engage in modes of consumption that have a markedly homoerotic component, although they are typically characterized in terms of (heterosexual) 'puppy love' [. . .]" (32). Again the notion of homoerotic bonding as a stage on the way to heterosexual maturity creates a context within which both subcultural activity and queer desire can be dismissed as temporary and nonserious. Gayle Wald's careful excavation of the sources of social scorn levied at teenyboppers and her contextualization of the boy band phenomenon within popular culture opens up new and important questions about youth cultures and femininity, and it makes possible a consideration of the queerness of even the most heterosexually inflected pre-adult activity.

I never invested much hope of queer alternatives in the performance of boy bands, I must admit, until I was present at the World Premier of New York's drag king boy band: The Backdoor Boys. When the Backdoor Boys took the stage as A.J., Nick, Kevin, Howie, and Brian, I saw at last the butch potential of the boy band phenomenon. The queer audience screamed as each boy was introduced, picked their favorites and began the ritual ecstatic fan worship that we associate with teenage girls but that seems to be fun at any age. The current between the stage and the packed house was electric. At least part of the appeal of the Backstreet Boys depends upon the production of seemingly safe and almost unreal masculinities—the boys croon about what they would do for their girls, about being there for her, buying her flowers, giving her gifts, doing everything that other boys supposedly won't do. The boys, in short, offer themselves as a safe alternative to the misogyny and mistreatment that many girls find and expect in adolescent relationships. Here, in a drag king context, the space of the alternative is taken back from the realm of popular culture and revealed as proper to the subcultural space. As the Backdoor Boys went into their version of "I Want It That Way," and they began to act out the barely concealed homoerotic implication of the lyric, the queer crowd went wild; the source of pleasure for the queer fans had as much to do with the acting out of the song's homo potential as with the sexual appeal of the drag kings. The Backdoor Boys' performance of "I Want It That Way" speaks to the purpose of what Wald calls "the deliberate sublimation of sexual explicitness" in Backstreet Boys' lyrics and dance moves. The fan desire and ecstasy can only be maintained by keeping at bay the erotic relations between the boys on the one hand and the potentially erotic relations between the screaming girls on the other. As the boys sing together, the girls scream together and the whole fragile edifice of heterosexuality could come tumbling down at any moment if the homosocial structures of desire are made explicit. The drag king impersonation of the faggy boy band, finally, recognizes the act as neither a performance of male heterosexuality nor a performance of gay masculinity—this is rather an intricate performance of butch masculinity, queer masculinity that presents itself to screaming girls as a safe alternative to heteromasculinities.

Finally, all of these representations of teen and youth genders offer us a space within which to think through the alternatives that young people create for themselves to the routine and tired options recycled by adult culture. When the Backstreet Boys croon "I want it THAT way" and the girls scream, we think for a moment that it does not have to be *this* way and that just maybe girl and boy partial identities can be carried forward into adulthood in terms of a politics of refusal—the refusal to grow up and enter the heteronormative adulthoods implied by these concepts of progress and maturity. The boy bands in particular allow us to think of boyhood, girlhood, and even tomboyhood and riot girlhoods, not as stages to pass through but as pre-identities to carry forward, inhabit and sustain.

Conclusion

In his powerful study of a disappearing sexual subculture in New York City's Times Square, queer legend Chip Delany describes queer subterranean worlds as "a complex of interlocking systems and subsystems" (xviii). The unimaginably precious meaning of these systems are of no consequence to the city planner who sees only ugliness and filth where Delany sees a distillation of the promise of radical democracy. The porn theaters that Delany visits and learns from offer him and other men, he claims, one of the last opportunities in urban America for "interclass contact and communication conducted in a mode of good will" (111). Counter-publics, as his book shows, are spaces created and altered by certain subcultures for their own uses. Since lesbians and women in general partake so little in public sex cultures, we, much more than gay men, need to develop and protect counter-publics for subcultural uses. In the Bay Area, San Francisco, and Oakland in particular, there is a long history of subcultural activity; counter-publics abound here and new bands, spoken-word artists, and performers appear weekly at different shows in different venues. These counter-publics have survived the dot.com explosion and the latest recession, the yuppies and the businessmen; they have also survived so far the new patriotism of a post–9/11 culture and the new "homonormativity" of the recent lesbian baby boom. To return to Judith Butler's question from "Agencies of Style for a Liminal Subject": "What sorts of style signal the crisis of survival?" (36), we can now answer that the crisis of survival is being played out nightly in a club near you. The radical styles crafted in queer punk bands, in slam poetry events, in drag king boy bands do not express some mythically pure form of agency or will, but rather, they model other modes of being and becoming that scramble our understandings of place, time, development, action, and transformation. And for a more concrete example of how the "crisis of survival" may play out, we can go to the Bitch and Animal website (www.bitchandanimal.com) where Bitch and Animal present fans with a hard-hitting politics of transformation in their "Pussy Manifesto"; and they counsel listeners as follows: "Wise, old, kick-up-shit-chicks and chick lovers alike: Be not afraid to take up space! Manifest this Motherfuckers and let the Pussy rule!"

NOTES

1. Thanks to Glen Mimura for the formulation of an "epistemology of youth."

2. For work on queer space see Gordon Brent Ingram, Anne-Marie Bouthillette, Yolanda Retter, eds., *Queers in Space: Communities, Public Places, Sites of Resistance* (Seattle, WA: Bay Press, 1997); David Bell and Gill Valentine, eds., *Mapping Desire: Geographies of Sexuality* (New York: Routledge, 1995); Joseh Boone, et al., eds., *Queer Frontiers: Millennial Geographies, Genders, and Generations* (Madison, WI: University of Wisconsin Press, 2000).

3. See Joshua Gamson, *Freaks Talk Back: Tabloid Talk Shows and Sexual Nonconformity* (Chicago, IL: University of Chicago Press, 1999).

4. For an article on the fate of the queens and children featured in *Paris Is Burning*, see Jesse Green, "Paris Has Burned," *New York Times*, "Styles of the Times" Section 9, Column 5, page 1 (Sunday, April 18, 1993). Green documents the death of Angie Extravaganza and Kim Pendarvis among others. Drag queens are interviewed for the article, and Green reports on the anger that many in the ball world feel about Jennie Livingston's film. Green reminds us that: "the film's critical and financial success should not therefore be taken for the success of its subjects." While Jennie Livingston became a filmmaker as a consequence of the circulation of *Paris Is Burning*, the film's subjects continued to live in poverty.

5. See *Resistance Through Rituals: Youth Subcultures in Post-War Britain*, ed. Stuart Hall and Tony Jefferson. London: Routledge, 1975, rpt. 2000.

6. Paul Gilroy, for example, was a DJ while working on black expressive cultures; and nowadays, many public intellectuals straddle the worlds of cultural production and theory. Josh Kun, for example, writes about Rock En Espanol and hosts a radio show. Patrick Johnson is a theorist of black performance art and he himself performs in a one-man show.

7. For a great article on feminism and rock music see Gayle Wald, "Just a Girl? Rock Music, Feminism, and the Cultural Construction of Female Youth," in *Signs* 23 (31): 585.

8. For Alix Olson's poetry see *Only the Starving Favor Peace* (Brooklyn: Feed the Fire Productions, 1998).

9. See Muñoz, "Ephemera as Evidence: Introductory Notes to Queer Acts"; Lauren Berlant, *The Queen of America Goes to Washington City: Essays on Sex and Citizenship* (Durham, NC: Duke University Press, 1997); Ann Cvetkovich, *An Archive of Feelings: Trauma, Sexuality and Lesbian Public Cultures* (Durham, NC: Duke University Press, 2003).

WORKS CITED

Becquer, Marcos, and Jose Gatti. "Elements of Vogue." In *The Subcultures Reader*, ed. Ken Gelder and Sarah Thornton. New York and London: Routledge, 1997.

Chin, Staceyann. "Dykepoem." *Wildcat Woman: Poetry*. Self-published, 1998.

Delany, Samuel. *Times Square Red, Times Square Blue*. New York: New York Press, 1999.

Du Plessis, Michael, and Kathleen Chapman. "Queercore: The Distinct Identities of Subculture." *College Literature* 24, 1 *Queer Utilities: Textual Studies, Theory, Pedagogy, Praxis* (February 1997).

Foucault, Michel. "Friendship as a Way of Life." In *Foucault Live: Collected Interviews, 1961–1984*, ed. Sylvere Lotringer, trans. Lysa Hochroth and John Johnston. New York: Semiotext[e], 1996.

Hebdige, Dick. "Posing . . . Threats, Striking . . . Poses: Youth, Surveillance, and Display." In *The Subcultures Reader*, ed. Ken Gelder and Sarah Thornton. New York and London: Routledge, 1997.

Kearney, Mary Celeste. "The Missing Link: Riot Grrrl, Feminism, Lesbian Culture." *Sexing the Groove: Popular Music and Gender*, ed. Sheila Whiteley. New York and London: Routledge, 1997.

Leblanc, Lauraine. *Pretty in Punk: Girls' Gender Resistance in a Boys' Subculture*. New Brunswick, NJ: Rutgers University Press, 1998.

Lipsitz, George. "Cruising Around the Historical Bloc: Postmodernism and Popular Music in East LA." In *The Subcultures Reader*. 1990.

McRobbie, Angela. "Settling Accounts with Subcultures: A Feminist Critique." *Feminism and Youth Culture*. New York: Routledge, 1991; 2000.

———. "Different, Youthful, Subjectivities: Towards a Cultural Sociology of Youth." *Postmoderism and Popular Culture*. London and New York: Routledge, 1994.

———. "Introduction." *Postmodernism and Popular Culture*. London and New York: Routledge, 1994.

———. "Shut Up and Dance: Youth Culture and Changing Modes of Femininity." *Postmoderism and Popular Culture*. London and New York: Routledge, 1994.

McRobbie, Angela, and Jennie Garber. "Girls and Subcultures." *Resistance Through Rituals*. Ed. Hall and Jefferson. London: Routledge, 1975; 1993.

Muñoz, José Esteban. "Ephemera as Evidence: Introductory Notes to Queer Acts." *Queer Acts: Women and Performance, A Journal of Feminist Theory* 8:2, 16 (1996): 5–18.

Nancy, Jean-Luc. "The Inoperative Community." *The Inoperative Community*, ed. Peter Connor, trans. Peter Connor, Lisa Garbus, Michael Holland, and Simona Sawhney, foreword by Christopher Fynsk. Minneapolis: University of Minnesota Press, 1991.

Thornton, Sarah. "General Introduction." *The Subcultures Reader*, eds. Ken Gelder and Sarah Thornton. New York and London: Routledge, 1997.

Wald, Gayle. "I Want It That Way: Teenybopper Music and the Girling of Boy Bands." *Genders* 35 (2002): 1–39.

CHAPTER 2

"THE GALAXY IS GAY"

EXAMINING THE NETWORKS OF LESBIAN
PUNK ROCK SUBCULTURE

Angela Wilson

In 2000 Angela McRobbie made the sobering proclamation that feminism was dead among young women, and she complained about the
lack of an "organized lobby" because there were no "campaigns or
demonstrations by young women, no new magazines, and barely a
handful of explicitly feminist books" (212). While postfeminism and
third wave power feminism have made great impressions through mainstream media outlets, and the institutionalized feminist organizations of
the second wave are apparently on the decline, there have always ex-
isted lesser known groups of young women concerned with gender
politics and exemplifying the new grassroots approach to feminism
adopted by younger generations. Indeed, Jane Long and Anita Harris
posit that "young women's feminism is expressed in a cultural space, for
example by constructing Internet sites, publishing ezines, playing in all-
women bands" (qtd. in Bulbeck 1). This chapter will explore the past
and present of lesbian punk rock, a music youth subculture emerging
out of a feminist tradition but reflecting a dynamic way of thinking
about gender politics that draws from second and third wave feminism
but that also integrates innovative ideas of queer politics to create a new
brand of gender activism that has gone largely unnoticed by mainstream

media outlets. As such, lesbian punk rock subculture offers up a space for the discussion of gender, sexuality, queer activism, and intergenerational relations.

THE FEMINIST ROOTS OF DYKECORE

Lesbian punk rock was pioneered in the late 1980s and the early 1990s by bands such as Sister George, Huggy Bear, Tribe 8, and Team Dresch. The music style has since been carried on in the United States by bands like The Butchies, Le Tigre, The Gossip, and The Need. These groups have worked in association with such independent, queer-positive record labels as Mr. Lady, Kill Rock Stars, and Chainsaw Records. The music varies from band to band, but is primarily punk and features the driving rhythms, aggressive guitar solos, and the sharp, often angry vocals so characteristic of the genre. The sound also includes softer ballads that erupt into faster hardcore tempos. The early dykecore bands developed alongside riot grrrl bands, and musicians often identified with both subcultures. Both styles revel in disrupting gendered rock stereotypes that dictate that women by nature play soft music while men naturally incline to be swaggering rock virtuosos. Lesbian punk rock also draws inspiration from the lesbian feminist folk music tradition of the 1970s, which featured songs with politically charged lyrics that alternately criticized and offered alternate visions to the existing social structure and its constraints.

To better understand the cultural context within which dykecore emerged, we need to look at the development of the lesbian feminist musical subculture of another era. Cynthia Lont suggests that the integration of feminist thought into rock music during the 1970s threatened male performers because it encouraged women to move beyond female musical stereotypes and to assert their place in the industry (91). Typically women were seen as either fans or muses. At the same time, the reluctance of some in the established rock industry to accept gender equality drove many women to create their own independent music networks. One such network was the lesbian folk scene. This scene grew out of the radical lesbian feminist community and reflected many of the same political and social priorities. As part of this movement, Olivia Records formed in 1973, bringing together several small independent American record labels and the lesbian artists they represented. The politically motivated, nonprofit collective produced albums by folk singer–songwriters, including Meg Christian, Alix Dobkin, and Kay

Gardner, while smaller independent labels also produced lesbian artists. Musicians were encouraged to participate in all levels of production, including writing, recording, distribution, and promotion. Artists even had financial control of the labels (Lont 93). In terms of content, the sound differed from popular music in several important ways. For example, its lyrics were based on the assumption that any person in a relationship is independent and strong. This view challenged what Cynthia Lont calls the " 'If you leave me, I will surely die,' syndrome" (93) that was prevalent in popular love songs of the era. In a 1981 study of forty lesbian love songs, Mary Hornby found that their lyrics offered women a space for "female notions of love and relationships" (qtd. in Lont 93). In this way, lesbian folk music provided an alternative to mainstream popular music and its focus on the male experience of love and relationships. Today, as it explores the complexities of female relationships, dykecore continues the tradition begun by lesbian folk music.

Dykecore traces its musical heritage to punk rock. When it comes to lesbian relationships, however, dykecore presents some very real challenges to the parent movement. With songs like "Screwing Yer Courage," and "She's Amazing," Team Dresch moves beyond the gender binary of male and female and deals directly with female relationships by removing the constraints of patriarchal influence. Such songs move past the male gaze and into a space concerned with the practical issues of female-female relationships. "Screwing Yer Courage" is simply a love song: it contains no reference to homophobia or to the many obstacles to be overcome by lesbians. The song's lyrics present the lesbian experience as both natural and complex. Like the early lesbian folk music, Team Dresch deals with female love and desire without reference to patriarchy.

Given Team Dresch's outspoken goal to educate young people on the challenges inherent in being lesbian, songs like "Screwing Yer Courage" simply cannot ignore the difficulties lesbians face in society. In a direct nod to the earlier generations of lesbians like those involved with Olivia Records, Kaia Wilson's liner notes from Team Dresch's 1996 album *Captain My Captain* stress the importance of remembering the struggles lesbians have faced through time. She writes that "It [. . .] sucks that people think it's never been a big deal for a girl to kiss a girl. People have been beaten down in everyway [sic] and killed because they cared about liberation and that's a big [. . .] deal" (Team Dresch 1996). Team Dresch's songs do not ignore homophobia, but they deliberately move past a preoccupation with the lesbian community's relation to patriarchy and create new spaces for young women to explore important dimensions of their lives. In the same liner notes Wilson—currently of dykecore band The Butchies—explains that the song "I'm Illegal" is about how she and her girlfriend were asked to leave bars because of their displays of affection. Such lines as "I'm afraid to walk down the street holding hands with my girlfriend" and "sometimes I even think I'm doing something wrong, make me feel safe," express the experiences and the struggles of many lesbians. Wilson directly addresses her young female audience and adopts a mentor's role in her communication with them. Through lyrics and liner notes Wilson, like many dykecore musicians, sets out to inspire and to comfort her fans. Indeed, the *Captain My Captain* cover features letters from young fans discovering their sexual identities. In this way the lesbian punk rock scene makes sure to acknowledge the struggles involved in the history of the lesbian community, and it also takes on the responsibility of educating young fans through discussions on sex and gender. This represents an empowering shift for all queer-identified youth, most especially because it reveals the lifestyle alternatives that arise when a community challenges traditional gender stereotypes.

Independent record label Mr. Lady, begun in 1996 by dykecore musician Kaia Wilson and feminist scholar and filmmaker Tammy Rae Carland, demonstrates that the lesbian punk subculture has also made efforts to offer women the opportunities they are less likely to find with major labels. When Carland and Wilson created the Mr. Lady label and video distributor in Greencastle, Indiana, they insisted it was a "community service, not just a business" (Grossman 1). The label—which shared 50 percent of its profits with its artists—aimed to remedy the failure of the entertainment industry to dedicate financial and other resources to lesbian feminist issues. Carland recalls that "we decided that we needed a label like this. See, I got involved in the punk scene in the early '80s in Boston, and it wasn't very queer friendly or girl-friendly. For all punk's liberal meanderings, it was an entirely homophobic space" (qtd. in White 1). The label put out new releases from The Butchies, Le Tigre, and Vaginal Cream Davis, and established itself within the young lesbian and (male) homocore queer communities through music compilations. For example, the collection *Calling All Kings and Queens* features tracks from Indigo Girl Amy Ray, Sleater-Kinney, The Butchies, and queer cabaret artists (White 1). Mr. Lady also sponsored "speak-outs" across the United States, and, according to Carland and Wilson, many gay teens, looking for advice and support on sexual identity, called and sent e-mails. The two relocated the label to California in 2003 and continued to work on all aspects of music production from pressing CDs to designing album covers and promoting releases, until it folded in 2004. Like the Olivia Records collective in the 1970s, Mr. Lady brought a lesbian-feminist sensibility to current independent music making, and it also provided a valuable network of resources for teens. Unlike the separatist lesbian feminist artists, however, Mr. Lady musicians, as part of a larger punk rock subculture, collaborated with people in the broader punk community through independent labels like Olympia's Kill Rock Stars and K Records.

DYKECORE AS QUEER MUSIC SUBCULTURE

Kaia Wilson's description of her sound as "emo-core," or "Husker Du done the dyke way" (Schade 4), demonstrates the extent to which dykecore situates itself within broader punk rock subculture. In the 1990s the style was able to forge strong connections with various offshoots of the subculture through local communities and self-published fanzine networks. The queercore musical movement (also known as "homocore") which is considered by some to contain dykecore music, is described by D. Robert DeChaine as "a queer(ed) punk rock," but also as "queer identity politics with punk rock as its vehicle" (3). It is mainly represented by gay male bands such as Pansy Division and Limpwrist. The queercore music style is closely associated with the community of young punks who, beginning in the mid-1980s, self-published zines dealing with issues faced by gay men and lesbian women. Donna Dresch of Team Dresch was involved with the gay fanzine *Homocore* in the early 1990s and brought dykecore to a wider audience through the publication. However, while dykecore is closely related to queercore musically, and while both subcultures fight for an end to homophobia in both punk and mainstream society, dykecore differentiates itself from queercore through a heavy focus on feminism and, in some cases, separatist feminist politics. Even as a queer youth subculture, dykecore differs from the broader category of queercore because it retains some elements of lesbian feminism, and represents a space in which issues common to lesbian feminism are still debated. As Annamarie Jagose asserts, while there is tension between "queer" and "lesbian feminist," it is impossible to maintain that queer culture represents a clean break with history (75). Dykecore participants tend to embrace the concept of queer identity because it questions gender identities as natural constructs, but there is a continuity between lesbian feminism and this subculture as it retains feminism as one of its main tenets. This tendency does not exist within the larger genre of queercore.

A defining characteristic of any musical subculture is its artists' political and personal interaction with their audience. Dykecore musicians actively engage their fans and urge them to examine issues related to being gay, to negotiate the relationship between the queer experience and society at large and ultimately to move beyond patriarchy to a place safe for the female experience of desire, love, and relationships. Bands have used music making and a variety of media to educate and facilitate the experience of the young lesbian woman in a male-dominated culture. In turn, the bands are supported by a loyal following, and receive letters and critical feedback from young fans. Jessica Ocasio, who maintains the website Girlpunk.net—a showcase for female-fronted punk bands—says that "the support among [dykecore] bands is probably the strongest in the entire music scene" (qtd. in Pike 1). Indeed, Toastacia Boyd of the now-defunct lesbian-identified band the Automaticans recalls that "we had a built-in crowd wherever we went. [. . .] People would come to our shows without even hearing us first because we were on the Chainsaw label [known for its dykecore acts]" (qtd. in Pike 1). In creating a reciprocal relationship between bands and their fans—who are often themselves artists and activists within the same community—these groups are following in the footsteps of the close-knit lesbian folk scene. They are also demonstrating that the do-it-yourself (DIY) feminist political activism found in riot grrrl subculture of the 1990s is still alive and well.

CONTEXTS: PUNK ROCK AND RIOT GRRRL

The riot grrrl musical subculture has been examined by many music scholars over the past decade, so much so that it has become one of the best-known music histories in academia. In fact, the subculture's origin story has taken on a mythical quality to rival that of the birth of the rockabilly music style in the 1950s. As scholars have argued, riot grrrl is an important development in popular music and in feminist and gender politics as well. Riot grrrl provides the historical and political context for the majority of current feminist bands. As the legend goes, at the beginning of the 1990s, young women in Olympia, Washington, and Washington, DC, began speaking out against the male-dominated nature of the punk rock community. They formed feminist bands whose music aggressively and intelligently challenged female stereotypes. They advocated awareness of gender politics and sexual discrimination, intimidation and assault, and created a subculture reflecting the feminist message that they quickly spread across punk scenes in North America and Europe.

As part of the genesis of riot grrrl, young women, both straight and gay, became united in making and circulating fanzines that expressed their frustrations at the male dominance of punk subcultures. As a result, riot grrrl pioneer Kathleen Hanna met dykecore pioneer and zinester Donna Dresch in the early 1990s through each others' self-publications. Zines were just one of the connections between queer female punks and riot grrrls, who often were part of the same punk rock communities. Indeed, it is in many ways impossible to separate dykecore and riot grrrl because both groups were determined to stimulate discussion on gender and sexuality, homophobia and sexism within the punk community.

Mary Celeste Kearney has suggested that the media's refusal to acknowledge any association between lesbian feminism, dykecore punk, and riot grrrl is a somewhat obvious attempt to distance the "radical female youth subculture [of riot grrrl] from the taint of homosexuality" (222). True, a 1992 *L.A. Weekly* article on riot grrrl and zines did not address the fact that most riot grrrls were also involved in the queer punk community. This oversight is especially important since Kathleen Hanna insists she urged the author to also interview her friend Donna Dresch (Juno 88). The general failure to draw connections between the different punk subcultures has made it difficult to gain an understanding of just how closely the various punk scenes are interconnected and how much overlap there exists among the communities. Indeed, the community surrounding lesbian feminist punk makes explicit attempts to defy gender boundaries, and for this reason has made the connections between feminism and queer politics impossible to overlook.

DYKECORE AND THE POPULAR MEDIA

The riot grrrl style offered a highly marketable and less controversial message of "girl power" that could easily be transformed into merchandise.[1] The music emerging from dykecore, on the other hand, was more of a challenge to the mainstream. In the mid-1990s, while watered-down versions of the riot grrrl message (and to a lesser extent the actual music) were being brightly packaged for young girls, a dubious version of lesbianism was being addressed in popular culture through

the phenomenon Danae Clark has termed the "commodification of
lesbians" (qtd. in Hennessy 721). Clark suggests that the "intensified
marketing" of lesbian images was "less indicative of a growing acceptance of homosexuality than of capitalism's appropriation of gay 'styles'
for mainstream audiences" (721). In the liner notes to the 1996 Team
Dresch album, Kaia Wilson pointed to this fantastical appropriation of
"gayness" when she asked fans not to "let the media make you think
that homosexuality was invented last night just to sell magazines" (3).
Like many in the lesbian and gay communities, Wilson was alarmed by
the fact that while homosexuality was "in fashion," many important
elements of gay culture were being overlooked, even ignored. During
this time, the innovative music being produced by dykecore bands
remained under the radar of the popular media, this despite its close
connection—in sound and politics—to riot grrrl. In the end, just as
commercial interest in riot grrrl did not go much beyond the flashy
slogans that appealed to a ripe market of "teenyboppers," the commercial interest in lesbianism tended not to stretch far beyond the male
fantasy ideal. As a result, the subculture of lesbian punk rock did not
reach the mainstream, and the queer-positive stance of riot grrrl subculture was ignored by the popular media. In this way, important and
groundbreaking aspects of two young female music subcultures, namely
their inclusivity and their support for queer youth, were overlooked.

Since 2002, Olympia, Washington, has hosted Homo A Go Go, a
queer music, art, film, spoken-word, and radical activist festival that is
part of a nonprofit organization, Queer Arts in Action. The biennial
event continues in the tradition of other music festivals including Ladyfest,
Yoyo a Go Go, and the International Pop Underground Convention.
These events are aimed at "providing a venue for underground, DIY
and independent artists" ("About HAGG"). While the Homo A Go Go
festival situates itself within the broader North American independent
music community, and more specifically within the Olympia scene, it
places emphasis on fostering a welcoming community for queer-
identified youth who remain outside of popular culture. Organizers
express their wish to create their "own cultural landscape and community": "The community we hope to create overlaps yet exists outside
of the mainstream queer community and the independent music/arts
community. We hope to encourage anti-war, anti-capitalist, anti-racist,
anti-sexist [and] anti-classist ideals while providing a venue for non-
mainstream queer culture" ("About HAGG"). Events like Homo A Go
Go demonstrate a conscious effort within the queer punk rock scene

to remain outside a mainstream culture they and many others see as misrepresenting or overlooking queer subculture. Therefore, while mainstream perceptions of queer youth subcultures may be skewed or even nonexistent, dykecore communities have forged their own connections with other underground political subcultures—the indie and punk music communities, for example—and in so doing are creating cultural networks and support systems beneath the surface of popular culture.

FEMINISM AND DYKECORE SUBCULTURE

While dykecore follows in the tradition of lesbian feminist folk music, which emerged out of lesbian feminism, some vital differences exist between the two subcultures. While the notion that biological sex and gender identity are one and the same is commonly associated with second wave feminism, Judith Butler's exploration of the social construction of gender identity has led many of the younger generation to reject gender dichotomies that characterize lesbian feminism and to embrace the concept of gender variance related to queer cultures. The resulting tension is apparent in the controversies that have sprung up over the Michigan Womyn's Music Festival. The festival, established in 1976 by a radical separatist feminist group, has created a venue for women to discuss the politics of their lives and what it means to be female. Each August a temporary "village" is construction on some 650 acres in Walhalla, Michigan. It becomes the site for hundreds of workshops, over forty musical performances, a film festival, and is a showcase for hundreds of artisans and their crafts. Organizers describe the event as "a female generated alternative culture where [women] envision the world [they] want to live in," and as a "radical, chaotic, inspirational, exhausting and magnificent" experience providing "fertile ground for controversies, transformations, and many amazing personal and community revelations" ("General Festival Information").

In 1994, the members of San Francisco's veteran all-lesbian band Tribe 8 performed at the Michigan Womyn's Music Festival as the first punk act. Typically, the line-up is composed of folk, "world beat," and pop acts associated with the womyn's music scene. During their performance Tribe 8 unapologetically and aggressively explored traditionally taboo aspects of female relationships including S/M and incest, as well as the question of abusive lesbian relationships. While they come from a strongly feminist perspective, the band members pride themselves on "pushing the boundaries of lesbian feminist music and politics"

(McDonnell 1). They write songs that challenge what it means to be a feminist and they strive to expand the definitions of gender and sexuality. The band faced much apprehension leading up to their performance. Some attendees flew a banner declaring "Tribe 8 promotes violence against women" (Juno 40). There was also much discussion on how the crowd of "grey-haired women, Midwestern couples in purple t-shirts, and women's music pioneer[s] like Alix Dobkins" would react to the band's infamous mid-performance enactment of a castration using a sex toy (McDonnell 1). In the end, their performance was well received and they paved the way for more lesbian punk acts at Michigan. However, Tribe 8 and their younger feminist music fans were not in the least surprised by some continuing protest against their appearance at the festival: they believed that the festival presents idealized and "limited images of feminist behaviour" (McDonnell 2). As Tribe 8 sees it, the audience tends to shy away from punk rock in favor of the softer folk music with its lyrics on the idealistic potential of female community and relationships.

Tribe 8's 1994 performance was interpreted by some women at the Michigan Womyn's Festival as overly aggressive, violent, and disruptive to the safe environment festival organizers have tried to nurture. Singer Lynn Breedlove maintains that their aggression does not put them into the same category as male performers: "A lot of people say, 'You're just trying to be like men,' or 'You are just like men,' or 'You're being just like the patriarchy' [. . .]. I'm a woman, and I feel aggro, and that means that my aggression is not male" (Juno 41). Tribe 8's difficulty at fitting into the Michigan Womyn's Festival's softer, less aggressive atmosphere points to a deeper issue: a generational divide between feminisms. At the root of this gap, however, is the dykecore criticism of what they see as second wave radical feminism's adherence to the idea that there is a clear-cut, historical, or natural difference between men and women. Indeed, the essentialist viewpoint of radical second wave feminism has been increasingly challenged with the integration of queer politics into feminism that characterizes many dykecore participants. Lynn Breedlove expresses her frustration at being criticized for demonstrating her power on stage "like a man": "women having power are not being like men. Women having power are women having power" (Juno 41).

For over a decade, the festival has been the focus of another controversy involving younger women. This controversy has caused a rift within the lesbian punk rock community as well. In 1991, the event's admission policy was altered to include a "womyn-born women only" clause after attendee Nancy Burkholder and a friend were forcibly evicted from the site. As the now-famous story goes, during a workshop, Burkholder identified herself as transgendered[2] (Van Gelder and Brandt 1). The festival's trans-exclusionary policy maintains that as a designated women's space, participants must have lived their lives as women "both physically and psychologically" (1). For example, an individual born with male sex organs who has identified as a woman for her entire life but has not had a sex-change procedure is barred from the festival. Similarly, a female-born individual identifying as a man is also refused entry. In a 1997 interview, festival cocreator Lisa Vogel said that transsexual and transgendered individuals would be welcome on festival grounds "over [her] dead womyn-born body" (qtd. in Van Gelder and Brandt 1). She declared that the festival staff would not become "gender police" by demanding gender checks. Rather, they would operate on a "don't ask, don't tell" basis (1). In other words, transsexual and transgendered women may attend so long as they are not vocal about their identities. Since the first expulsion, groups calling themselves "gender activists" have camped on public property across from the festival grounds to hold Camp Trans, an annual cooperative effort to educate the Michigan festival's attendees about what they call the "inconsistent application of a discriminatory policy" ("Eight Young Attendees" 1). In 2000, eight Michigan festival attendees identifying themselves as "trans" were ejected from the festival after they disclosed their biological identities to staff. The Michigan festival's decision to ban all transsexual and transgendered women reflects what Lisa Vogel calls her "political and personal feeling of spirit that femaleness is not something that's particularly ambiguous—or created" (Van Gelder and Brandt 1). If Vogel argues that femaleness is not created, and men who identify as woman can never truly be women, she contests the view that gender is socially constructed. By their policies with the sex-gender essentializing assumptions, the Michigan Womyn's Music Festival adheres to the brand of feminism limited by dichotomies and has difficulty addressing transsexual experiences.

The festival's trans-exclusionary policy has become a major point of contention in the dykecore community. Lynn Breedlove of Tribe 8 has pledged support for trans-inclusion, and she has stated that infighting between women is counterproductive:

Whether we're dykes or not, S/M or not, incest survivors or not, been beaten or not, we've all been oppressed by the same system. That's the enemy, not each other. As long as we keep being distracted by that bullshit, which is what they have created—they've created the divisions among us then we're going to be controlled by them. (Juno 39)

In 1999 Kaia Wilson spoke out in support of the trans ban on her record label's Internet community discussion website. Her record label, Mr. Lady, released many bands who played at the festival, and she herself has played the event in recent years with The Butchies. The implications of such a legendary figure supporting the policy were enormous: given Wilson's high profile and her outspoken activism, many were outraged that she aligned herself with a policy that many in the community consider trans-phobic. The fact that the pro–Womyn-only comment came from a woman who in the liner notes of Team Dresch's album *Captain My Captain* described her song "The Council" as being "about feeling unfairly judged within a community where we hope for and encourage solidarity and communication" did not temper the response within the scene. On the Internet message board, fans accused Wilson of denying transsexual people's right to self-identification and described her rationale as intolerant and hateful. However, Wilson maintained that while she supported trans-inclusion in the queer community at large, she did not think that women's space need include transsexual women. The ensuing controversy highlights the fact that the lesbian punk rock community is by no means homogeneous, and that there are networks in place to foster debate within the scene.

In April of 2003, Strap-On.org, an online community that was extremely critical of the Mr. Lady bands for supporting the Michigan Womyn's Festival, reported that Wilson's band, along with label-mate Le Tigre, had pulled out of their commitment to play the festival that summer (Van Gelder and Brandt 1). This development demonstrates how the lesbian punk rock landscape is in constant flux. Artists, it seems, are continually repositioning themselves in the gender debate. Such controversies within the subculture need not be seen in a completely negative light. The constant working-out of issues signals a refusal to commit to what Sandra Harding calls a feminist empiricist view of social structure (240). Instead, the scene makes use of 'standpoint theory' as it takes into account various points of view on the forces at work within and on queer communities (240). The very fact that there exist public venues for such a debate (accessible by all young women with Internet access or ties to the community) means girls are being exposed to complex and important issues.

Indeed, since the controversy began in 1991, Eminism.org has kept an online archive of discussions about the issue. Curious web surfers can access documents and forum discussions, including the completer archived text of the Chainsaw Records message board discussion thread where Kaia Wilson first spoke out in favor of the trans ban in 1999. Also accessible on the archive site is a joint statement by the creators of the Michigan Womyn's Festival addressing the trans issue. Discussion of this issue continues on the Camp Trans main website, as well as on the Strap-on.org online message forum, which provides a secure space for transgendered, transsexual and gender variant people to communicate with each other. Through such resources, young participants have access to the online archives and history pertaining to important developments in the representation of queer-identified people. Most importantly, though, they are able to draw a clear line between earlier debates and controversies and the current actions, such as the annual Camp Trans and multitude of queer cultural events. The online forums create a sense of community and continuity that is valuable to the continued existence of the queer subculture. The fact that these debates center around musicians and musical events speaks to the importance of dykecore music to the community.

Whereas the feminist standpoint represented by Michigan Womyn's Music Festival organizers tends to equate sex with gender and does not take the transsexual predicament to a deeper level of analysis, the lesbian feminist punk rock community has acknowledged the shortcomings of a binary view of gender and has tried to look beyond it. While the staunch supporters of womyn-born-women-only policies see gender identities as clear-cut, many in the lesbian punk rock community take a less rigid approach to identity. This view is reflected in their gender politics. The continuing debate within that scene represents a working-out of what it means to be a woman, and, on the question of gender politics, a certain self-reflexivity. Wilson's ongoing negotiation with the transsexual's place in the community exemplifies these efforts, as do the artistic endeavors of more recent bands such as Le Tigre. Through their multimedia performances and through their aggressively queer-positive lyrics and feminist political activism, Le Tigre blurs the boundaries. Young fans of the bands involved in such controversies are able to take part in debates they would not otherwise have witnessed.

QUEER POLITICS IN DYKECORE SUBCULTURE

The New York City band Le Tigre has made great strides in the punk rock world toward the inclusion of queer-identified people in the subculture. Emerging from the riot grrrl and dykecore communities,

they are dedicated to informing fans about the challenges faced by
young gay, lesbian, bisexual, and transsexual people. Through discussion
and by voicing a variety of opinions on issues such as trans inclusion,
Le Tigre's JD Samson, along with the other band members Kathleen
Hanna and Johanna Fateman, have inspired even more young feminist
fans to explore queer politics. In interviews, on the band's website, in
lyrics, and through gender-bending choreography in Le Tigre's live
performances, they hold frank discussions of androgyny, transsexuality,
and lesbian feminism.

As a film student, Samson became frustrated by the separate theory
of each artistic medium she studied and she was determined to challenge
media boundaries by creating "wall films" that, she says, broke down the
" 'inherent boundaries' of the film medium by forcing the film out of the
projector and onto the walls" ("JD Samson" 2). The wall films—composed of a variety of media including pencil, charcoal, ink, Xerox transfer,
and paint—are what Samson sees as "queer art." They challenge the
traditional media boundaries in art: "I think of it in terms of breaking the
boundaries that one artistic medium can be constrained by" ("JD Samson"
2). Samson brings her concept of "queering art" to Le Tigre, and sees a
parallel between blurring the boundaries of artistic media and challenging the traditional gender binary of male and female.

On the band's website, Samson and Hanna draw deliberate par-
allels between "coming out" as queer and being a survivor of sexual
abuse. The section entitled "Keep on Living" provides fans with information and links to resources that will help a young person who is
"coming out of the closet as a sexual abuse survivor and as queer" (*Le
Tigre World*). The website brings issues of feminism and queer politics
together. While it offers support for young women struggling to come
to grips with their sexuality, it also gives young heterosexual women a
way of understanding the challenges that young queer-identified people
face. In this way, the band is both supporting queer youth and exposing
straight fans to the realities of being queer in an attempt to promote
unity. Le Tigre's song "Fake French" also articulates the band's commitment to challenging gender stereotypes and expresses their inclusive
attitude toward feminism. The lines "I've got a deviant scene" and "I've
got post-binary gender chores" (Le Tigre 2001) demonstrate the band's
awareness of issues related to gender definitions, while the lines "I've
got extensive bibliographies" and "I've got multiple alliances" express
their dedication to an inclusive feminism. The major efforts of Le Tigre
to give young lesbian, gay, transsexual, and bisexual people, as well as

abuse survivors, a stronger voice can be seen in their blurring of the boundaries of feminism and queer politics.

In the end, lesbian punk rock subculture is fertile ground for some of the main projects of queer theory. This involves "not just the questioning of the content of collective identities, but the questioning of the unity, stability, viability and political utility of sexual identities even as they are used and assumed" (Gamson 404). Lesbian punk rock is an example of a subculture that works against the dichotomy of gender while it offers an alternative representation of the female in music. By looking past and by challenging socially constructed notions of gender, dykecore transforms a stereotypically masculine genre into a site of female agency. Within the traditionally male-centered punk rock subculture, dykecore moves past what Esther Leslie describes as the "dialectical imagery" of male/female interaction (116) toward a nuanced perspective that includes various subjectivities: what Haraway refers to as "situated knowledges" (253).

CONCLUSION

The dykecore music community is still going strong and was conceived by women passionate about their own rights and the rights of those who are discriminated against. Like riot grrrl, dykecore and the larger genre of homocore have been seen by the popular media as fleeting trends and, in the late 1990s, were "very quickly regarded as passé" (White 2). However, Tammy Rae Carland challenges this assertion, and in a 2001 interview she maintained that those active within the subculture "weren't necessarily feeling that anything was over. We were just getting started" (qtd. in White 2). Certainly, the fact that for Homo A Go Go 2004, dykecore pioneers Team Dresch reunited for a performance to benefit the Olympia-based Gender Variant Health Project—a nonprofit organization "devoted to health issues and healthcare needs of [people whose] gender identity differs from the gender assigned to [them] based on [their] biological sex" ("About HAGG" 1)—demonstrates that the new spirit of lesbian feminist subculture is thriving.

Deborah L. Siegel has observed that contrary to popular perception, within the past two decades there has been a "remarkable resurgence of grassroots student activism, young feminist conferences, and a host of new or newly revitalized social action organizations and networks led largely by young women" (51). The young women involved in dykecore subculture are vital examples of this resurgence of feminist engagement. Using alternative media such as zines, web pages, message boards, and song lyrics, women in these subcultures have forged new directions in feminist thought. They do so by integrating into discussions of gender and sexuality their own diverse stories of their interactions with mainstream culture, punk subcultures, misogyny, sexual abuse, homophobia, and queer identities. As a result, young artists have revamped feminist theory and activism by making music that challenges the boundaries of performance and politics, second and third wave feminism, and queer politics and feminism. In so doing, they have succeeded in creating a new, exciting brand of feminism that makes the inclusion of queer politics and identity a main priority.

NOTES

1. A yearly summer feminist music festival established in 1976 as a safe space for feminists and lesbian feminists to gather and share cultural activities. In addition to live music performances, the festival features discussion groups, activities, and workshops on feminist-oriented topics.

2. In the late 1990s, the pop music group the Spice Girls embodied the mainstream fascination with the Girl Power trend, which Jennifer Harris describes as "fun tied to conventional definitions of femininity that is often dependent upon consumption." Harris warns that girl power should not be confused with feminism because as "less 'serious' than feminism, Girl Power is playful and does not 'threaten boys.'"

3. The history of the term "transgender" is complex and controversial. As I use it here, "transgender" refers to an identity category and "a sense of belonging to all those who have been excluded from gender identity programmes and denied access to surgery, and to all those who have felt marginalized by heteronormative values and institutions more generally" (Sullivan 95).

WORKS CITED

"About Homo A Go Go [HAGG]." *Homo A Go Go Festival*. 4 June 2004. <http://www.homoagogo.com/2004/about.html>.

Beasley, Chris. *What Is Feminism? An Introduction to Feminist Theory*. London: Sage, 1999.

Bulbeck, Chilla. "Feminism by Any Other Name? Skirting the Generation Debate." *Outskirts: Feminisms Along the Edge*, ed. Delys Bird. Volume 8. May 2001. January 2004. <http://www.chloe.uwa.edu.au/outskirts/archive/volume8.htm>.

Chainsaw Records. Chainsaw Records official website. <http://www.chainsaw.com> 1999. Archived site: <http://www.geocities.com/snarkles/chswmwmf.htm>.

De Laurentis, Teresa. "The Techology of Gender." *Technologies of Gender: Essays on Theory, Film, and Fiction*. Bloomington IN: Indiana University Press, 1987.

DeChaine, D. Robert. "Mapping Subversion: Queercore Music's Playful Discourse of Resistence." *Popular Music and Society* 21, 4 (Winter 1997): 7–31.

"Eight Young Attendees Thrown Out of Michigan Women's Festival." *Camp Trans Online*. Camp Trans website. 14 April 2003. <http://www.camptrans. com>.

Freedman, Estelle B. *No Turning Back: The History of Feminism and the Future of Women*. New York: Ballantine Books, 2002.

Gamson, Joshua. "Must Identity Movements Self-Destruct? A Queer Dilemma." In *Queer Theory and Sociology*, ed. Steven Seidman. Cambridge, MA: Blackwell, 1996.

"General Festival Information." *Michigan Womyn's Music Festival Info*. 14 April 2003. <http://www.michfest.com/General/general112.htm>.

Haraway, Donna. "Situated Knowledges: The Science Question in Feminism and the Privilege of Partial Perspective." In *Feminism and Science*, ed. Evelyn Fox Keller and Helen E. Longino. New York: Oxford University Press, 1996.

Harding, Sandra. "Rethinking Standpoint Epistemology: What Is 'Strong Objectivity?' " In *Feminism and Science*, ed. Evelyn Fox Keller and Helen E. Longino. New York: Oxford University Press, 1996.

Harris, Jennifer. "Betty Friedan's Granddaughters." In *Turbo Chicks: Talking Young Feminisms*, ed. Lara Karaian, Lisa Bryn Rundle, and Allyson Mitchell. Toronto: Sumach Press, 2001.

Jagose, Annamarie. *Queer Theory: An Introduction*. New York: New York University Press, 1996.

"JD Samson." Interview. *Voiceout*. Issue 1. *Solanas Online*. 2002. 20 November 2003. <http://www.solanasonline.com/html>.

Juno, Andrea, ed. *Angry Women in Rock*. Vol. 1. New York: Juno Books, 1996.

Kearney, Mary Celeste. "The Missing Links: Riot Grrrl—Feminism—Lesbian Culture." In *Sexing the Groove: Popular Music and Gender*, ed. Sheila Whitely. New York: Routledge, 1995.

Leslie, Esther. "Space and West End Girls: Walter Benjamin versus Cultural Studies." *New Formations*. 38: 110–124.

"Le Tigre." *Chicks on Speed Records* website. 6 May 2003. <http:// chicksonspeedrecords.com/site2/display/index.php?what=artist&artist_id =7.html>.

Le Tigre World. Le Tigre official website. <http://www.letigreworld.com>.

Longhurst, Brian. *Popular Music and Society*. Cambridge, UK: Polity Press, 1995.

Lont, C. M. *Between Rock and a Hard Place: A Model of Subcultural Persistence and Women's Music*. Diss. University of Iowa, 1984. Ann Arbor: UMI, 1985. 8428265.

McClary, Susan. *Feminine Endings: Music, Gender, and Sexuality*. Minneapolis: University of Minnesota Press, 1994.

McDonnell, Evelyn. "Queer Punk Meets Womyn's Music." *Ms.* Arlington: November 1994. 5, 3: 78–83.

McRobbie, Angela. *Feminism and Youth Subculture.* New York: Routledge, 2000.

"Michigan/Trans Controversy Archive." Eminism.org. 19 May 2006. <http://eminism.org/michigan/documents.html>.

Namaste, Ki. "The Politics of Inside/Out: Queer Theory, Poststucturalism, and a Sociological Approach to Sexuality." In *Queer Theory and Sociology*, ed. Steven Seidman. Cambridge, MA: Blackwell, 1996.

Pike, Laurie. "Three Chords and a Rolodex." *The Advocate.* 16 Apr. 2002: Issue 861. 60–61.

QueerKit. Official QueerKit website. May 2006. <http://www.queerkit.org/aboutus.php>.

Salih, Sarah. *Judith Butler.* New York: Routledge, 2002.

Siegel, Deborah L. "The Legacy of the Personal: Generating Theory in Feminism's Third Wave." *Hypatia* 12, 3. (Summer 1997): 47–75.

Strap-on.org. 31 May 2006. <http://p083.ezboard.com/bpseudochainsaw.htm>.

Sullivan, Nikki. *A Critical Introduction to Queer Theory.* Ediburgh: Edinburgh University Press, 2003.

The Butchies Tour Bands, Record Labels, Magazines, and Organizations. The Butchies band website. <http://www.thebutchies.com/links.htm>.

Van Gelder and Brandt, eds. *The Girls Next Door: Into the Heart of Lesbian America.* 1996. 12 April 2003. <www.strap-on.org/mwmf/policy.html>.

White, Dave. "A Home for Homocore." *The Advocate.* Issue 840. 19 June 2001: 105–107.

Discography

The Butchies. *Are We Not Femme?* Durham, NC: Mr. Lady Records, 1998.

Le Tigre. *Le Tigre.* Durham, NC: Mr. Lady Records, 1999.

Le Tigre. *Feminist Sweepstakes.* Durham, NC: Mr. Lady Records, 2001.

Team Dresch. *Personal Best.* Portland, OR: Chainsaw and Candy Ass Records, 1994.

Team Dresch. *Captain My Captain.* Portland, OR: Chainsaw and Candy Ass Records, 1996.

CHAPTER 3

REDEFINING REALITIES THROUGH SELF-REPRESENTATIONAL PERFORMANCE

Jama Shelton

The quality of light by which we scrutinize our lives has direct bearing upon the product which we live, and upon the changes which we hope to bring about through those lives.

—Audre Lorde, "Poetry is Not a Luxury"

When given the freedom, queer youth have the ability to create their own cultural practices and to alter the ways in which they are conceptualized by people and institutions. It is important that they are provided a means through which they can develop a language of their own and are given space in which they can join with other youth in the articulation of identities. Self-representational performance is one means through which queer young people may begin to develop and utilize languages of their own, focusing and strengthening their unique voices. When the goal of creation is self-representation, that voice is sharpened and clarified in order to reflect personal experiences and desires. These experiences and desires, specifically for queer youth, are rarely included in mass media representations or within dominant cultural theory and practice. Through the creation of self-representational performance pieces, a power shift occurs in which queer young people become the authors of their own lives and the creators of their own culture. Creating work that is self-representational removes the necessity to identify with pre-existing, often inaccurate portrayals of young people. Whereas mainstream media and other institutions representing dominant culture accentuate the need for queer young people to adapt to heteronormative society, *Turned Up Volume*, a national video/performance residency project, seeks to bring queer youth voices and desires to the forefront in order to challenge already existing models of sexuality, gender, desire, politicism, and conformity.

Queer young people continue to be a marginalized group in American society, denied public language with which to articulate their experiences, to name themselves, and to frame their needs. It is imperative that queer young people are provided the tools with which they can explore and express themselves in a manner that is consistent with their subjective and collective desires and are also offered safe spaces in which to do so. A safe space is a neutral meeting ground where individuals are allowed and encouraged to present multiple aspects of themselves, free from judgment and emotional and physical harm. This type of space is created through collective decision making around ground rules, in which participants specify the type of language and/ or behaviors that will be used there. In a sense, those present are creating democratic modes of communication that will enhance their personal and social powers and freedoms. Through safe spaces in which they can explore and define themselves, articulating their identities openly, outwardly, and publicly, queer youth have the potential to become an empowered and community-minded group of young people. *Turned Up Volume* is an example of one such space, created through the efforts of youth participants, artists, social workers, community volunteers, and institutions. As a practice-based youth project geared toward self-representation and community development, young people were given value as artistic collaborators and authorities on their programmatic needs. As a result, the project was successful in meeting the needs and expectations of the young people involved. The individual and collective benefits of creating an artistically driven youth-friendly space will become evident in the following account of the project.

Turned Up Volume (TUV) is a video/performance residency project for queer young people that video artist/social services provider Barbara M. Bickart has directed at DiverseWorks Artspace in Houston, Texas, since 1999. I have been the assistant director for this project since its inception. For the past five years, we have worked with young people from a Houston-based LGBTQ youth service organization, the New York City Lesbian, Gay, Bisexual, and Transgender Community Center and DiverseWorks Artspace. *TUV* residencies take place over a ten to fourteen day period. The residency consists of group-building exercises, writing assignments, movement and performance exercises, and instruction on composition, shooting, and editing digital video. The final product is a full-length, multimedia performance involving all participants, including live performance and their completed video shorts. Following the performances, the audience is invited to participate in a panel discussion with the participants and directors. It should be noted that the majority of audience members stay for the post-show discussion, and we have rarely had time to address all of the questions and comments from the audience.

DECONSTRUCTING MEDIA/RECONSTRUCTING IDENTITY

Fliegel states that adolescents search for identity as much as they seek an environment in which they can articulate their identity. Rothenberg suggests that the developmental tasks and psychological and biological conditions of adolescence give rise to creativity, and that turning to creative work as a means of examining and resolving issues of identity is a fundamental feature of the adolescent phase. *TUV* provides a space in which these things are possible. Unlike other environments that may require young people to hide parts of themselves in order to be accepted, *TUV* works to support the whole person and the many ways in which one person identifies. Material is generated during the residency as the participants work collaboratively and intensively exploring the intricacies of what it means to be a queer young person living in America. Participants ask the following questions, from the perspective of an American, and from the perspective of a queer person: What do I fear (as an American, as a queer person)? What do I expect? What do I value? What do I dislike? What do I need? What is my privilege? In what ways am I discriminated against? In a country of contradictions, the combination of queerness and Americanness is complex. The two identities don't fit easily together. Participants analyze the complex relationship of living in a country in which part of who they are is considered by some to be un-American; a country in which the president advocates for an amendment to the constitution to specifically deny them the right to marry; a country in which sodomy laws specific

to same-sex couples were in existence until the year 2003. Messages
such as these from the government, reinforced by many religions and
schools, and institutions such as the Boy Scouts of America, directly and
indirectly tell queer people that they are second-class citizens and that
their way of life is not valid. Many participants expressed the desire to
dissociate from their American identities, resulting from the rejection
they feel from American society. They often did not feel pride in their
identity as Americans. Likewise, it was difficult for them to feel pride
in their queer identities when they had been taught it was unnatural
and undesirable to be queer. Goldstein states that a primary concern of
queer adolescents is the awareness of their membership in a stigmatized
and marginalized group, and that when individuals learn at an early age
that they are a part of a stigmatized group, the development of an
affirmative sense of identity is more difficult. An affirmative sense of
identity is one in which a person feels safe, nurtured, and recognized:
"It is very difficult to grow up with a positive self-image when one's
identity carries a stigma. People who are unable to conform to the
standards society calls normal are disqualified from full acceptance and
are, therefore, stigmatized" (Hunter and Schaecher 1990: 300, qtd. in
Appleby and Anastas). Examining this reality is the first layer of exploration in the art-making process of the *TUV* residencies.

In addition to examining their queer and American identities,
issues surrounding race, gender, class, sexuality, and the ways in which
they intersect and overlap are explored. Participants in *TUV* come from
various socioeconomic backgrounds, races, and ethnic groups. This
complicates their experiences as Americans and as queer people. Acknowledging and examining these diverse experiences create a dialogue
and a level of understanding that encompasses all the "isms" that directly affect their interactions with the world. Not only do they develop a better understanding of where they fit on the spectrum of class,
race, sexuality, and gender, they also begin to deconstruct their assumptions and judgments concerning those whose experiences differ from
their own. I have witnessed queer young people participate in discussions about specific cultural practices, finding the commonalities and
acknowledging the differences in growing up in Hispanic, African
American, Caribbean, and white households. They analyze the ways in
which culture plays a role in their identification as queer people, and
the implications of being queer in their familial groups and ethnic
communities. They discuss what it's like growing up dependent on food
stamps, living in urban communities and suburban communities, iden-

tifying as male, female, or anywhere on the spectrum of gender. Young people whose only commonality is their identification as queer people come together to understand one another, to understand their world, and to push through the limits imposed on them by discriminatory practices. Through this reflexive and critical process, they learn to celebrate their differences. They learn to work beyond and through their personal histories as they build an awareness of society's perception of difference as otherness. They join around their experiences as "other" and create a community of inclusion in which each has his/her own individual niche and where each voice is valued. When queer young people begin to appreciate and feel pride in their uniqueness, they no longer accept the position of less than. Being validated and accepted cultivates in them the strength to move further away from the margins. When queer young people feel confident and comfortable with who they are, they are more likely to actively speak out and act against oppression and injustice. They become creatively mobilized. They become agents of change: "Young people need to become critical agents able to recognize, appropriate, and transform how dominant power works on and through them [. . .]. They need a pedagogy that provides the basis for improvisation and responsible resistance" (Giroux, n.d., qtd. in Ashworth and Jensen 12).

The *TUV* residencies provide a basis for responsible resistance through creating opportunities for queer young people to make video/performance work that communicates how they feel and what they need, as individuals and as members of a marginalized community existing in American society. Art has long been utilized in this way, as a tool for social change. Colleen Jennings-Roggensack, former president of the Association of Performing Arts Presenters, has said, "Art is an ongoing notion which commands, 'I am here, I am present, recognize me' " (Cannon). The first step in making social change is recognizing that change needs to happen. Once that is done, a dialogue can be created and different perspectives can be presented. This is what happens through *TUV* residencies. First, participants examine who they are, where they fit (or don't fit) in the larger society, acknowledging the ways in which they are marginalized. The next step is creating video/performance work that articulates their perspectives and presents it to a broader community, who either share and support that perspective or are seeing it then for the first time. This creates a presence and a dialogue that continues long after the performance ends. Implicit in this dialogue is the opportunity for education and activism.

TUV is effective in creating dialogues within the communities of people who experience it. The primary reason for this success is because the voices heard are coming directly from their sources. Participants in *TUV* do not rely on manufactured media images. Rather, the work they create is self-representational, meaning that it is their own unique expression of themselves rather than character-based fiction. This expression is multilayered, going beyond stereotypes, societal expectations, and imposed ideals. Participants are given the flexibility to formulate their own opinions about issues that may have previously been presented to them as black and white. For example, many of the young people we meet come to us with the internalized belief that they are unworthy. Often they have never been told that their queer identity is okay. Adolescents take cues from their environments and learn from institutions and people in power. Without the opportunity to freely and safely conduct self-exploration and self-representation in a nonjudgmental setting, queer adolescents are more likely to succumb to the reductive one-dimensional images of queer people handed out by media groups, religious organizations, and governing bodies.

Representations of queer people in mainstream media construct a narrow range of socially acceptable roles. These normative roles are caricatures, fragments of the better-developed characters of their heterosexual counterparts. Queer characters are funny, often single, and asexual. Queer women are very rarely presented, and queer people of color are nonexistent. *Queer Eye for the Straight Guy* has perfected the reduction of gay men to finely groomed interior designers, hair stylists, and experts in the kitchen. And, ironically, they are utilizing their expertise toward the greater goal of helping the guy get the girl. Even *Will & Grace* is presented in a heteronormative way—Will and Grace set up house together and are interdependent like a married couple would be. While these shows have gained popularity and have been long running (a surprise post-*Ellen*, which rapidly went off the air following the main character's disclosure of her sexuality), they do not provide inclusive and dynamic representation of queer people. It can be argued that all characters on prime time television are inaccurate caricatures of the groups they represent, regardless of their sexual identity. However, heterosexual characters range in age, relationship status, profession, class, and gender (variation in race is practically nonexistent). Heterosexual characters freely discuss their sex lives, are often caught in bed with a lover, and their relationships tend to be the focus of the shows they inhabit. The heterosexual relationship in *Will & Grace* is the one around which the show revolves. True, the show does address the friendship of two gay men, Will and Jack. However, the presence of two gay male leading characters can only be represented as a friendship. Furthermore, both men fit into stock characterizations of gay male sexuality; one is egocentric and materialistic while the other is the court jester or the effeminate gay clown. These are the reasons the show is palatable to the larger public. It can be argued that the groundbreaking wave of queer visibility in mainstream media is a step in the right direction. What it does, though, is teach the general public to tolerate gay people, constructing and reinforcing the roles that they can be tolerated in. Toleration is a positive thing when compared to condemnation, but not when acceptance and equality are goals. The reality is that it continues to be acceptable to openly demean and ignore queerness in mainstream media, and the majority of Americans are strongly influenced by the values depicted in mainstream media.

When asked how they see themselves in mainstream media, participants in *TUV* said simply that they do not see themselves there at all. There is very little, if any, representation of queer young people. Judging solely by what is portrayed on prime time television, all queer people are single white men nearing their fortieth birthdays, with an occasional appearance by their very masculine lesbian friend or a beefy bodybuilder cruising the locker room for a one-night stand. Variation of this form is a rare occurrence. Queer young people often find themselves represented by the media in ways that are shame based, disempowering, and detrimental to the development of a strong identity formation of which they can be proud. For some, gay and straight alike, mass media representation is their introduction to and only exposure to queer people. It directly affects queer young people who are searching for someone with whom they can identify. Queer young people deserve enriching representations of queer people and of queer culture.

Gay and lesbian identities in mass media are normalized and tucked neatly into mainstream culture. They exist within a framework that is heterofriendly and nonthreatening to the majority. They are accepted only if they fit into pre-existing structures of gender, sexuality, achievement, and the pursuit of the "American Dream." In order to "queer" these representations, they would have to include a much broader account of gender expression, sexual experimentation, family structure, and political dissonance. Each portrayal of gay and lesbian people in mass media affirms a system of binary gender, monogamous relationships, materialism, and conformity to already existing models of family and success. It teaches that gay people can have a place in the world as long as they are focused on and working toward similar things as their heterosexual counterparts. It does not accurately represent the reality of queer lives, nor does it make an attempt to do so.

In *TUV* residencies, there is much discussion around the word "queer." The term is used to describe something or someone who does not follow the constraints of dominant culture and who does not wish to conform to those constraints in order to gain entry into the dominant culture. Rather, queer people seek to live out their desires independent of majority approval, actively articulating their own culture that does not rely on or strive for dominant status. Many of the young people participating in *TUV* have echoed this idea, with statements such as "Queer is someone who is not normal, and who wants to be normal?" and "Queer is a word that includes everyone we want it to include—if you're gay or if you just don't want to get married—anyone who doesn't follow the 'rules' can be called queer."

RESPONSIBLE RESISTANCE: *TUV* WORK SAMPLES

The pieces created by *TUV* participants elaborate representations missing from mainstream media. They embody queerness in their honest and complex instances of nonconformity. The following example illustrates that when given artistic tools, queer young people clearly articulate their desires in ways that resist rigid standards of gayness. Larry, a young Hispanic gay man, struggled with finding his place among the previously mentioned stock characters. He did not have an adult role model with whom he could identify. Hispanic people are nearly nonexistent in mainstream media, much less young gay Hispanic men. Larry's creative writing within the *TUV* program centered around wanting to be seen, and on rebelling against the idea that he had to be a well-built, drug experimenting, promiscuous young adult, distorted assumptions that pressured him when he came out. Larry created a satirical animation commenting on the belief that young gay men must adopt those characteristics. In an interactive performance, he instructed audience members on how to be a perfect gay boy. The following is an excerpt from that piece:

"Each person is unique and special in their own way." This is the filth that has been fed to us since our childhood. These thoughts are out of date. Any modern day gay boy can tell you that it is best to conform. The following information will help you become a gay boy that will fit perfectly into your average gay community.

Three types of gay boys:

1. Standard Gay Boy:
This is your average gay boy, commonly known as a "Twink." They range from age 14 to 20 years old and have smooth, lean bodies with 28"–30" sized waists. It is a Twink's own responsibility to get his very own fake ID and drive a Honda Civic. He also must keep up to date with the latest trends in fashion and music, and attend a gay club or bar at least twice a week.

2. Flamer Boy:
A flamer boy is also known as a Queen, and a boy can keep his Queen status up to the ripe old age of 30. Queens usually weigh about 95–120 pounds and their clothing can either be the latest high fashion, or a simple t-shirt with a playful cartoon print. A Queen must be known by everyone in his community, and must also keep up with the latest gossip. Queens are never afraid to be loud or silly. They must always, always be the center of attention.

3. Abercrombie Boy:
Abercrombie Boys are also known as straight acting boys. They don't have to be tops, but they must always keep a high school jock image. They usually wear (you guessed it) Abercrombie and Fitch or American Eagle brand clothes. They also drive trucks or SUV's. It is important to keep a macho image. They don't talk unless they need to and they don't dance unless they're drunk . . . and if they keep their act up and do it right they'll never have to think again.

Review

Basic Do's and Don'ts:
DO . . .
>*Get a fake ID*
>*Keep up with the latest trends*
>*Keep your weight down*
>*Go out at least twice a week*

Be well known in your scene
Take drugs, especially when they're free
DON'T . . .
Talk to ugly people
Waste your time in relationships
Talk to people unless they talk to you first
Seem strange or different, people are watching

Larry conducted the audience in a recitation of the "rules" of fitting into the gay community. His piece was a smart and provocative critique of the ways he felt invisible in the world. The response from the audience was overwhelming.

Video is a productive medium for confronting "isms" because it is the medium most people are consistently exposed to on a daily basis. It is crucial for young people to develop the skills necessary to critically dissect media, and to analyze the ways in which media messages are constructed. In doing so, they can begin to recognize the impact media messages have on the formation of their own ideals, desires, standards, and ethics. They then may become active participants in the creation of their lives. Through examining media and developing a skill set that will enable them to create their own media, they are refusing to allow their thought processes and beliefs to be shaped by someone else. For queer youth, media literacy has a direct impact on their self-concepts and media making is crucial for engaged cultural involvement. Media literacy and media making provide queer young people a way to inventively represent themselves and control their self-image, rather than leaving that power in the hands of the dominant culture. In American culture, media equals power. Therefore, it makes perfect sense for marginalized groups to utilize media as a tool for empowerment. Vitiello reports that her students became empowered by their abilities to deconstruct media, to discuss issues of power in relation to media, and to construct their own realities through the use of media. She further states that through the making and viewing of personal videos people are able to learn about themselves, to lay claim to their lives, and to bring about collective change.

I have witnessed firsthand the empowerment that results when participants in *TUV* have utilized video and performance to define their realities, to lay claim to their lives. Every young person we have worked with has emerged from the residency with an enhanced sense of self and a stronger, more confident voice. Participants have joined one another and found commonalities among myriad experiences, creating community bonds that have driven them to work alongside each other throughout the year in various LGBTQ organizations. They have become critical thinkers, analyzing media images and information before simply digesting them without question, moving on to make their own representations. Most participants have returned year after year, and each year they continue to build their critical thinking skills, their sense of self, and their community-mindedness.

The fact that *TUV* participants return year after year is evidence that queer youth need more spaces and more programs through which they may safely explore and express themselves, where their struggles are not pathologized. A very basic tenet of such programs is trust building. Through creating a nonjudgmental environment in which queer young people can vocally lay claim to their unique experiences in the presence of other young people and adults, they begin to find validity in their own lives and to trust their own voices. From this place, confidence grows. When young people are confident in their voices, they begin to take more risks in expressing themselves and stating their needs and desires. Through *TUV*, young people learn to trust themselves, their peers, and adult members of their community. What results is an increased ability to express themselves outwardly—at their schools, at their jobs, within their families—as agents of change, actively constructing their lives and making a place for themselves in the larger community. The following example is a testament to the power of self-representational performance as a tool for building one's self-concept and sense of personal power.

The first year Rae participated, his words were hardly audible. He never smiled. He was tentative in sharing his work with the group, even though his artistic sensibilities were incredibly well developed for a fifteen year old. His piece told the story of being harassed by a group of kids at his school. His words were difficult to understand and hard to hear. It was challenging for him to be seen and to take up his space on stage, a metaphor for how he felt in his life. Imagine the difficulty in taking to the stage and telling his story when previously, every time he was noticed at school he was ridiculed. Being given permission to tell his story within an environment that encouraged Rae to creatively express his outrage and defiance was vital in promoting his sense of personal power, and the following summer when we returned to Houston to begin the residency, he was transformed. Pinderhughes perceives power to be a critical factor in the functioning of a group, and states that for people to feel they have a certain amount of power to control their own lives is crucial to their mental health and their level of social engagement. Through his participation in the *TUV* residencies, Rae began to feel comfortable and passionately engaged in communicating his narrative. When he spoke, people listened. Not only did they listen, but also they accepted him. This was a new experience for him.

The following year, Rae created a sophisticated multimedia performance piece commenting on the binary gender structure American society unquestionably adopts. When he felt free to express himself without being judged, he began to more closely articulate who he is, in his own unique voice. What emerged was a complex video self-portrait in which Rae alternated imagery of himself standing in front of a urinal with close-ups of himself applying make-up, and a whispered soundtrack repeating variations of the following sentences: "At school, I'm not allowed to use the bathroom. I have to hold it all day." On stage, Rae wore a suit, and delivered a monologue while tying his tie. The monologue discussed the reasons he sometimes dresses as a woman and articulated how he felt doing so. Through this piece, he challenged the audience's notions of masculinity and femininity, while sharing a poignant story of discrimination and communicating a need most people take for granted—a safe place to use the restroom. In addition, by his second year as a *TUV* participant, Rae became more involved in the city's LGBTQ youth organization, serving on advisory boards and speaking more at the meetings. The program director reported that she had witnessed monumental change in Rae since the previous summer, confirming the idea that through self-exploration and expression queer young people become more empowered and more engaged in their communities.

The importance of community mindedness among the queer youth population is twofold. First, the establishment of oneself in a broader community is one of the tasks characteristic of a healthy transition from adolescence to adulthood. Being a part of a community in which a person feels comfortable, accepted, and a sense of belonging is crucial in the development of self-esteem. This is especially important for queer youth, who face difficulties within other communities with which they associate, such as their religious, familial, educational, and/or vocational communities. In addition, when young people are able to identify and take up a role in a community in which they feel comfortable, they become more invested in developing and participating in that community. This provides an active way to transform themselves and foster the conditions for change for future generations of queer young people. There is strength in community, and the more active a community, the more likely they are to be recognized and reckoned with.

Self-empowerment and community building are directly related in the *TUV* residencies. Before a person can identify oneself outwardly as a member of a community, s/he must be able to comfortably identify and accept oneself inwardly as a valuable individual. Through this media project, participants deconstruct shame-based ideas surrounding their queer identities and begin to reject the notion that they must fit themselves into fixed roles of gender and sexuality in order to legitimatize their lives. One participant expressed pride in his gay identity, whereas previously he recognized it as something to be ashamed of and despised. He stated, "*TUV* constantly brings me to embrace, love, and nurture that which has been slandered and used to shame me—my homosexuality." When shame is stripped from one's identity, s/he feels worthy of a voice and claims the power to use that voice. The result is a person who can define oneself accurately and begin to interact with others in an authentic way. Rae is an example of the ways in which *TUV* has enabled young people who have previously been unable to represent who they perceive themselves to be in the context of the larger society to create moving works that communicate their identities and their needs while simultaneously challenging derogatory messages they've received about this aspect of their identity.

Millie's history with *TUV* is a testament to the transformative power of self-representational performance. Over a three-year period, she discovered the power to challenge ideas of normative bodies, relationships, race, and class. Her process, like many others, began with recovering from judgment and the internalization of shame. Millie was eighteen the first summer she participated in *TUV*. She was soft-spoken and self-conscious, refusing to participate in the live performance aspect of the residency. That summer she sat on stage with her back to the audience as her video played. The following year, her face was visible to the audience, but she did not speak. The focus of these two residencies was self-discovery and the articulation of her identity. After being given the opportunity to express herself as an individual, she was then able to examine her role within a larger societal context. She began to analyze and reject aspects of mainstream culture that did not correspond with her identity. Rather than pushing herself to find a place to fit into the mainstream culture, she began to create her own vision of culture that did not mirror normative standards she had previously adopted. She became fearless in her critique of the dominant culture and in her examination of privilege and power. By the end of her third summer as a participant, Millie wrote and performed several bold performance pieces detailing her experiences as a lesbian,

a Hispanic woman, and an American. The following is an excerpt
from one such piece:

> Being greedy, closed off and selfish makes me feel American.
> We will own you, we will do what we please, we will pretend
>   to be free.
> Democracy is a crock of shit.
>
> I am
> female–
> Queer–
> Women
> Vaginas
> Questioning
> Girl who likes girls
> breasts
> nipples
> chemical make up
> Whatever I want
>
> I am having trouble identifying what my privilege is.
> I have the privilege to express myself—but not necessarily
>   sexually.
> To become skinny.
> To become educated.
> To become heard.
>
> What pisses me off??
> Having the opportunity to be white.
> Our ignorance as we consume everything we touch and exploit.
> Don't paste my mouth shut, don't sweep me under your rug.
>
> I am repulsed by our lack of clean untouched places.
> I am repulsed by being for sale . . . body, country, cultural values
> I am repulsed by out need to perpetually build, up and out up
>   and out
>
> What do I fear?
> I fear appearing white
> I fear I have become one of them

I fear being poor, I fear being forgotten
I fear being left behind
I fear my own need to perpetually build, up and out up and out

Millie is currently the peer mentor for *TUV*, and represents the Houston LGBTQ youth population on multiple community boards and organizations. She plans to study film and would like to pursue a career in politics. She was recently featured in the local LGBT magazine's annual "People to Watch" issue. When we first met her, she was a young woman who, like Rae, was not completely comfortable being seen. The transformative power of self-representation is evident through her growth. Her experience demonstrates the effectiveness of performance as a tool for identity formation, empowerment, self-esteem building, community involvement, and cultural development. When asked how the *TUV* residencies have affected her life, Millie said, "I know more and see more and think more; *TUV* has opened endless doors for me."

At the core of *TUV* is the belief that creative self-representation has the power to transform the world in which we live, one person at a time, one community at a time. In creating a safe space for queer young people to explore themselves and providing an artistic medium through which they may articulate their identities, their lives are altered. Further, sharing their works with the public has the power to engage and empower young people in new ways. They are given license to speak, they are listened to by a room full of people, and they become the experts of their own lives. No longer deferring to people or institutions in power for answers or guidelines on the "correct" way of living, they *become* the people in power as they develop a new sense of ownership and pride in their own lives. This is the way in which performance is transformative—both for those who do it and for those who witness it. Participants in performance can learn through their response as spectators or through their artistic experience as performers and creators (Gay and Hanley). By witnessing people who have historically and systemically been marginalized and stigmatized take the stage and become the authors of their own lives, the perceptions of the audience members are altered. Following the *TUV* 2003 performance, a preteen girl stood up in the audience and said, "I don't understand why people hate. My sister is gay and I'm very proud of her and I love her very much." The same evening one of the participants publicly thanked his mother and her partner for their support, calling them down onto the stage. They cried together as they received a standing ovation. The president of the city's LGBT Chamber of Commerce developed a youth membership program; he was so moved by his experience as an audience member. Community businesses and organizations ranging from a catering company to a public school came forward, offering support and services for the queer youth community.

As previously mentioned, the panel discussions following *TUV* performances have consistently exceeded the time allotted them. The conversations that take place there are honest, intimate, and energizing. Adult audience members often compare the young people's work to their own lives. They tell stories about their own experiences as queer young people, some of which were similar and some that were not. Several audience members have told stories of their own coming out processes and attempts to assimilate into mainstream society. Age divisions become irrelevant as audience members and participants share personal accounts of joy and struggle surrounding queer identity. An open dialogue takes place in which adults and young people share information on a level playing field, where the experiences of the participants are valued. Every person present is actively listening and learning, openly questioning in order to gain a deeper understanding of both the participants' lives and their art. What results is an opportunity for the participants to create and represent their own version of queer youth culture, one that is relevant to their lives. Youth speak publicly and educate others, often enlightening audience members and playing an active role in the development of awareness and the opening of minds. Through the sharing of stories, commonalities are identified and bonds are formed, establishing a broader, stronger sense of community. The enrichment of the individuals leads to the empowerment of the community. From this place, the focus of the discussion shifts as ideas are shared about ways to further the visibility and strength of the queer community while continuing to foster and support the voices of its youth.

The impact of *TUV* residencies has been colossal. It is undeniable that engaging queer young people in the process of creating self–representational performance work and engaging audience members in the presentation of that work is an effective method for building an empowered community. It is clear through the previous examples that when given permission to openly explore and express themselves, queer young people emerge with a more complete sense of self and stronger, more confident voices, which will ultimately be used to move queer people away from marginalization and toward equality. Through investing in and cultivating the strength of our young people, we are taking active steps toward social change. *TUV* illustrates the change that occurred among one community of queer people in one city in the United States. If similar opportunities are created for queer young people, the result will be replicated in other locations, and the number of actively empowered and imaginative queer young people will grow exponentially.

I end with inspiring words by Margaret Mead. "Never doubt that a small group of thoughtful, committed citizens can change the world. Indeed, it is the only thing that ever has." Mead's idea became a reality for a small group of queer young people in Houston, Texas. When given the tools for self-expression and performative representation, *TUV* participants became agents of change within the larger community. Through the outward articulation of their identities and desires, they took up their own space and laid claim to their own lives and their own version of culture. They refused to be measured against dominant ideals, and refused to allow others' perceptions to shape their lives, to mold themselves into already existing models of youth sexuality.

In order to continue altering the ways queer youth are represented and perceived in mainstream society, queer youth must be recognized and listened to as representatives of their own experiences. For practical application, this would require creating safe spaces in which queer youth are free from pathologization, regulation, and judgment. When we abandon the assumption that queer youth desire assimilation into the heteronormative world, we will be better able to hear and understand their desires as individuals and as members of a community. This must start as a grassroots effort in the field of queer youth work with the creation of projects that emphasize media literacy and self-representation. These skills play a crucial role in the ability of queer youth to recognize and deconstruct the ways in which mainstream media plays on them and through them, and how to turn that information into action as they create media of their own.

WORKS CITED

Appleby, G. A., and J. W. Anastas. *Not Just a Passing Phase: Social Work with Gay, Lesbian, and Bisexual People*. New York: Columbia University Press, 1999.

Ashworth, J., and A. P. Jensen. "Pedagogy, Process Drama, and Visual Anthropology." *Stage of the Art* Spring (2003): 11–13.

Cannon, L. "Art as an Agent of Social Change: A Conversational Snapshot." Lincoln Center Graduate School, n.d.

Fliegel, L. S. "An Unfound Door: Reconceptualizing Art Therapy as a Community-Linked Treatment." *American Journal of Art Therapy* 38, 3 (2000): 81–89.

Goldstein, E. *Ego Psychology and Social Work Practice.* New York: The Free Press, 1995.

Lorde, A. "Poetry Is Not a Luxury." *Sister Outsider: Essays and Speeches.* Freedom, CA: Crossing Press, 1984.

Mead, M. Institute for Intercultural Studies: Margaret Mead and Gregory Bateson. n.d. 9 January 2005. <http://www.interculturalstudies.org.>.

Pinderhughes, E. "Significance of Culture and Power in the Human Behavior Curriculum." In *Ethnicity and Race: Critical Concepts in Social Work*, ed. C. Jacobs and D. Bowles. Silver Spring, MD: NASW, 1998.

Rothenberg, A. "Creativity in Adolescence." *Psychiatric Clinics of North America* 13, 3 (1990): 415–434.

Vitiello, M. "Echoing Voices: Crossing Boundaries through Personal Videos." *Afterimage* November/December (2001).

CHAPTER 4

MY IDENTITY IS FLUID AS FUCK

TRANSGENDER ZINE WRITERS
CONSTRUCTING THEMSELVES

Jackie Regales

I've concluded that my identity is as fluid as fuck.

—Izz, *the wicked which*, 3

If self-representation in some form is a creative aspect of leaving childhood behind and becoming an adult, then studying how young people
represent themselves seems an obviously fruitful field for those looking
to understand who young people are, who they want to become, and
how they plan to accomplish such a transition. The subject of this study
is a loosely affiliated group of young people who are struggling to make
such transitions on several different cultural fronts. These youth are zine
writers, who self-publish small-circulation magazines within channels
of distributions that cross DIY subcultures, who want to make their
voices heard in alternative public contexts. They are transgendered people
writing themselves into a theoretical discourse dominated by academic
writers, and they are doing it with wit and eloquence, as their own
words will demonstrate throughout this chapter. Within the safe space
of their zines, transgender youth are engaged in an amazing variety of
political and cultural strategies, mostly centering on identity construction,

construction of sexuality, and the culture of queer-identified people in the United States. They are using their zines as a safe space for talking and thinking about sexuality, gender, theory, and performance, and how these issues play out in their lives, relationships, and communities.

The project these writers are engaged in is deeply personal and vitally important in their daily lives. For transgender youth, it is an especially pressing concern that they not be misrepresented or "cut" into smaller "pieces" to prove an academic point, since forcible fragmentation and invisibility in mainstream society confronts and frustrates them. To avoid becoming part of that system, I attempt to include excerpts from the original zine text as often as possible, so that their voices are not only honored and included, but given the foreground in explaining to you, their readers, who they are and how they think about their lives and culture. Page numbers are given whenever I could find them. I have also tried to honor the pronoun choices the writers made for themselves in the issues of their zines that were available to me. The importance of pronouns, proper names, and language is another issue that transgender zine writers have clearly identified as a major concern, and so I either use the traditional pronouns they use for themselves, or when noted, newer pronouns like "hir" and "zhe." Sometimes, no pronouns were used for the writer within the zine, and so I either used the proper names as a guide or avoided pronouns altogether.

Transgender zine writers speak again and again of trying to "make sense" out of themselves and who they are or want to be, and just as often of making sense to others. Micah's rage is directed at those who do not see him the way he is trying to see himself, and that invisibility inhibits the existence he is trying to construct for himself. When Izz speaks of the genders and sexuality that zhe lives, zhe seems to feel the same sense of trying to make something fit in a certain system, a certain pattern:

> Because I've concluded that my identity is fluid as fuck. Some-
> times I feel like a femme fag, sometimes like a butch dyke,
> sometimes like a cocky teenage boy, sometimes like a girly girl.
> And those are only the binaries I inhabit, there are so many
> more feelings I can't yet articulate.

The constructions or identities that Izz seems to alternately in-habit are not only constructions of gender but also of sexuality. Whether to be feminine or masculine, as well as whether to be male or female, is a question transgender zine writers wrestle with in their own articulate ways, but many operate with the cultural toolbox that mainstream American society has allowed them, the system of binaries that Izz identifies when zhe speaks of femme and butch, cocky teenage boys and girly girls. The first step for these writers sometimes is trying to place themselves in a classification system of gender and sexuality that intuitively they know is not made to include people like them but also is the site of cultural acceptance and rewards, providing the initiative to attempt to reside somewhere in that system.

"A HAVEN FOR MISFITS": TRANSGENDER ZINES WITHIN THE ZINE WORLD

Zines have traditionally been a means of expression for people who feel shut out of mainstream society to connect with each other and find a community of like-minded people, whether they are linked by identity, politics, or cultural tastes. In *Notes from Underground*, a landmark text in the scholarly study of zines, Stephen Duncombe finds that zine writers and readers are trying to "form networks and forge communities around diverse identities and interests" (2). Some of the more cohesive and identifiable communities that feature zines at the heart of their communication strategies are science fiction fans and punk rock fans, but a genre of zine known as the "per-zine" or personal zine has flourished in recent decades as a particularly popular style for both readers and writers. Almost every zine I used in my sampling is clearly a per-zine, a zine written by a single author, on extremely personal subjects, attempting to enter a conversation with others who share interests or identities. In *DIY: The Rise of Lo-Fi Culture*, Amy Spencer describes zine writers who use the per-zine form "as a voice with which to explain their situation and a way to turn to others for support" (25). In fact, the writers Spencer studied believed that "the fundamental purpose of zine-making is to reach out to others" (27). The tradition of the personal zine and the strategy of using zines to form support networks shows us partly why many personal zines serve easily as safe spaces for transgender zine writers in which to discuss their thoughts of sexual and gender identities and communities.

As we have seen, zines can be useful tools for those invested in constructing a new and authentic identity that they feel is true to their own experiences. While the ages of zine writers varies from pre-teens to grandmothers, a preponderance of per-zines are written by youth, which is logical in view of youth culture's preoccupation with identity construction. Figuring out who you are and who you want to be is a crucial element of the transition from adolescence to adulthood, and zine writers are especially invested in this process because they realize that their emerging identity will not be welcomed in mainstream culture, by virtue of interests, politics, or ideology. Duncombe found in his extensive survey of zines that those writing "use their zines as a means to assemble the bits and pieces of their lives and interests into a formula that they believe represents *who they really are*," a process that grants their new identity authenticity because they retain control over its construction (37). For most zine writers, the only power they have is "the interpretations they give to the circumstances and conditions that surround them, and the ideals and character traits they possess" (20). Spencer found that "many writers create their zines as a conscious reaction against a consumerist society" (16). The act of writing a zine and trading it for others often involves small sums of money, but it is a rare zine writer who makes a profit after expenses, and those who do risk being deemed a sellout. Rejecting commercial media and embracing the underground press sends a clear message that "you can create your own space" as an alternative to mass-produced culture (16). For marginalized people, cultural power is rare and limited, and thus zines become a crucial tool in their identity construction.

Amy Spencer's work on zines within lo-fi culture shows the evolution of the form and how specific subcultures developed. The practice of trading, rather than asking for money, establishes the zine as a "gift more than a product, as it typically bypasses the profit motive" (15). From the beginning, zines have been the source of personal networks, rather than profit, establishing the subculture's anticonsumerist practices. As zines became part of punk culture, Spencer found, "networks are forged which serve to support not only the zine community, but also activist and artistic endeavors" (27). Zines have always been crucial in forming far-flung networks among individuals who feel isolated for particular subcultural reasons within their geographic locations. In the subcultural worlds of punk and zines, explicitly queer zines began to appear for the first time as well. Partially, this was a reaction to the greater mobilization of gay men for social change and civil rights, but Amy Spencer traces a parallel development in punk, as "the queer zine rapidly evolved and, accompanying the growing numbers of punk individuals in punk music, became a force to be reckoned with in DIY culture" (39). By the late 1980s, with the rise of hardcore music and culture within punk, the terms "homocore" and "queercore" were used to describe the body of gay-themed zines, films, and music that included zines like *Holy Titclamps* and bands like Pansy Division and Team Dresch. The queercore culture was not only aligned with punk dissent against mainstream society, but also the "homogenous" gay culture that had evolved, including "gender segregation and strict codes of dress and behavior" (40). Queercore created a space within punk culture, using many of the same tools and strategies favored by punk and DIY communities for creating an alternative culture outside of mainstream society. In the 1990s, punk culture was questioned and challenged by a movement of riot grrrls, who also developed the "distro," which Spencer found "were staffed by individuals who sometimes didn't even run zines, who simply wanted to 'help the cause' and work towards getting the information out" to other riot grrrls (33). Before distros, most zine readers and writers found zines almost haphazardly, being passed out at a music show or protest or on the racks of the local alternative bookstore.

"THEY TELL ME IN CHINESE THE PRICE OF THREE BANANAS": RACE, ETHNICITY, AND PASSING

While the majority of the zine writers I chose for this essay either identify as white or do not mention their race, several not only discuss their racial or ethnic identities, but connect it to their experiences as a transgendered individual. The most vivid example of this is a passage from Lauren's fourth issue of *Quantify*, though it is important to mention here that Lauren never identifies as transgender, but instead calls herself asexual in this issue of her zine. Nevertheless, her experience with both racial and sexual passing is illustrative of greater concerns for youth who also inhabit identities that are racially and/or sexually ambiguous.

If I keep my mouth shut, I can pass. It always happens when I am shopping. They say "Can I help you, sir?" or they tell me in Chinese the price of three bananas. If I keep my mouth shut, I can pass. If I try to answer back, my trickster façade fades away and they are forced to do a double-take, to peer closer at this incongruous person with the too-high voice & the Staten Island accent. "Oh, I'm sorry, ma'am," they'll reply, or they'll cluck their tongues and rephrase what they were saying English.

If I keep my mouth shut, I can pass. When the clerk asks if he can help me, I look him in the eye, and slowly shake my

head until he walks away. I don't want to shatter the illusion.
In this moment, I remain boy.

If I keep my mouth shut, I can pass.

When the cashier names a price in words I don't understand, I bypass the change in my pocket and silently fumble in
my wallet for a dollar bill. I don't want to shatter the illusion.
In this moment, I remain fully Chinese. Words and voice, language and timbre, they always give me away; but if I keep my
mouth shut, I can pass.

Later in the zine, Lauren discusses her Chinese/Jewish heritage and
growing up "a member of an upwardly-mobile interracial immigrant
family who has always lived in working-class, middle-class and people
of color neighborhoods." Clearly, in this description of her experiences
in public spaces, Lauren experiences a sense of pleasure when she
successfully passes, either as a Chinese-born immigrant or as a boy, and
she is reluctant to destroy the image of herself as both of these identities, possibly because they place her in a known category, identify her
as a known quantity, rather than being "anomalous, androgynous, at
times even amorphous."

Finding a home within Judaism is the main subject of Micah's
zine, which is subtitled "A TRANS JEW ZINE." Micah desperately
wants to find a way to reconcile his identity construction with his
religious and familial heritage. Eventually, Micah wants to make
the medical transition to live in a male body, and compares this to the
Jewish tradition of having a bar mitzvah:

> Some times I think, if I do transition medically, that physical
> adolescence would be the appropriate time for a bar
> mitzvah [. . .]. In some ways, having a bar mitzvah would feel
> like stepping up and taking my place at the gates of gender
> privilege—privilege which I don't and will never have.

Becoming a physical man is linked for Micah with becoming a man in
the religious tradition in which he has grown up. He also connects the
experience of passing as a transsexual to the experience of assimilation
for Jews:

> I am thinking about the term "passing." As a Jew, it means
> assimilation. Passing always means being accepted into a more

dominant group: white, Christian, non-trans, etc. It involves proving that you are not something supposedly inferior.

Also, Micah feels much more anxiety and pain over the question of being accepted within Jewish communities than even being accepted by mainstream societies. He attempts to become a part of a few congregations, but feels a "palpable discomfort" at each one, which is especially "jarring to feel so un-welcome after participating in such a moving shared experience." While Micah feels separate from mainstream society for political and ideological reasons, as do many zine writers, "A betrayal by other Jews feels like an internal organ rupturing when I'm already knocked down." When discussing the bar mitzvah concept and the possibility of his own participation in the ritual, he says, "Any spirituality is about wholeness, healing and honesty. How could I do something sacred, how could I do something in the names of my ancestors without being whole, without being honest?" Identity construction is especially painful and awkward to negotiate when also navigating the tricks and turns of another facet of your identity, such as race or ethnicity, when the differing facets may come into conflict.

"I AM NOT YOUR EDUCATIONAL OPPORTUNITY": INCLUSION AND SUBCULTURES

Transgender zine writers often identify the need for a safe space in which to work out or articulate their experiences as a result of the exclusion or lack of support that they feel from certain subcultures and communities that otherwise they would identify with, if not for their transgender identity. In the third issue of *the wicked which*, Izz writes a letter to "the girl from Louisiana," who appears to be a riot grrrl:

> I am not your educational opportunity. . . Damn you for making me into your hip points, damn you for making me feel wrong . . . You say to yourself *I know this many weirdoes. But they're not weirdoes to me, no, because they are my friends. I am radical, see? I listen to riot grrrl.* Yeah well, me too, kid. This freak riots, dammit, so go fuck your well-intentioned self. This freak is putting hir queer shoulder to the wheel.

Even though Izz recognizes that the girl may seem well intentioned, zhe also recognizes that the girl may be collecting token "weirdoes" in her friendship circles to assure herself that she is a radical, open-minded person, despite the contradiction inherent in seeing these friends as tokens or only as part of who they are. In certain circles, it is considered correct to espouse radical gender politics, or to be allies to queer and transgender people, but transgender zine writers are astute in recognizing that calling a transgendered person your friend does not give you an automatic free pass on gender issues.

The question of how best to become an ally to those who identify as transgender in progressive or radical communities is one that is often symbolized by the debate over the Michigan Womyn's Music Festival (MWMF), a long-running summer festival of music that has clarified its policies in recent years to only include "womyn-born womyn" in the population it welcomes to the festival. Controversy has raged in radical and feminist communities since then over the appropriateness of the policy, the exclusion felt by transgendered women, and the question of supporting bands that continue to play the festival despite what many consider a transphobic policy. Anna of *Getting Louder Everyday* does not appear to identify as transgender, but does identify as queer, and addresses the controversy thus in the third issue of her zine:

> the individuals and bands and record labels that we as feminists, as queer people put on a pedestal should be called on their shit (or their fans need to be called on their shit) if these artists or groups are going to continue to be portrayed as having radical gender politics or as being allies to transgendered people.

In the first issue of *Rock Star with Purses*, Connie addresses the issue from a transwoman's blunt, incisive, and angry perspective:

> Here's another tranny hint for you festies out there: If you fucking go to the fest, wear a shirt, wear a sign, a button, FUCKING SCREAM that all Womyn ARE WOMYN. We are not some masquerading fags, we are not closed into the boundaries of heterosexuality. We are womyn, we are queer, we are straight, we. are. womyn, and the MWMF's exclusionary policy is like the biggest blow to me.

Connie's rage speaks to the idea that marginalized people often expect to find support and understanding in communities of other marginalized people, and the rejection or ostracism they face from those groups may be an even deeper and more painful blow than that they experience from mainstream society.

While the Michigan festival is only one experience, many transgender zine writers seem to echo this experience in different communities or subcultures. Micah of *Tim-Tum* dismisses some of the "members of the 'gay community'—people who claim to be Trans Allies in a political sphere, but who actually know nothing about FTM experience." When speaking of discrimination in healthcare practices that transgendered people often face, he adds, "However, all this is not unconnected to the painful every day stuff, often coming from people 'in the community' who should know better." Micah's disdain for those who identify as queer but make no effort to educate themselves on the particularities of transgender experiences echoes Izz's anger at being made to be someone's "educational opportunity." Just as people of color often speak with anger of having to represent all people of color or answer ridiculous questions from well-meaning white people, transgender zine writers recognize the lack of self-education they see in the very communities that should ostensibly welcome them. For Connie, the question arises again in "the dyke community," where she often sees lesbians partnered to trans men who still identify as being in a homosexual relationship. For Connie, this presents a "clear picture of trans men discrimination," and advises, "Hey girlies, if you are in a relationship with a TRANS-MAN who identifies as a man, then you are in a heterosexual relationship." Whether or not those lesbians agree with her statement, Connie is calling on them to examine their own constructions of gender and sexuality.

"DEAR MOTHER, I'M NOT YOUR SON": PASSING, LANGUAGE, AND PERCEPTIONS

Because most of the zines I include in my project are written by transgender people who are rather new to identifying as transgender, many spend a good deal of time and space discussing the spectrum of trans experiences they now find themselves defining, adopting, or processing. Choosing a new name to suit the identity they are discovering or building is often a first step in the process, and identifying the pronouns with which they feel comfortable is a complementary process as well. For many youth, the primary relationship in their lives is with their parents, and so the process of coming out to their parents and dealing with the aftermath and/or fallout is a consuming and painful one. None of the zine writers I included in my sample seemed to have parents who were accepting of their "new" identities, and negotiating those relationships and struggling for understanding is a key component of their trans experience.

Greenzine is a compilation zine, mainly composed of writings and artwork by its editor, Cristy Road, and often featuring letters from her friends. The thirteenth issue features a letter from Darby, writing to a mother who seems to feel that being transgender is "a phase" Darby is working through, rather than a true transformation. The letter is unique because Darby's mother actually shares memories of wishing she were a boy in her youth, because she often transgressed social notions of femininity and paid certain prices. Darby remembers a mother who "would cut down trees for firewood, built the cabin we lived in for years, drank heavily, was very extroverted and outgoing." However, Darby's mother still does not seem to accept that Darby is truly experiencing an identity shift, leaving Darby to wonder, "does that mean part of who I am is to be uncomfortable with this body, this societally imposed gender? And then where do I go from there?" Darby's mother, the only parent who seems to even partially understand a child's coming out as transgender, still does not recognize Darby in a different gender, leaving Darby feeling both uncomfortable and still misunderstood.

In subject to change, 12, toby writes, "the short story is that i changed my name to toby because i wanted a name that was less definitely recognized as a girl name & more ambiguous. And i changed pronouns from she to he because it felt better." Part of the longer story involves toby's family, who may or may not be aware of the change. Later in this issue, toby speaks of "twenty-one years in florida, hiding all the important parts of my life from my family and everyone else there." It is not clear from this issue how aware toby's family is of his gender or sexual identity.

In the second issue of Casa de los Trucos, Tricky Martin writes that "My mom doesn't understand that I'm not a girl. She won't accept Mateo as my name or even Tricky as my nickname." For Tricky, his mother's denial not only affects his family relationships but also negates some of the confidence he feels when he is recognized for he who believes himself to be. In the same issue of his zine, Tricky says, "Tricky Martin, the sexy confident boy who flirts with reckless abandon & doesn't think about things like dirty dishes or laundry piling up, is who I really am." For Tricky, choosing a new name is part of his self-constructed identity, and for his mother to evade or deny that denies who he is, or is trying to become. Micah recounts several dreams in which various characters recognized and named him as Micah, which became the name he uses by choice. For Connie, choosing her name is tied to how many of her friends and acquaintances use it for and to her. She writes: "When a tranny tells you the name, when they tell you their selves it's a person inside that they believe they are against a whole world of nay sayers. If they're not out yet, and it's just you two, say it to them." Izz recounts with frustration in the fourth issue of *the wicked which* that since coming out to hir parents, "in the intervening time, I have become a lesbian, apparently." The identity of lesbian seems to be the only construction hir parents want to acknowledge, perhaps because it is a "new" sexuality for their child but not an entirely "new" gender, which for many in mainstream culture is still a radical and abnormal possibility. In this way, even Izz's attempts to come out to hir parents are negated, since hir parents choose, for whatever reason, to deny what zhe has said, just as Tricky's mother does when she denies Tricky's name and self-identified gender and as Darby's mother does when she refers to it as a "phase." Micah writes to his parents, "I am your daughter I am your son. I was your daughter first now I am your son," echoing Darby's "Dear Mother, I am not your son." For most queer people, coming out to their parents is a difficult, anxiety-creating process, but for transgender youth, they often face more ignorance and denial from parents who choose not to accept even the possibility, much less the actuality, of transgenderism.

Tricky of *Casa de los Trucos* also writes of his coming out to his partner, a lesbian whom he has been dating since before he began to identify as transgender. This process comes with its own complications:

> Late last year, I decided to be honest with myself and come out to my partner as transgender. It's something I've known for a good long while & have strategically hidden out of fear. I was afraid I had used all my coming out cards. Abuse Survivor, Queer, Sex Worker. Every one of them inescapable truths & every one of them a huge weight lifted off me. So I really fucked myself up over the coming out process. Imagining all possible scenarios, thinking my girlfriend would be freaked out—after all, she had fallen in love with me in this girl body I can't avoid.

Happily, Robin, Tricky's girlfriend, is fully supportive and encouraging of Tricky's revelations, even though their relationship has ended by the time this account appears in the second issue of the zine.

Transgender zine writers also experience the anxieties of passing in public arenas, especially when they feel that they will not be "successful" or fit the image of transgendered people who do pass. Izz writes of becoming increasingly aware of "bodies and perceptions" when zhe writes in hir third issue of the first time zhe "successfully" passes as a boy in a public space. Micah attempts to find mirrors for his experience in the existing literature on transgender life, such as Leslie Feinberg's *Stone Butch Blues*, a landmark text in queer and transgender literature. For Micah, he finds that *Blues* is a "fictional account of the life of one transgendered butch lesbian—it is not a handbook on the diversity of trans experiences." The main point of difference for Micah is that "the protagonist's life is very different from mine in her ability to pass. Her trans-ness is more physically apparent . . . The experiences of transpeople who pass and those who don't are very different." Later, Micah talks about first attempting to pass and trying to buy clothing that would allow him to pass as a boy or man. "Shopping sucks in general (fuck consumerism!)" he writes, "but shopping with gender anxiety is even more fun. And when you're trans and your body is extra 'wrong' it sucks even more ass." Connie of *Rock Star with Purses* believed that passing as a trans woman would "simply never be a possibility, a viable path for ME." After all, she says, "I wasn't like the others I had seen: lean, long hair, shorter than me. I didn't have narrow feet and I grow far too much facial hair and I was fat and didn't think I ever wanted to have long, straight hair." Connie's anxiety over being able to fit into traditional cultural expectations for femininity inhibited her belief that she could ever pass as a woman in our culture. For Micah, this anxiety is a chance for people to "break down their gender conditioning." The answer is to create more possibilities, to "get used to (and excited about) bearded ladies and dudes with cunts. Short boys with 'dessert hands' and big-boned gals with deep voices." Toby says, "if i pass as male it is as a very young boy," which leads him to question how passing will change as he grows older. These concerns and answers echo the rage and frustration many zine writers express over the gender binary system that conflicts with their construction of identity.

For Tricky, performing in public in drag was a way for him to experiment with a transgender identity on his way to recognizing himself in the process. In fact, performing in drag becomes such a positive experience for Tricky that he says in his first issue, "I have never felt sexier than when I do drag." Tricky's first performance, at the Southern Girls Convention in 1999, began with this process:

I would slick my (already short) hair, leaving a little crest of boy bangs at the top. Dress up in a tight black button down dress shirt (after having the breasts bound and gagged behind a trusty ace bandage and once even duct tape) and loose fitting gray pants and go out there with my hottie dancer and perform the raunchiest version of "la vida loca" anyone has ever seen.

By the second issue of *Casa de los Trucos*, Tricky calls drag "a religious type experience," adding:

it always made me cry to remember how comfortable I felt doing the drag performances & I was wrong when I said that it was the performing high, the girls in the crowd, the lights/camera/action/music/ etc of it all. Because I've played with bands & done the exact same thing only not presenting & passing as male & it was never the self-same experience.

Tricky refers later in the zine to drag as something that can "open doors," and it seems clear that the experience of successfully passing as male and the jolt of confidence and pleasure that afforded helped Tricky begin to recognize the emerging transgender identity he later claims as his own. Just as passing can be a source of anxiety, it can also serve to liberate feelings that young queer people are unaware they were feeling or were not willing to examine.

Several of the transgender zine writers have college educations or are in the process of acquiring them, but others are not, and yet almost every writer attempts to apply cultural and feminist theory to their experiences as a transgendered person. Some, like Izz, find it restricting and inadequate, leading hir to say, "I can't find accurate language anymore, and so I have begun to resent theory intensely." Micah of *Tim-Tum* discusses the Continuum of Violence model often used in self-defense classes and in discussions of violence against women, and connects to it to his experiences thusly: "It illustrates the idea that individual, small acts of violence are related to and enable the most systemic and destructive ones. . . . Knowingly referring to a transperson by the wrong pronoun is DISRESPECTFUL and a step on this continuum."

Lauren of *Quantify* chooses to counter her theoretical readings with "the TOUGH GIRL PERFORMANCE PROJECT, a funky fresh short slideshow performance about the construction of gendered identities through manifestations of toughness." Lauren also edited an accompanying compilation zine entitled *Hard As Nails: the tough girl comp zine*. While toby of *subject to change* finds limitations in theory, saying dryly, "it is not really realistic for me to quote judith butler when someone demands to know if i am a boy or a girl," he still reads extensively, as evidenced by the included reading list. Also, toby sees an opening in theory for his own writing, saying, "i am writing myself into existence. I am theorizing more space, more genders, more ways of perceiving interacting with & being in gendered bodies. it feels better. it feels good." Clearly, zine writers are elaborating their own theories on gender and sexuality, drawing from their daily lives, conversations, and other zines, thus adding to the complex modes of representation offered by scholarly theoreticians.

Including a reading list at the back of a personal zine is a common device in the world of per-zines, and transgender zine writers use their reading lists to show us that they are also drawing on a wide and varied body of literature to help formulate some of the theories they put forth in their zines. Often these lists include scholarly works, fiction, graphic novels, and other zines, but are usually separate from zine reviews. Lauren's list in the back of *Quantify*, 4, includes the autobiographies of Angela Davis, Assata Shakur, and Lorraine Hansberry, which Lauren places side by side with work by Ralph Ellison and Sherman Alexie. Amber Hollibaugh's *My Dangerous Desires* and Michelle Tea's *Valencia* provide some examples of current work on sexuality, both fiction and nonfiction. In the back of *Casa de los Trucos*, 2, Tricky lists "articles of inspiration" and includes Tony Kushner's *Angels in America* and Aurora Levin-Morales *Remedios: Stories of Earth and Iron from this History of Puertoriquenas*. For Micah of *Tim-Tum*, the "inspirational reading list" includes Kate Bornstein's *Gender Outlaw*, Mab Segrest's *Memoir of a Race Traitor*, and a mention of *Bridges: A Jewish Feminist Journal*. The direct mention of "inspiration" in both lists allows us to infer that Tricky and Micah used ideas and theories from these works to inform their own discussions of sexuality and gender. Toby's reading list shows that he is not only reading scholarly texts on gender and sexuality, but that he is looking to studies of race and ethnicity for help as well:

sexing the body (anne fausto-sterling)
how sex changed (joanne meyerowitz)
genderqueer (nestle, howell & wilchins)
push (sapphire)
sula (toni morrisson)

caucasia (danzy senna)
black like me (john howard griffin)

As I mentioned earlier, it is difficult to ascertain the level of college education of a writer unless the text specifically refers to it, like toby of *subject to change*, who mentions "four years of college." I found no mention in any of these zines of university-level courses on gender and sexuality, which opens up the possibility that these zine writers are conducting independent studies, reading widely in fiction, nonfiction, and scholarly work to find theories and images that resonate with their own lives and thoughts.

"WRITING IS THE PASSAGEWAY": CONCLUSIONS AND THOUGHTS

The writers of these zines are indeed trying to write themselves new lives, writing toward a life where they can be the people they feel they are, regardless of how others see them. The act of envisioning that future, setting it down on paper, and sending it out to potential readers imparts a kind of power, a kind that Carolyn Heilbrun describes as "the ability to take one's place in whatever discourse is essential to action and the right to have one's part matter" (18). Transgender zine writers are writing themselves into several discourses at once and asserting the importance of their voices. They are creative, innovative, skilled writers, who use a variety of strategies and techniques to tell their own stories and construct their own identities. They engage with dense cultural theory, situate themselves on a spectrum of gender they are in the process of building, and compare different facets of their experiences to those shaped by other aspects of their identity, such as ethnic or religious heritage. Like thousands of young people, the writers of these zines are invested in discovering who they are, who they have been, and who they want to become, and in figuring out how to reconcile those points in time and in their own histories. Zines are the safe space in which they negotiate all the various ways in which young people are distinguishing themselves from each other, their families, and the children they used to be. Queer and feminist theorists have much to learn from what these writers tell us, in their own vivid and urgent words. In *Feminist Theory: From Margin to Center*, bell hooks wrote that "just as our lives are not fixed or static but always changing, our theory must remain fluid, open, responsive to new information" (xiii). Clearly, the words of transgender youth, as read in their zines, give theorists crucial new modes of self-representation to explore.

NOTES

1. One difficulty in studying zines is their ephemeral nature. Distros appear and disappear with some regularity. However, there are some "reliable sources" by which readers of this chapter may still be able to get zines by the time this chapter is published. They include Atomic Books, Baltimore, MD, www.atomicbooks.com; Quimby's Books, Chicago, IL, www.quimbys.com; and Zine World, www.undergroundpress.org, also available in print as *The Reader's Guide to the Underground Press.*

2. I've chosen not to include contact information for these zines either because only a home address was available, no information was given, or because I was unable to reach the author and get his or her permission.

3. The books cited by zine writers are often well-known texts in critical race studies, feminist and queer theory. However, writers also exhibit a preference for novels, memoirs, and autobiographies, that dovetail with their own styles of storytelling and political thinking. Authors of texts cited by zine writers often include poets, scholars, and activists, suggesting that zine writers draw from fiction and nonfiction alike, placing no primacy on scholarly material. I found no way to discern, but am curious about, how zine writers come across these texts—whether they are books from courses, recommendations from friends, or from scholarly journals.

WORKS CITED

Duncombe, Stephen. *Notes from Underground: Zines and the Politics of Alternative Culture.* New York: Verso, 1997.

Heilbrun, Carolyn. *Writing a Woman's Life.* New York: Ballantine Books, 1988.

hooks, bell. *Feminist Theory: From Margin to Center.* 2nd ed. Cambridge, MA: South End Press, 2000.

Spencer, Amy. *DIY: The Rise of Lo-Fi Culture.* New York: Marian Boyars, 2005.

Works Referenced by Zine Writers

Bornstein, Kate. *Gender Outlaws: On Men, Women and the Rest of Us.* New York: Vintage, 1995.

Fausto-Sterling, Anne. *Sexing the Body: Gender Politics and the Construction of Sexuality.* New York: Basic Books, 2000.

Feinberg, Leslie. *Stone Butch Blues: A Novel.* Los Angeles: Alyson Books, 2004.

Griffin, John Howard. *Black Like Me.* Reissue. New York: NAL Trade, 2003.

Hollibaugh, Amber. *My Dangerous Desires: A Queer Girl Dreaming Her Way Home.* North Carolina: Duke University Press, 2000.

Kushner, Tony. *Angels in America.* New York: Theatre Communications Group, 1993.

Levins Morales, Aurora. *Remedios: Stories of Earth and Iron from the History of Puertoriquenas.* Cambridge, MA: South End Press, 2001.

Meyerowitz, Joanne. *How Sex Changed: A History of Transsexuality in the United States.* Cambridge, MA: Harvard University Press, 2004.

Morrisson, Toni. *Sula.* Rpt. New York: Vintage International, 2004.

Sapphire. *Push.* Rpt. ed. New York: Vintage, 1997.

Segrest, Mab. *Memoir of a Race Traitor.* Cambridge, MA: South End Press, 1994.

Senna, Danzy. *Caucasia.* New York: Riverhead Books, 1999.

Tea, Michelle. *Valencia.* Seattle: Seal Press, 2002.

CHAPTER 5

ARTICULATING SISSY BOY QUEERNESS WITHIN AND AGAINST DISCOURSES OF TOLERANCE AND PRIDE

David McInnes and Cristyn Davies

INTRODUCTION

Over the past fifteen years, significant developments have been made in Australian schools in relation to gender and sexuality education describable as a pedagogical discourse of homophobia. This pedagogical discourse has evolved through research and through educational policy, teaching resources, and training. Young men and boys who do not conform to standards of gender (whom we strategically and rhetorically refer to as sissy boys) participate in research focused on homophobia through processes of interview, analysis, and interpretation. The experience of "sissy boys" is potentially queer/ing. We will explore what is made of this queer potential when sissy boy experience is understood/ shaped/accounted for within the discourse of homophobia. Reworking ideas of "normal," this pedagogical discourse arrests the disruptive possibilities of gender nonconformity and, instead, strives for ontological certainty, a central component to the formation of masculinity.

The *discourse of homophobia* is drawn from a complex arena, including gay liberation, discourses of diversity, tolerance, and acceptance. This discourse is produced across a range of fields, including legal, legislative, political, and community bodies. The discourse of homophobia is a second order discourse, a pedagogic discourse about *homophobic discourse*. *Homophobic discourse* is understood to be that set of things that are possible to say about sexuality and those things that cannot be said because they are "homophobic," statements, ideas, ideals, principles, omissions, silences, and repudiations that marginalize, vilify, ostracize, abuse, demean, humiliate, and render as other those who have same-sex sexual attachment or desire (characterized by Butler, *Excitable Speech* 13–41 as "hate speech" following Matsuda). The discourse of homophobia has developed as a pedagogical discourse, a second order discourse that shapes understandings of and attempts to change the first order homophobic discourse.

ENACTING A PEDAGOGICAL DISCOURSE OF HOMOPHOBIA

In the state of New South Wales, Australia, the discourse of homophobia is enacted in anti-homophobia education in schools. Family Planning Australia Health (FPAH) is a community health organization in New South Wales and, along with other organizations, participates in an anti-homophobia interagency. We attended a round table conducted by the interagency group in Sydney in 2003. Lynne Hillier is a significant contributor to this research field in Australia and was the first to address the roundtable. Her presentation was representative of one of the ways in which the discourse of homophobia is produced in Australia through research. A panel discussion at the round table was kicked off by a testimonial speech by a young man. He is one of a number of trained young people who participate in FPAH's education and teacher in-service training by giving accounts of their experience. His speech was representative of a key educational technique used to enact the discourse of homophobia.

Throughout our discussion, it is important to keep in mind that masculinity is intolerant of ambiguity and ambivalence and resists ontological uncertainty by producing closures around narratives of identity, selfhood, and becoming. Masculinity, conceptualized as phallic masculinity, is understood to be built on a bedrock of defensive autonomy and a resistance to ambiguity and is written through boys and girls lives in the drive to be "big and winning" (Corbett). We hold throughout our analysis that it is the strength of masculinity's underpinning defensive autonomy and resistance to ambiguity that permeates liberal educational ideals of pride and tolerance in the educational discourse of homophobia.

Focusing on sissy boys, as our project does, means paying attention to the performative moments of declaration, in social contexts, in which young men and boys are othered because of their nonconformance to the standard performances of masculinity. The sissy boy's uncomfortable becoming/becoming known is one that has at its core the intense semiotic and interactional labor that is required to sustain the realness of masculinity and its *authentic* relationship to male bodies.

THE SAFE SPACE IMPERATIVE

The idea of safety is a recurring theme in the research and educational interventions in the field of gender and sexuality in schools (Hillier et al 1996; Hillier et al. 1998; Harrison et al.; Dempsey et al.; Ollis et al.). This imperative is argued for by Hillier and her colleague Lyn Harrison (2004) where they claim that their "research highlights the need for same-sex attracted young people to have access to spaces in which they are free to explore their sexuality and people with whom they feel safe to be themselves" (91). The idea of safe space is figured here as an educational/social aim. But, we want to trouble the idea of an *authentic* self underpinning the notions of "exploration" and "being," and this means questioning the notion of "freedom." Same-sex attracted young people or those who are gender nonconforming should not be abused or vilified. However, we are keen to illuminate the intricacies of power in the process of subject formation, and how notions of freedom or liberation are, in practice, processes of subjection. We will explore below how the kind of shaming involved in declaring a boy a "sissy" is an attempt to shut down the presence of ambiguities related to gender. Boys who "act like girls" or sissies need to be shamed and tamed so that the normative ideals of masculinity, wherein boys act like boys and girls act like girls, can be reiterated and made real.

Declarations of the self, who you are, Hillier claims, give power back to these young people by reclaiming the category of the normal. Underpinning the notion of "being yourself" within the safe space imperative is a sense of certainty that there is a self to be and, by inference, to know and to make known. In the Hillier and Harrison article (2004) this valuing happens by way of an uncritical and unproblematized engagement (even though this work is presented under the rubric of critical discourse analysis) with young people's ideas (presented in interview) of being open about "who" they *are*. Liberal technologies that privilege ideas of "authentic" identity assist in keeping the discursive process of pedagogical production and regulation opaque, reality producing, and, therefore, resistant to critique and change. An unreflexive and too-sure-of-itself account of gender and sexuality within pedagogical discourse also risks the reproduction of normative ideas of gender and the operations of power. Claiming normality shores up the space of the speaker and works toward a *fixity* of subjectivity that disavows precariousness. This reclamation of the category of the normal is also voiced in the teaching resources developed for in-school use by teachers.

WORKING TO NORMAL

Yes You Are: A Guide to Educating Young People and Adults about Healthy Relationships, Sexual Diversity and Anti-Homophobia is produced by FPAH and was published in May 2000. Much of the material used in *Yes You Are* is inspired by *Affirming Diversity*, which is a resource produced by Family Planning New Zealand. Many of the learning activities in this resource seek to change the representation of gays, lesbians, and bisexual and transgender people. However, rather than resisting already established discourses around sexuality, some of these tasks participate in assimilating sexual difference into categories marked as normative.

Consider Marco. He doesn't like to play sport, he talks and walks "like a girl," cries when he is injured or insulted, hangs out with girls, and enjoys reading and participating in school theater projects. He's a sissy. Understanding Marco as and declaring him a sissy does not mean he is outside discourses of gender, but that his gendered performance confounds the normative ordering of gender. The supposed biological "fact" of his body is misaligned with a feminized performance. That he confounds the normative ordering of gender can be used (as is often the case) to suggest that he is disordered (Sedgwick, "How to Bring Your Kids Up Gay"). However, what is more profoundly pedagogically and politically useful is that Marco, as a sissy boy, disorders gender, revealing through his very sissiness the impossible-to-maintain fiction of gender and normative ideals of masculinity.

In unit 2 of *Yes You Are*, "Sexuality and Coming Out" (39), the first task students are required to undertake is titled: "Homosexuality—it's only natural." While this choice of title subverts normative narratives wherein heterosexuality is the only "natural" sexual orientation, this title maintains the binary structures homosexual/heterosexual, natural/unnatural, normal/abnormal, and so on. A binary structure creates a discursive hierarchy wherein one term occupies a more privileged status than the other. Rather than inverting or extending these terms, we suggest that it is more productive to make transparent the power relations normative categories encourage. With this perspective in mind, let us return to the resource in question.

One of the tasks in *Yes You Are* requires the class to be divided into three groups and that each group take up a different rhetorical position. Students are required to respond to a news item suggesting that "Scientists discover that sexual orientation is genetically predetermined" (40). These are:

- Gays and Lesbians against Discrimination (GLAD)

- The Moral Minority—A conservative religious/political group who believes homosexuality is a sin and lobbies for the banning of the promotion of homosexuality

- Your Baby's Chromosomes R Us (a chain of fertility clinics where you can choose features of your baby, like gender)

While this is a useful task for students to adopt different rhetorical positions with regard to a current media debate, students are encouraged to accept sexual difference by assimilating this difference into normative discourses. Similarly, task 2 "Reality Checks" requires students to burst balloons that carry a myth about homosexuality and bisexuality on the balloon's exterior, while a message within the balloon's interior reveals the "reality" (41). Although this task effectively debunks myths about sexual categories and practices, the main messages and key themes for discussion are that homosexuality and bisexuality are as "normal" and "natural" as heterosexuality and sexual diversity is not a problem—homophobia is (41). So, the category "homosexuality" is subsumed into discourses of what is normal and natural while these more foundational categories remain uninterrogated. This kind of rhetoric expands the category of "normal" and maintains binary distinctions rather than offering a new framework through which to think about sexual difference.

TESTIMONIALS

Testimonials are given by young people in schools to teachers or to students as accounts of their experience of homophobic discourse. Pablo's testimonial, analyzed as follows, comes from *Skool's Out! A Report from the Skool's Out Forum on Homophobic Bullying and Harassment in and around Schools, 2002* (NSW Attorney General's Department). Pablo began his testimonial with an introduction that positions him and his fellow speaker, Michelle, as "representatives" of queer students.

> We feel it's our duty to represent the queer students within our schools, and as part of that obligation, we are here to share some of our experiences, struggles, and triumphs in our jour- ney of discovery of our identities and places in the world as queer students and people. (8)

Pablo begins with an account of finding out that he was different. He had assumed and treated as natural his attraction to boys until he went into the first year of high school, from which point he experienced vilification, abuse, and learned to fear going to school. In response, Pablo developed strategies for secrecy and he hid in the library where: "By reading ancient myths of heroes and gods, I escaped my terrible reality. Somehow I also related to the great men in the stories, and they filled me with hope, that things would get better in the end" (8).

In response to this, Pablo decided to excel academically, to be "as great as those heroes." Curiously, the narratives Pablo chose to read were constructed within a culture in which male homosexuality was crucial to the practice of homosociality, or relations between men. These ancient Greek narratives also position male protagonists as hypermasculine, so that the contemporary reading of the male homo- sexual body as one that panics gender is not articulated through these images of masculinity. Pablo attempts to interweave these narratives of success, and of overcoming difficult circumstances, into his own narra- tive of "self." This strategy was successful for Pablo. He succeeded aca- demically, but he also, as he describes, continued to hide and shun "that part of him that was gay and wrong." Pablo describes the duality of this experience through metaphors of "inside and outside," where the "real" Pablo was on the inside accompanied by feelings of "hatred" and emptiness, and on the outside was "a brave face of a confident pupil that made everyone laugh." These multiple and competing discourses of masculinity and sexuality have serious material effects. Pablo also de- scribes self-hatred and gives an account of self-harming. These feelings are mapped spatially, and are unable to be contained by the body as they "swelled" and "burst," leading Pablo to attempt suicide. After his suicide attempt, a counselor was crucial in setting Pablo on his "journey of self discovery." "Through counselling sessions I became aware of my true self, the 'me' that had been hidden so long since that time I decided to shun it to oblivion. Slowly I came to terms with the fact that yes, I was gay, and that didn't mean I was bad or wrong . . . slowly I trotted along, accepting a little of myself every step of the way" (9).

Pablo then describes a coming out process in which his "fears of rejection" and concerns with "what others thought of me" gave way to declarations that "yes, I was a fag, and totally proud of it!" The taunts now "bounced off" him and he "tried to demonstrate to [his] younger peers that the weakness generally associated with homosexuality was only a myth and that I as a gay person could do anything a straight and " 'normal' person could" and, as Pablo explains, "it wasn't easy, but I succeeded, all the while being 'gay' " (9).

Pablo uses a passage from the biography of Ian Roberts, an "out" Australian Rugby League football player (Freeman, qtd. in NSW Attorney General's Department) to sum up what he had learned:

> If you dare to be different and you do not join the crowd,
> If they laugh at your honesty, and taunt you if you're proud
> When they talk of you in whispers and criticise the things you
>   say and do
> Do not fear them but forgive them for they are more afraid
>   than you. (9)

Ian Roberts's biography, suggestive of a process of self-discovery, is subtitled *Finding Out* and is, as the publisher's introduction describes it, "the story of an ordinary man with an extraordinary talent and the courage to finally live his life honestly" (Freeman). Mike Gibson, a tabloid commentator, best sums up this discursive space that was simultaneously opened and contained by Ian Roberts's coming out when, in accepting and tolerating this gay footballer, he contrasts what he describes as the "real man" version of gay—Ian Roberts (courageous, with a belief in himself and with a strong character), to the feminized version of gay, or in his words "those fairies who flap around Oxford Street in their lipstick and tights."

Pablo's and Ian's stories are stories of self-discovery, liberation and authenticity hinged on essentialist notions of selfhood. They are stories of pride built on ideas about *normal* masculinity. Both stories foreclose, by producing ontological autonomy and certainty, uncritically claiming pride in the qualities of success, competent public performance, certainty about who one is, inner strength and a sense of self-coherence and being "true" to oneself. Probyn suggests that the demonstration of pride is a defense against other affects, notably shame and that "as a form of body politics, paradoxically the move to pride stifles the power of our bodies to react: to be, as Deleuze puts it, a judge to ourselves" (129). The pride-produced avoidance of shame also avoids the reflexivity that it may afford to those shamed, those shaming, and those witness to shame. Pablo and Ian are heroic, capable, and "true." These valued ways of being men depend on understandings of identity in which there is a "true" self, available to be discovered and made known or to be displayed to others. The experience of sissy boys, who may or may not be gay, unsettle this kind of authenticating, ontological certainty and disrupt the self-evidence of masculinity as written onto male bodies. This unsettling or discomfort offers an opportunity for reflexivity. Reflexivity is made possible because the sissy boy experience is one of shameful becoming and an attendant melancholy.

Heterosexuality demands the loss of primary homosexual attachments and, because of the power of normative sexuality, this loss cannot be mourned because of the prohibition of same-sex attachments (Butler, *Psychic Life* 132–159). Heterosexuality, and the formation of the properly masculine and feminine subjects that it demands, is, therefore, dependent on melancholy—ungrieved and ungrievable loss. Butler offers gay men in the military and the "don't ask, don't tell" debate as an example (132–159). The presence but unspeakability of male homoerotics in a homosocial context exemplifies the unspeakability of a surrendered attachment. The only way to maintain the fiction of a heterosexual masculinity in an intense homosocial context like the military is if same-sex desire remains unspoken. The sissy boy's presence in the school is like that of the gay man in the military—it exists as a "speaking" of that which should be kept silent. For the sissy boy, that which must be denied (while being lost) is the nonconformity of their gender performance, that they act like girls.

So far we have looked at the experience of Pablo. We have attempted, in foregrounding the sissy boy rather than the proto-gay youth, to make salient the ways in which gender nonconformity for boys (acting like girls) calls forth a set of considerations that are too easily and too early foreclosed by the invocation of a pedagogical discourse of homophobia. The foreclosure operates, we argue, by obfuscating the question of gender (nonconformity and messiness), overriding it with ideas about sexuality propelled by notions of pride as we have seen in Pablo's narrative.

We want to enact the same maneuver again with a different pedagogical moment. A well-regarded and significant resource emerging from research into homophobia in Australia is *Safety in Our Schools* (Ollis et al.). In a case study section designed to aid teachers in intervening in homophobic situations, the following is offered:

> You are conducting a continuum activity with year 8 students responding to the statement "girls get it easier in school than boys." One boy goes to the "strongly agree" end of the continuum. You ask him why and he replies, "some boys get it easy too, Matt gets it easiest but he acts like a girl."

We reclaim Matt as a sissy boy, not because we think this is a more authentic or accurate account of who Matt is but because it is a way of preventing the moment from being absorbed into a discourse about sexual knowledge (*Matt's gay and you are being homophobic, learn to be tolerant and accept diversity*) and retaining its significance as a moment of gender recognition, a moment when the idea that a boy acts like a girl is recognized through vilification in an attempt to keep ordered the way bodies (boys' and girls' bodies) align with gender (masculinity and femininity respectively).

The same kind of moment is enacted when Marco tries to bowl a ball in a cricket match at his school: "Marco prepares to bowl. He hates this moment. He knows what's coming. He takes off, running in as controlled a fashion as he can. He makes it to the crease, lets go of the ball and it's 'no ball.' He hears it again as he moves off to try again, 'Fucking Sissy.' " Taking our lead from Butler's use of the performative, we see these moments as enacted by circuits of recognition (we develop this description from an insight of Benjamin's). Performatives require declarers (Matt's school mate), declared (Matt) and witnesses (teachers and other students) operating with the semiotic and discursive resources of the context (here, this is most directly observable as the ordering and management of gender in the school). In these moments, the students declare Matt and Marco disordered. This declaration not only disorders Matt and Marco but it does this to (re)order the way gender should be organized—"we're boys because we act like boys and you're not because you act like girls." The declaring students have an investment, as all in circuits do, in the reproduction of "ordered" gender (involving boys acting like boys and girls acting like girls). The declaration, its recipient and the witnesses are all woven into the reproduction of masculinity's "logical," "essential" split from the feminine. It is this circuitry of performatives and the recognition they make manifest that make this logic "real," that make boys masculine and girls feminine. It is also this circuitry that needs to be shorted if the disruption that Matt and Marco make manifest is to be used as reflexive educational resource. We will return to these moments later in the chapter.

The recognition of the melancholy that forms gender must also recognize that gender is formed relationally, by the negotiations of and performances of desires and body/gender alignments and must be variously and differently performed, silenced, avowed, or disavowed. Given that under the normative organization of gender and sexuality these losses must be kept silent and invisible, recognizing gender melancholy means surrendering "the notion of ontological autonomy" (Salih 134; Butler, *Psychic Life* 197) and involves accepting one's "Otherness." Acknowledging melancholy as formative of gender demands a recognition of ambivalence, ambiguity, incoherence, and a lack of ontological certainty. This incoherence is disavowed by masculinity in order to produce itself as certain, autonomous, and knowable. This disavowal also requires the obfuscation, overcoming, or removal of shame and instead works toward the production of pride in much the same way that Pablo's and Ian's narratives do.

This drive to the avoidance or removal of shame to which we refer is encapsulated in a poem used by Hillier and Harrison in their article:

A Little Sense of Solidarity

How in the name of heaven can I escape
That defiling and disfigured shape
The mirror of malicious eyes
Casts upon my eyes until at last
I think that shape must be my shape?

—William Yates

"Escape" suggests freedom and safety; freedom from the "defiling" and disfiguring of one's shape in and through the eyes of others. How else do we "know" ourselves, except through the "threat" and damage that make possible our being in and through discourse? Avoiding this or making it silent is one of the principal ways in which the "fiction" of gender sustains itself as "real." And, there is also in the Yates poem an implicit juxtaposition between the "real" shape of oneself and an "unreal" shape, cast by the eyes of others, encoding another appeal to essentialism.

SHAME, MELANCHOLY AND QUEER PERFORMATIVITY

What are the concrete discursive effects and implications of shaming the sissy boy through a declaration of his "disordered" gender performance? Who benefits from the reproduction of the normative gender in the splitting of the masculine from the feminine enacted in moments of sissy boy recognition? What might happen if the melancholic presence of the sissy boy in schools is considered as a lively point of reflection rather than as a call to tolerance of homosexuality?

If we consider the circuits of recognition involving Matt and Marco earlier, it is useful now to extend the analysis of these experiences through noticing how shame operates to police and regulate gender. Both Matt and Marco are recognized as disordered. The declaration of their sissiness ("Matt acts like a girl," "Fucking Sissy") are shaming techniques—they thwart social contact and involvement, enacting in those who are shamed a retreat from social contact, an incomplete withdrawal of social interest or involvement (Tomkins 123). What could happen in these situations is that Matt and Marco would withdraw from participation in areas of school activity in which their gender nonconformity calls forth shaming circuits of recognition or they "tone down" their excessive behavior to stay more comfortable within the normative bounds of masculinity. The research literature concerned with boys, gender, and homophobia in schools indicates that boys who experience such vilification tend to move into less stressful and "risky" areas of school life and school space (Martino 1998, 1999, 2000; Renold) or choose to excel in alternative ways that ease the tension produced by their gender nonconformity thereby rendering themselves more acceptable or compensating for their disorder. Pablo did the latter.

In Pablo's testimonial his response to shame was spatially organized—he hid in the library. He also "hid" within himself. This hiding removes the shamed from the spaces in which their disordered selves draw attention and shaming recognition. But it also means that the "reality" of gender alignments (boys acing like boys; girls acting like girls) on which normative gender is built remain unscathed, unaltered, unpolluted by the performances of those that do not conform.

Many educational strategies seek to avoid shame and propel pride. The *Safety in Our Schools* pedagogy is an example of this. However, the move to pride stifles the reflexivity available in shaming circuits. What *Safety in Our Schools* suggests is management of this situation via NAC— a strategy whereby the teacher names the problem of a student using a put-down, makes reference to a group agreement not to use put-downs, and then presents the consequence of such an action if continued— discipline. This strategy, as one that is shame-avoiding/shame-quelling, offers a punitive response without the capacity for reflection or disruption. It makes no educational use of the circuit of recognition.

Our offering of the circuit of recognition, we think, provides a way to engage with these moments of sissy boy recognition that sees shame as an educational resource not as something to be avoided or replaced by pride. We are not saying that sissy boys should feel shame and live the pain of this. But, making shame an observable element of school interaction might offer some capacity for reflection. Why does Matt's classmate shame him, what is his investment in enacting a normalizing split from the feminine through shaming Matt? How is an investment in capable, strong, and winning masculinity remade by Marco's schoolmate's declaration?

These are not just analytical questions for those who research education. They are essential questions to ask students and teachers involved in circuits that make gender "real" in school contexts. However, these questions cannot be asked if the *liveliness* of sissy boy gender nonconformity (his acting like a girl) is not visible and available for reflection. If he hides, if he withdraws in response to shame, or if he simply and only becomes prideful about his alternate achievements (enacting a competitive dynamic), then the conditions of an autonomous masculine subjectivity remain unaffected and the reality-producing split from the feminine on which masculinity depends remains unquestioned.

Shamed because of gender nonconformity, the sissy boy has a particular relation to the order of the school world. The declaration "sissy" (and words like it) others the sissy boy from the masculine. This shaming marks the value of *appropriate* masculinity/male body alignments. It is part of a process of producing a proper world in which boys act like boys and girls act like girls: to be properly masculine demands a non-articulation of same-sex attraction and the non-articulation of a self other than that predicted by biological sex. The sissy boy is a melancholic figure because he is an expression of what should be inexpressible. He is a presence of disorder—not of himself but of an order in which boys act like boys. The presence of this melancholic figure is, on one hand, produced to cement the naturalness of gender/body alignments in the school and, on the other, is a continuing discomfort to the school, often managed by continuing shame. The fragility and mobility of the ordering of gender is made visible in the declaration of "sissy."

Following directly from Sedgwick (*Touching Feeling* 64), we suggest that the sissy boy as a melancholic figure offers schools the opportunity of queer performativity. " 'Queer performativity' is the name of a strategy for the production of meaning and being, in relation to the affect shame and to the later and related fact of stigma" (61) and "it [. . .] offer[s] some psychological, phenomenological, thematic density and motivation to [. . .] the 'torsions' of aberrances between reference and performativity, or indeed between queerness and other ways of experiencing identity and desire" (62).

We would like, in the context of this discussion, to ask who or what is being protected by safe space imperatives or shame-silencing strategies? If shame is residual and integral to the formation of identity, then boys who recognize sissies and the masculinities such boys enact are allowed to appear real, autonomous, unambiguous, and valued because the split-producing shaming of others necessary for the production of their masculinity is avoided or silenced. While we might imagine that protecting sissy boys from shame is a positive thing to do (and, of course, protecting young people from harm is vital) it produces an impasse in any attempt to critique gender because it makes boys like Marco and Matt responsible for the production of an autonomous pride which mimics that of defensive, split-producing masculinity, cementing the realness and value of defensively produced, autonomous, and unambiguous masculinity.

TOWARD A SISSY BOY EDUCATIONAL ETHIC

We would like, in drawing our discussion to a close, to consider what the theoretical maneuvers made in this chapter can offer in terms of an educational approach to gender and sexuality. This section attempts to answer both theoretically and practically how it is we might engage ethically and in an educationally effective way with the gender nonconformity of sissy boys without surrendering too quickly to liberal ideals of autonomous selfhood.

Butler (*Precarious Life* and *Undoing Gender*) suggests a critical "ethics" building on the work of Emmanuel Levinas. Key to Levinas's development of an idea of the ethics that might pertain between people in the production of peace and the reduction of violence is the idea of the face. "The face," he explains, represents or stands "as the extreme precariousness of the other." So, "Peace" is understood "as awakeness to the precariousness of the other" (Levinas 167, qtd. by Butler, *Undoing Gender* 134).

The face might be for us the presence of the sissy boy's gender nonconformity, his confounding of gender because he, a boy, acts like a girl. The ethical question then becomes what do we do as students and as teachers when "faced" with the sissy boy? Our attempt throughout has not been about offering a new label for these kinds of boys or of a new strategy for tolerance, but to offer a view of circuits of recognition so as to open a space for reflexivity. How might this operate?

Butler offers a way for us to think about what might be educationally available for Matt's, Marco's, and Pablo's classmates and teachers when "faced" with their confounding gender performances: "To respond to the face, to understand its meaning, means to be awake to what is precarious in another life or, rather, to life itself." But she cautions that "this cannot be an awakeness, to use his [Levinas's] word, to my one life, and then an extrapolation from an understanding of my own precariousness to an understanding of another's precariousness. It has to be an understanding of the precariousness of the Other" (134).

Butler and Levinas's warning resonates with the educational imperatives of the discourse of homophobia in that they do not suggest empathy because empathy rests on knowing the other. In fact, their call is to resist sure knowledge of the other so that when Matt is declared to "act like a girl" it is vital to actively resist knowing him as gay or homosexual, to thwart the sublation of his gender performance necessary for the hate speech to be regarded as homophobic. Instead, Butler and Levinas would want to challenge teachers and students with the demand of recognizing one's own precariousness in the face of the sissy boy. This would compel students and teachers to ask, what do you and your experience suggest about me and my experience? What does how I make sense of you and your gender nonconformity suggest about what is at stake for me? The very possibility of this question is avoided if Matt or Marco or Pablo are framed as gay and interpellated into discourses of pride.

Levinas and Butler compel us to recognize that the fate of those who recognize and witness gender nonconformity is in the hands of the sissy boy. The very masculinity of a recognizing male student and any witness's investment in the ordering of gender depend on the split made possible in part by the shaming recognition of the sissy boy's gender nonconformity. Any declarer's or witness's self-recognition as masculine or as properly ordered in terms of gender is not possible without the disordered; their fate rests in the sissy boy's disorder.

The "face" of the sissy boy is a key component in what might be considered a circuit of recognition, in which the possibilities of self/ other representation hinge on a mutual and interdependent process, a binary production of gendered selves hinged on normative, essentialist links between bodies and genders and also dependent on processes of address and recognition. These processes of representation, address, and recognition are very crucially unstable and impossible to *fix*. Any fixity is an unethical (in that it is partial and unresponsive) rigidity, ignores the precariousness of others, and assumes a lack of precariousness for the self. The fiction "boys act like boys; girls act like girls" attempts to fix what is unstable in the pretense that gender is stable and that masculine subjects can be autonomous and unambiguously masculine.

Homophobic hate speech forecloses and shores up the place of the *I* by producing the (abject) non-I, an other. However, the deployment of a discourse of pride and tolerance also shores up the place of the I (gay/lesbian/queer) subject by producing the non-I, the other (homophobe, heterosexual)—this is what happens when Pablo seeks to pridefully defend and succeed as "normal" and patronizingly "forgive" those that vilified him. He knows who they are; they are homophobic and ignorant, and he, therefore, can know who he is. These kinds of interaction (address/declaration and return address/declaration) work to fix recognition in an axis that moves from self to other (I know who/ what you are and can make such claims because through them my *self* appears stable), shutting down reciprocal address and ignoring (and therefore cannot attend to and make ethical judgment dependent on) the interdependencies within circuits of recognition. An ethical engagement with circuits of recognition (representation and address) would be one that is resistant to foreclosures typically deployed to shore up the subject/author, the *self*. It would involve approaching the sissy *as* a valuable confounding manifestation of a gender order that is impossible to fix and in which no one can have sure footing.

For queer people (and sissy boys are queered people), "shame is simply the first, and remains a permanent, structuring fact of identity: one that has its own powerfully productive and powerfully metamorphic possibilities" (Sedgwick, *Touching Feeling* 64–65). There is ethical educational potential in the metamorphic possibilities offered by shame within circuits of recognition. Folding the sissy boy experience, that is, the experience of gender nonconformity for young men and boys in schools, under the discourse of homophobia resists shame or moves quickly on from shame and, in so doing, eliminates the opportunity for reflection that shame makes available. The sissy boy experience as a shame motivated melancholic negotiation of gender means that Matt, Marco, and Pablo offer the opportunity for reflection and a resistance to the drive to autonomy and independent selfhood. Seeing the sissy boy as the constitutive outside to masculinity foregrounds Matt, Marco, and Pablo as like and different to their masculine recognizers and foregrounds masculinity's dependence on them. The observance of Matt, Marco, and Pablo's vital link in the formation of gender (seeing them as powerfully necessary for masculinity's authenticity) offers the chance to initiate reflections and to value the unstable and precarious place we all have in gender.

WORKS CITED

Benjamin, Jessica. *Bonds of Love: Psychoanalysis, Feminism and the Problem of Domination.* New York: Pantheon, 1988.

Butler, Judith. *Excitable Speech: A Politics of the Performative.* New York: Routledge, 1997.

———. *The Psychic Life of Power: Theories in Subjection.* Stanford, CA: Stanford University Press, 1997.

———. *Precarious Life: The Powers of Mourning and Violence.* London: Verso, 2004.

———. *Undoing Gender.* New York: Routledge, 2004.

Corbett, Ken. "Faggott=Loser." *Studies in Gender and Sexuality* 2, 1 (2001): 3–28.

Dempsey, Deborah, Lynne Hillier, and Lyn Harrison. "Gendered (S)explorations Among Same-Sex Attracted Young People in Australia." *Journal of Adolescence* 24 (2000): 67–81.

Family Planning Australia Health. *Yes You Are.* New South Wales: Family Planning Australia Health, 2000.

Freeman, Paul. *Ian Roberts: Finding Out.* Sydney: Random House, 1997.

Gibson, Mike. "Gay Idol a Model for All Men." *Telegraph Mirror.* 19 September 1995.

Harrison, Lyn, Lynne Hillier, and Jenny Walsh. "Teaching for a Positive Sexuality: Sounds Good but What about Fear, Embarrassment, Risk and The 'Forbidden' Discourse of Desire?" In *Schooling and Sexualities: Teaching for Positive Sexuality*, ed. L. Lasky and C. Beavis. Geelong/Victoria: Deakin University, 1996.

Hillier, Lynne, Lyn Harrison, and Deborah Dempsey. "Whatever Happened to Duty of Care? Same-Sex Attracted Young People's Stories of Schooling and Violence." *Melbourne Studies in Education* 40, 2 (November 1999): 59–74.

———, et al. *Writing Themselves In: A National Report on the Sexuality, Health and Well-Being of Same-Sex Attracted Young People.* Melbourne: National Centre in HIV Social Research, La Trobe University, 1998.

———, D. Warr, B. Haste. *The Rural Mural: Sexuality and Diversity in Rural Youth.* Melbourne: National Centre in HIV Social Research, Program in Youth/General Population, La Trobe University, 1996.

———, Lynne, and Lyn Harrison. "Homophobia and the Production of Shame: Young People and Same-Sex Attraction." *Culture, Health and Sexuality* 6, 1 (2004): 79–94.

Levinas, Emmanuel. "Peace and Proximity." In *Basic Philosophical Writings*, ed. Adrian T. Peperzak, Simon Critchley, and Robert Bernasconi. Bloomington: Indiana University Press, 1996.

Martino, Wayne. " 'Dickheads,' 'Poofs,' 'Try Hards,' and 'Losers': Critical Literacy for Boys in the English Classroom." *Aotearoa* (New Zealand Journal for Teachers of English) 35 (1998): 31–57.

———. "Mucking Around in Class, Giving Crap, and Acting Cool: Adolescent Boys Enacting Masculinities at School." *Canadian Journal of Education* 25, 2 (2000): 102–112.

NSW Attorney General's Department. *Skool's Out: A Report from the Skool's Out Forum on Homophobic Bullying and Harassment in and around Schools 2002.* Sydney: 2002.

Ollis, Debbie et al. *Safety in Our Schools: Strategies for Responding to Homophobia.* Melbourne: Australian Research Centre in Sex Health and Society, n.d. (published 2002).

Probyn, Elspeth. *Carnal Appetites: FoodSexIdentities.* New York: Routledge, 2000.

Renold, Emma. " 'Other' Boys: Negotiating Non-Hegemonic Masculinities in the Primary School." *Gender and Education* 16, 2 (2004): 247–267.

Salih, Sara. *Judith Butler.* London: Routledge, 2002.

Sedgwick, Eve Kosofsky. "How to Bring Your Kids Up Gay." In *Fear of a Queer Planet*, ed. Michael Warner. Minneapolis: University of Minnesota Press, 1993.

———. *Touching Feeling: Affect, Pedagogy, Performativity.* Durham and London: Duke University Press, 2003.

Sedgwick, Eve Kosofsky, and Adam Frank. *Shame and Its Sisters: A Silvan Tomkins Reader.* Durham, NC: Duke University Press, 1995.

Tomkins, Silvan. *Affect, Imagery, Consciousness, Vol. II: The Negative Affects.* New York: Springer, 1963.

CHAPTER 6

HOW TO BE A REAL LESBIAN

THE PINK SOFA
AND SOME FICTIONS OF IDENTITY

Anna Hickey-Moody, Mary Louise Rasmussen,
and Valerie Harwood

This chapter draws upon, and critically considers, select textures of a contemporary queer youth cultural formation. We focus on the production of a particular lesbian youth subculture on the World Wide Web, via a site called *The Pink Sofa*. Building upon Giroux's ("Making the Pedagogical More Political") assumption that culture plays "a central role in producing narratives, metaphors, and images that exercise a powerful pedagogical force over how people think of themselves and their relationship to others," we read *The Pink Sofa* as a popular and accessible kind of public pedagogy. We explore some situated examples of queer/lesbian identity construction online and consider how *The Sofa* produces and also inhibits the agency of young women who build online "Sofa identities." In so doing, we allude to the idea of being a "real" lesbian. This "real" lesbian identity is a powerful, yet often metatextual idea that haunts many discussions on *The Sofa* forums. In this chapter we are interested to take up these points and consider *The Sofa* as a kind of public pedagogy and site of cultural production that facilitates a range of performances of sexual and gender identity.

This brings us to an important contextualizing comment on the value and import of this virtual space. General discussion of young lesbian cultures is not facilitated by mainstream media sources such as print media or prime time television. As such, *The Sofa* provides valuable articulations of the cultural politics of being a young lesbian, and allows such processes to be understood, interrogated, and incorporated into contemporary cultural fabrics. *The Sofa* is one site in which young people are exposed to sexual and gender identity politics and various means of constructing lesbian identity. The community is primarily a commercial venture; profiting financially from those who pay to join the community and post a user profile. People may browse *The Sofa* without becoming members. However, only members may participate in forums, chat, and contact other users of *The Sofa*. User profiles, many of which feature photographs, allow members of the community to make contact via the Web. While *The Sofa* has many functions, it appears that its central purpose is Internet dating (this aspect of *The Sofa* is not the object of our analysis in this chapter).

The Sofa users engage with the idea of being a lesbian and the essentializing possibility of being a "real" lesbian in very different ways. While we do not want to depict this online community as having one specific relationship to lesbian identity, we do want to consider the practices of essentializing identity on *The Sofa*. Specifically, we wish to signpost essentializing notions of sexual identity as an enduring thematic that young women alternatively play with, subscribe to, subvert, and refute on *The Sofa*. To do this we undertake a topical textual analysis of a particular aspect of *The Sofa*, focusing on a community forum specifically designed for young women entitled "Teenage Chix."[1] Within this forum we identify key discourses pertaining to the aesthetics of lesbian identity that young women deploy in their online conversations. The issues covered here canvass a broad range of topics—from tongue piercing, to coming out, to favorite artists and hangouts. However, ostensibly the subject of conversation remains the same: the art of articulating the "real" or quintessential lesbian self.

The "Teenage Chix" forum can therefore be understood as offering a rich array of information regarding how some young women are scripting their identities, engaging with and learning about issues relating to gender and sexual identity. Drawing on the Butlerian notion of performativity, we perceive these young women's acts of creating online virtual identities as part of the ongoing production of their own subjectivities. After Butler, we also recognize the power of this site of identity production to inform the gender and sexual identity of all *The Sofa* users. As such, *The Sofa* can be considered a cultural site that is critically important in influencing the ways some young women are thinking about and producing identity and community.

PUBLIC PEDAGOGIES ONLINE

Although the term "pedagogy" has traditionally implied a school context, it is also thought of as a cultural practice in the social sciences, humanities, and the visual and performing arts (McWilliam). In the humanities, the interrogation of sites of communication and knowledge exchange outside the classroom have generated extensive debates on ways of understanding the pedagogical relationship (e.g., Gallop; Gore; McWilliam and Taylor). As Giroux argues, pedagogy can no longer be considered as confined to the site of schooling. It needs to be understood as applying to everyday political sites in "which identities are shaped, desires mobilized, and experiences take on form and meaning" ("Making the Pedagogical More Political").

Giroux's concept of "public pedagogy" draws on his belief that cultural studies as a field of inquiry, and a scholarly community, needs to:

> acknowledge the primacy of culture's role as an educational site where identities are being continually transformed, power is enacted, and learning assumes a political dynamic as it becomes not only the condition for the acquisition of agency but also the sphere for imagining oppositional social change. ("Responsibility of Intellectuals," 60)

For Giroux, culture is pedagogical. We learn about ourselves and understand our relations to others via our position in lived cultures. A more explicit consideration of how culture influences identity production and relations of power is, for Giroux, one of the intended outcomes of considering culture as pedagogical. In demonstrating culture's pedagogical role Giroux hopes that we will become more cognizant of the myriad effects associated with consumer media culture. For Giroux, this is an important task because such knowledge of the role of culture is intrinsic to acquiring agency and "imagining [. . .] social change" ("Responsibility of Intellectuals," 60).

For example, in his essay "Education after Abu Ghraib," Giroux draws attention to how the nature of photographs and the technologies that produce them enable particular meanings; how these meanings connect with broader discourses and relations of power; how these sites allow or disallow resistance and challenge. While acknowledging the differences in subject matter, we suggest that a similar analysis can be applied to considerations of other cultural spaces, such as *The Sofa*. Thus in this chapter we demonstrate how meanings related to sexual and gender identity are constructed, authorized, and deauthorized in one queer community forum focused on young lesbian identified women. Doing this provokes us to analyze the types of discourses such a forum supports; another study might also consider the discourses that rarely appear in the frame constructed by *The Sofa* and its members. Such an investigation allows us to consider how these discourses intersect with larger regulatory frames regarding sexual and gender identity with a view to considering how *The Sofa* impacts young women's capacity to imagine diverse ways of "doing" lesbian identity.

Our reading of the cultural significance of *The Sofa* critically extends extant notions of public pedagogy in terms of our focus on the lived politics of affect[2] and gender and sexual identity. Current literature on public pedagogy tends to focus on mass communication and popular texts, as for example, in Giroux's work on commodified cultural texts, such as Disney movies (*Breaking*) or the photographs from Abu Ghraib that were circulated in the global media ("Education after Abu Ghraib"). Referring to sex education in the mid-twentieth century, public pedagogy is conceived by Bashford and Strange in terms of mass communication via media and broadcasting. This raises significant questions. It asks, what counts as "public pedagogy" and more pressingly, what kind of public pedagogy is not being counted, and with what implications? Virtual communities such as *The Sofa* are, we argue, important and under-researched sites of public pedagogy.

Following on from this conceptualization of *The Sofa* as a culturally significant public pedagogy, it is necessary to adopt a theoretical framework to analyze this virtual space. As such, we juxtapose Judith Butler's notion of performativity (1993, 1999) alongside Giroux's notion of public pedagogy. Butler challenges the law of heterosexual coherence, proposing instead that we see sex, sexuality, and gender as denaturalized performances (*Gender Trouble* 175). The Butlerian notion of performativity thus extends Foucault's work on the regulatory practices that compel a particular set of performances relating to sexual and gender identities. Butler is careful not to suggest that these identities are easily undone, but rather that there are no authentic or essential renderings of sex, gender, or sexuality. Such notions are particularly germane to the analysis of discourses regarding sexual and gender identity on *The Sofa* as they allow us to demonstrate the constructed natures of sex, gender, and sexuality, and to consider ongoing processes of negotiation in the production of sexed and gendered subjects.

For Butler all is performance, continuously reiterated, and therefore continuously open to contestation. The possibility of momentarily rupturing and resignifying normative renderings of sex, gender, and sexuality may be read as agency. Though, as our discussion of the "Teenage Chix" community forum suggests, homo and hetero normalizing discourses relating to sexual and gender identity continue to be very persuasive in this context.

If gender and sexuality are configured through experiential relations then connections between certain ideas of self and associated or ensuing feelings, emotional affects and logical systems, it is important to consider how such ideas of self may be constantly reconfigured via *The Sofa*. The lived cultures of people's daily lives are filled with systems of feeling, response, and logic that are bound together as affective logics. Such affective logics are marked by connections between feeling, thought, and external stimulations. As Giroux deploys the notion of public pedagogy to pull apart relationships between media, logic, and embodied response (image-political thought-emotional response-action), we want to employ the concept to similar ends but with a specific focus on a specific queer youth culture.

Taking up this affective reading of public pedagogy, we contend that the construction of gender and sexual identity on *The Sofa* does not, to our minds, provide a window into the "real world" of queer youth cultures. Rather, the community forum we analyze is more appositely read as a space in which individuals take up and learn affective logics that link behavior and appearance to relations and ideas of self. It is in this respect that we consider public pedagogy a useful tool for thinking about the production of gender and sexuality. Such a focus can break up, or *show up*, the amalgam of image-political thought-emotional response-action that produces gender and sexuality. Yet, to say that connections between media, experiences, and identity are political and pedagogical is not enough. The connections themselves must be disturbed. Ways of reading other people must be made conscious rather than unconscious. Ideas of self and other must be fluid and sensitive. In order to do so, we must consider individuals and their identities in ways that afford a nuanced conception of self.

As a consequence, our analysis is sensitive to the intersections between the commodification of identities (Giroux, *Breaking*) and performative productions of subjectivity (Butler, *Bodies*) that shape and we would argue, constitute, our identities. This focus on the critical enmeshments of identity construction and commodification infuses Giroux's public pedagogy with a lived, subjective, and affective dimension. This allows us to hold the micro-politics of gender and sexual identity and the ways in which such processes are informed by publicly accessible media alongside each other.

THE SOFA AS A VIRTUAL ENVIRONMENT

In choosing to explore *The Sofa* as a form of public pedagogy we were (somewhat naïvely) hopeful that this site of queer youth cultures would be a virtual space in which young members' imaginings of gender and sexual identity might be indicative of their capacity to challenge normalizing discourses about lesbian identity. To a certain extent this was, and is, the case. There is no doubt that *The Sofa* offers something which traditional pedagogical settings do not—namely, a virtual space in which members have the opportunity to perform and construct lesbian identities. The opportunity to perform "lesbian" may be read by some as indicative of the acquisition of agency. Drawing on Butler's notion of performativity, we want to provide a more nuanced analysis of the public pedagogy constructed in the "Teenage Chix" community forum.

There is a range of publicly accessible community chat forums on *The Sofa*. These are categorized under the headings of "Music," "General," "Arts," "Sexuality," "Interests," "Support," "Work," "Parenting," and "Generation L." Not all of these categories are aimed at youth. Within "Generation L" there is a youth discussion stream called "Teenage Chix." The excerpts discussed throughout this chapter offer an indicative, but by no means exhaustive, selection of the discursive formations we observed in this forum.

Before moving to our analysis of the discourse of "Teenage Chix," we first need to provide a more detailed discussion of the virtual architecture of *The Sofa*. According to its website, *The Sofa* (2005) "is the world's most popular online lesbian meeting place—and it's comfortable, friendly and fun. You can make new friends, find a date or someone special, have a chat and find answers to your questions!" *The Sofa* connects members of lesbian communities across the globe and offers a range of services including chat rooms, community classifieds, accommodation and conversation forums for people of different age groups.

The Sofa is a cheerful and welcoming virtual environment. It is bright blue and purple and is filled with photographs of women smiling or looking into a camera lens. Images of a "hot pink" sofa with a love-heart-shaped back appear on every page. When a member has not loaded a photograph as part of their member profile, an icon of the sofa-heart occupies the position that could otherwise be taken up by their picture. This image of The Sofa is an aesthetic metaphor, an iconic representation of "love" (the heart-shaped couch back) and domestic comfort (a couch). These are two prominent themes in what people are ostensibly 'looking for' and what people talk about on The Sofa. However, our interest here lies in the processes of identity construction that are part of perusing and cruising on The Sofa.

Once you have joined the site, you get your own home page that indexes messages sent to you from other Sofa members and "smiles" that people have sent you. Here we find two potential bars to young people fully participating in the virtual community of The Sofa. You have to have money, or have a friend with money, in order to have an identity, and you must be over the age of eighteen. As a business enterprise, The Sofa is invested with an economic agenda—in order to have visibility on the site, you have to pay. However, those without the means or desire to become members may still peruse part of member profiles and browse, but not participate in, the numerous grrrltalk forums hosted on the website.

Every member's home page connects them to chat rooms and features themed ways to connect to The Sofa community, alongside a search engine that allows you to locate other members by age, interest, geographical location, or name. It is here that you write your description of self (the act of constructing your own profile), upload or change your photo, and talk about the kinds of relationships you would like to build on and through The Sofa. Your membership home page is your primary "seat" on The Sofa.

"TEENAGE CHIX" AND TECHNOLOGIES OF IDENTIFICATION

Through the virtual community of "Teenage Chix," the nature of lesbianism and the art of being a "real" lesbian are both implicitly and explicitly defined. Comments that imply a "real" lesbianism or being

able to tell if someone is or is not "really" lesbian abound on *The Sofa*.
Below are a few select excerpts of a discussion on "real" lesbianism and
how to pick a "real" lesbian taken from the "Teenage Chix" forum:[3]

Contributor #1

Ok first of all I don't think that the clothes or the hair or the
way that they walk shows anything. I'm the baggy clothes . . .
long hair . . . soft butch looking type . . . and no one can ever
tell just by looking at me. I personally think that you can tell
by the way that they carry themselves. Their movements will
hold some sort of answer and also the eyes . . . always watch
the eyes. That's how I knew my girl was gay . . . and she's
femme like no other. All I can say is . . . never judge a book by
its cover and the worst that can happen is your gaydar is off for
some odd reason and just embarrass yourself and get over it.

Contributor #2

I'm surprised that no one has mentioned a labrys. My partner
has one on a chain round her neck and I remember someone
coming out to me by showing a labrys pendant years ago. Are
they out of popularity?

Contributor #3

First of all . . . I have excellent gaydar. Second of all . . . it's all
in the jewelry. If they have a thumb ring, my god its almost a
given that they're a total dyke. Also it's in the walk . . . some
women also have an aura about them that just screams lesbian.
I don't know how to teach people this; its almost a gut feeling
that I get when I'm around certain people. Needless to
say . . . one of the main giveaways is jewelry and where it is.

Such discussions are interesting in relation to the mediated nature of
these young women's comments: we read these comments, and the fact
that they are published online, as a kind of public pedagogy. *The Sofa*
is a publicly accessible site where knowledge about gender and sexual
identity is generated and shared. What we are particularly interested in
is the types of knowledges that are generated.

Implicit and explicit in all of the aforementioned posts is a sense
that it is possible to *know* whether or not someone is a lesbian via their
eye movements, the jewelry they wear, the way they move, or by your
own "gut feeling." Together, we argue, such statements might be understood as constituting a particular technology of identity "[. . .] strategies that some people deploy and call upon in specific circumstances to
construct familiar and identifiable narratives of [. . .] their sexual and
gendered selves (Rasmussen, *Becoming Subjects* 54). Certain prescriptions
pertaining to sexual and gender identity manifest as members draw
upon and simultaneously construct familiar and identifiable narratives
of what it means to *be* a lesbian. Two of the aforementioned contributors, for instance, draw upon, and simultaneously construct, the familiar
notion of "gaydar." This device is a technology of identification par
excellence (a gay radar, presumably only available to people who are
gay and lesbian identified, enabling them to detect others who are gay
and lesbian identified). The invocation of such a device, often used in
fun, often presupposes an essential lesbian identity. Implied in the idea
of the gaydar, however, is the possibility that those who don't possess
"gaydar" might question their authenticity as lesbians. In this manner,
such conversations are part of constructing powerful "truths" about
what a lesbian *is*, and, equally importantly, what a lesbian is not.

Ostensibly, the forum for "Teenage Chix" constructs what might be
perceived as a participatory notion of engagement, potentially reflecting
an understanding of youth as agentive in their own change. The participatory nature of "Teenage Chix" also performs the understanding that
youth are potential consumers of this product and need to be addressed
directly. As such, *The Sofa* creates an environment quite different from
those institutional settings where young people are compelled by legislation and other social expectations (such as future employment) to participate. The pedagogical relation that this virtual environment sets up is
also quite different from that established in school contexts. For example,
unlike most schools, it is OK to initiate discussions about sexual relations
and same-sex relations on *The Sofa*. Same-sex acts are not considered
taboo topics of conversation on *The Sofa*. While young people in school
environments will often discuss sex in graphic ways, discussion of same-
sex sexual relations may be less likely, particularly as an authorized discourse, in compulsory school settings.

Given that *The Sofa* functions as a pedagogical space where participation is voluntary, outside schooling, it is possible to argue that the
technologies of identification we have discussed in the aforementioned

excerpts are highly persuasive. In their text *Consuming Children*, Kenway and Bullen argue about the strength of young people's affective investments in popular culture. For Kenway and Bullen, such investments are propelled, in part, by popular culture's status as something that is not sanctioned by schooling. Hence, we might consider that the technologies of identification embedded within public pedagogies such as *The Sofa* may also be the most influential in the identity construction of those who participate in "Teenage Chix."

Following on from this we wonder about young people's ability to question these technologies of identification constructed in places like *The Sofa*, particularly given their potential affective investments in such virtual communities. The difficulty of interrogating such technologies may also be heightened by the qualitative uniqueness of such online pedagogies. On *The Sofa*, contributors say they feel safe in discussing same-sex attractions and expressing their "true" feelings as they are not in physical proximity to others who may bully or tease them; an act that is common in school spaces. We do not wish to further exemplify the personal statements made by individuals. However, we would like to note that while *The Sofa* is a safe place in which same-sex attraction is expressed, it can also be a space where essentializing notions of subjectivity are invoked via ideas of "true" feelings or sexuality.

A PUBLIC PEDAGOGY OF GENDERED IDENTITY

In order to consider a public pedagogy of gender identity, it is important to first be specific about how we theorize the notion of gender. Following Butler (*Undoing Gender* 41) we argue that the gendered subject does not preexist regulation but rather is produced *through* regulation. In other words, the process of becoming a gendered subject is always tied to the regulations and modes of relation that produce gender. Here, Butler draws upon, and builds on, the work of Foucault. In linking the production of sexual subjectivities to regulatory discourses, Foucault (1990) writes against the notion that people can "be" straight or gay. In Foucauldian terms, one can never be the quintessential homosexual. For this reason Butler, following Foucault, argues against the notion that subjects are elaborations of an essential or "true" self. People are always in a state of becoming. Linking this point to public pedagogies, we contend that public pedagogies such as those produced on *The Sofa* simultaneously draw upon, reiterate, and disrupt regulations that together produce certain technologies of identification.

One familiar technology of identification frequently explored in the "Teenage Chix" forum pertains to the interrelations between gender and sexual identity. In the excerpts that follow, it is possible to see various understandings of the interrelationship between gender and sexuality. The different ways this interrelationship is interpreted suggest the underlying dissonance between gender and sexuality. Butler offers two reasons for insisting that gender and sexuality should be construed as separate:

> [. . .] the one seeks to show possibilities for sexuality that are not constrained by gender in order to break the causal reductiveness of arguments that bind them; the other seeks to show possibilities for gender that are not predetermined by forms of hegemonic heterosexuality. (*Undoing Gender* 54)

Butler's reading of gender as dissonant is instructive because it provides a theoretical framework for thinking through interrelations between gender and sexuality apparent on *The Sofa* without seeing one as irreducible to the other.

In the first of the following excerpts we can see some of the negative consequences that may be associated with reading gender identity as a marker of sexual identity:

> i always wondered about why people automatically think short hair equals gay girl. I have hair just past my shoulders and when people find out that im gay they always say they could never tell and i usually say how can i tell that you're straight. [Posted: 7 February 2005]

Initially this statement might be considered within the broader cultural context in which it has been constructed. Dominant popular cultural representations of heterosexual femininity as a gendered sexual identity are almost always focused on women having long hair. In light of such a contextual positioning, the previous quote shows a critical perspective on the notion that gendered identity, sexuality, and sexual identity are not the same things ("i always wondered about why people automatically think short hair equals gay girl"). It also indicates some ways in which many people who are *not* involved with GLBTI cultural formations still think these aspects of a person (gendered identity, sexuality, and sexual identity) are the same thing ("when people find out that im gay they always say they could never tell").

The previous excerpt addresses assumptions about sexual identity and hairstyle (gender identity) made by "straight" people. In the following posts on the same topic we can see that certain presumptions that see gender and sexual identity as irreducible are also influential in the discourse of members of the "Teenage Chix" community. Another post on the same theme reads:

> I have heard gay girls that can't get anyone to notice that their [*sic*] gay wanting to shave their heads. I think its the same as rainbow beads. I don't have short hair my hair is all the way down my back and I fix it so its just right. I am very girly and people usually think I am lieing [*sic*] when I say I'm gay. If I were [*sic*] to cut my hair I think alot [*sic*] more people would think I am gay. [Posted: 8 November 2004]

This post suggests that young women who have long hair are more likely to be read as "girly" and therefore not gay, and consequently not objects of the "lesbian" gaze. This offers an example of one way in which young women continue to make heterosexist assumptions regarding the interrelationship between gender and sexual identity in ways that are grounded in aesthetics. Other contributors to this thread of discussion perceive short hair (when paired with a butch gender identity) as somehow deficit because it reinforces hegemonic assumptions of lesbian identity. Both examples demonstrate the pervasiveness of the ties that bind together our performances of, and readings of, gender and sexuality.

While some are critical of conformity to "real" lesbian stereotypes, and others bemoan their struggle to be read as "real" lesbians, still others observe that there can be no consistency in the way that hair is read as a signifier of identity:

> Hrm. Y'know, this is a good topic! . . . I . . . uh . . . think it's the whole gender thing. Short hair is like . . . mimicking masculinity, and of course with the butch/femme thing in lesbian history, a woman embracing anything remotely masculine points to homosexuality. Although, currently, more and more straight girls are going for short hair, and other typical "male" characteristics such as boyish PRACTICAL clothing or a love for videogames etc. The rules no longer apply like they used to. But anyone that disagrees/agrees with my post, please reply.

I really could be talking out of my ass on this. I only just
turned 18, and yet I'm on about lesbian history. [Posted: 4
November 2004]

This forum contributor makes a number of interesting contributions to
this popular debate about short hair. First she attempts to historicize the
ways in which short hair has been, and is, currently interpreted. Interestingly, the "butch/femme" dichotomy is situated here as something
historic in this post, though any user of *The Sofa* will find that it is
replete with butch/femme references. Overall, the contributor seems to
be arguing that rules about gender identity no longer apply, that regardless of sexual identity, young women are now free to author their own
gender identity. Such a perspective is quite contrary to Butler's concept
of agency (*Psychic Life*), which emphasizes the difficulties of intervening
within/against majoritarian opinion.

   Drawing on Butler, one might argue that together these posts on
"short hair" reinforce her contention that gender norms are "always and
only tenuously embodied by any particular social actor" (*Undoing Gender* 41), therefore resisting the temptation to construe these young
women as authors of their own identity. Various regulation of gender
persists, and as the author of the previous post suggests, these regulations have complex histories and they are not constant over time. This
is a noteworthy point in relation to this form of virtual public pedagogy, that is, the contributors to *The Sofa* must navigate their own way
through these contradictory regulations.

   While we cannot know how influential such postings might be
for participants; we do know that these public pedagogies of gendered
identity deftly illustrate the types of gender regulations that are produced in virtual communities. Such an observation prompts us to
question any easy assumptions one might be tempted to make about
the transformative role of virtual queer youth cultures.

CONCLUSIONS

The politically and aesthetically grounded processes of knowledge and
power exchange that occur on *The Sofa* produce embodied affections.
Potentially, such emotional and aesthetic affects can support young
people in dissolving inflexible ideas of "sameness" or "the way things
are" (Gatens and Lloyd). Yet *The Sofa*'s capacity to dissolve ideas of
sameness appears to be more than matched by its capacity to reinforce

ideas of sameness. Such contradictory pedagogies are embedded in lived cultures that cannot be situated outside hegemonic regulations of gender and sexual identity. At the same time, the "Teenage Chix" forum may be read as an important site in the production of queer youth cultures for at least two reasons; first, because it exposes readers and contributors to diverse ways of "doing" sexual and gender identity. Second, publicly accessible forums that foreground issues pertinent to young women's sexual and gender identities at the very least provide a counterbalance to homophobic discourses that still infiltrate young people's lived experience.

In *Architecture from the Outside*, Grosz reflects on the production of virtual identity. She writes:

> The problem is that if you choose to perform a certain sexual identity, then you have not changed at all by undertaking that identity, you're just acting out. It would be nice to be able to choose an identity, but in fact it is chosen for us. Our agency comes from how we accept that designated position, and the degree to which we refuse it, the way we live it out. (22–23)

The debates we have examined can be read as both refusals and adoptions. One of the most interesting things about *The Sofa* for us is the extent to which people affirm some technologies of identification, and how much they refuse others. Regardless of the position that contributors take up, it is apparent from our fieldwork on *The Sofa* that considerations of questions of gender and sexual identity are often central to discussions in the "Teenage Chix" community forum. Furthermore, in the respect that it constitutes a publicly accessible, interactive text on youthful lesbian identity, *The Sofa* can be considered a kind of, and specific location for, public pedagogy.

As a site of public pedagogy, *The Sofa* promotes diverse relationships to gender and sexual identity, showing up their instability while reminding us that such identities can also be produced in hegemonic ways, regardless of the venue in which they are produced. Most saliently, *The Sofa* can be considered an important site of public pedagogy for queer youth cultures. We are happy to observe that there are many enthusiastic *Sofa* users ready to contribute to the dialogue offered on forums such as "Teenage Chix." In so doing, they are taking up the opportunity to participate in the ongoing *production* of a vibrant queer youth culture.

NOTES

1. These community forums are available in the public domain; you do not need to be a member of *The Sofa* community to read postings on the forums hosted by the website.

2. For an explication of "lived politics of affect," see Gatens and Lloyd.

3. The ensuing excerpts are available in the public domain of *The Pink Sofa*. We have chosen to remove the contributors' names.

WORKS CITED

Bashford, Alison, and Carolyn Strange. "Public Pedagogy: Sex Education and Mass Communication in the Mid-Twentieth Century." *Journal of the History of Sexuality* 13 (2004): 71–99.

Butler, Judith. *Gender Trouble: Feminism and the Subversion of Identity*. London: Routledge, 1990.

———. *Bodies That Matter*. New York: Routledge, 1993.

———. *The Psychic Life of Power: Theories in Subjection*. Stanford: Stanford University Press, 1997.

———. *Undoing Gender*. New York: Routledge, 2004.

Ellsworth, Elizabeth. *Teaching Positions: Difference, Pedagogy and the Power of Address*. New York: Teachers College Press, 1997.

Foucault, Michel. *The History of Sexuality, Volume 1: An Introduction*. London: Penguin, 1990.

———. *Discipline and Punish: The Birth of the Prison*. London: Penguin, 1991.

Gallop, Jane, ed. *Pedagogy: The Question of Impersonation*. Bloomington: University of Indiana Press, 1995.

Gatens, Moira, and Genevieve Lloyd. *Collective Imaginings*. London: Routledge, 1999.

Giroux, Henri. "Cultural Studies as Public Pedagogy Making the Pedagogical More Political." *Encyclopedia of Philosophy of Education 1999*. 15 May 2005. <http://www.vusst.hr/ENCYCLOPAEDIA/main.htm>.

———. "Postmodern Education and Disposable Youth." In *Revolutionary Pedagogies: Cultural Politics, Instituting Education and Discourse of Theory*, ed. P. Trifonas. New York: Routledge, 2000.

———. *Breaking in to the Movies: Film and the Culture of Politics*. Malden, MA: Blackwell, 2002.

———. "Public Pedagogy and the Politics of Resistance: Notes on a Critical Theory of Educational Struggle." *Educational Philosophy and Theory* 35, 1 (2003): 5–16.

———. "Cultural Studies and the Politics of Public Pedagogy." *Parallax* 10 (2004): 73–89.

————. "Education after Abu Ghraib: Revisiting Adorno's politics of education." *Cultural Studies* 18 (2004): 779–815.

————. "Cultural Studies, Public Pedagogy, and the Responsibility of Intellectuals." *Communication and Critical Cultural Studies* 1, 1 (2004): 59–79.

Gore, Jennifer. "Disciplining Bodies: On the Continuity of Power Relations in Pedagogy." In *Foucault's Challenge: Discourse, Knowledge and Power in Education*, ed. T. S. Popkewitz and M. Brennan. New York: Teachers College Press, 1998.

————. "Micro-Level Techniques of Power in the Pedagogical Production of Class, Race, Gender and Other Relations." In *Body Movements: Pedagogy, Politics and Social Change*, ed. H. S. Shapiro and S. Shapiro. Cresskill, NJ: Hampton Press, 2002.

Grosz, Elizabeth. *Architecture from the Outside: Essays on Virtual and Real Space.* MIT Press: Cambridge, 2002.

Jagose, Annamaire. *Queer Theory: An Introduction.* Washington Square, NY: New York University Press, 1996.

Kenway, Jane, and Elizabeth Bullen. *Consuming Children: Education-Entertainment-Advertising.* Buckingham, England: Open University Press, 2001.

Lusted, Deborah. "Why Pedagogy?" *Screen* 27, 5 (1986): 2–15.

McWilliam, Erica. "Introduction: Pedagogies, Technologies, Bodies." In *Pedagogy, Technology and the Body*, ed. E. McWilliam and P. G. Taylor. New York: Peter Lang, 1996.

Rabinow, Paul. *The Foucault Reader: An Introduction to Foucault's Thought.* Middlesex: Penguin, 1984.

Rasmussen, Mary Louise. *Becoming Subjects: Sexualities and Secondary Schooling.* New York: Routledge, 2006.

Rasmussen, Mary Louise, and Valerie Harwood. "Using Ethnography to Enhance Contemporary Understandings of Australian Youth Underachievement." *AARE Conference.* Melbourne: December, 2004.

Salih, Sara. *Judith Butler.* New York: Routledge, 2002.

The American Heritage Dictionary of the English Language. 18 April 2005. <http://dictionary.reference.com/>.

The Pink Sofa. 13 April 2005 <http://www.thepinksofa.com>.

Tyler, Ralph W. "Silent, Invisible, Total: Pedagogic Discourse and the Age of Information." In *Reading Bernstein, Researching Bernstein*, ed. Johan Muller, Brian Davies, and Ana Morais. London: Routledge/Falmer, 2004.

CHAPTER 7

PHOTO-ESSAY

Cass Bird

"Prospect Park" 2006

"Talk Normal" 2004

"Golden Shower" 2005

"Dusty and JD" 2005

"Dork" 2003

"Dork Jump" 2003

"I Look Just Like My Daddy" 2003

"I Look Just Like My Mommy" 2003

"Dirty Holiday" 2004

"K8 Hardy" 2004

"Oskar" 2004

"Eliza" 2006

"J.D." 2004

"J.D." 2005

"Isabelle" 2005

"Rhys" 2004

"Rhys" 2004

"Kerby" 2004

"Tire Rolling" 2003

PART TWO

DESIRING YOUTH AND
UN/POPULAR CULTURES

The previous part emphasized do-it-yourself representational practices, honing in on creative ways queer youth fashion identities through a broad range of performative languages. Adapting media technologies and formats to suit their specific and local needs, youth forge interactive and flexible modes of communication. In one sense queer youth cultures provide nuanced alternatives to mainstream commercial cultures, expanding the parameters through which youth signify their personal identities and generate social connections beyond scientific pathologization and media trivialization. At the same time, mass media have also emerged over the last decade in ways that complicate simple divisions between mainstream and independent cultural spheres within the lives of queer youth. Movies, television shows, music, and comics have opened up a much richer field of mediated images and stories that queer youth intimately and insightfully engage with. What is important is not only the increasing visual evidence of explicit textual inclusion of gay and lesbian youth as sympathetic characters and issue-oriented themes, but rather the convoluted interventions of young readers seeking enjoyment and meanings beyond the "straight" ideological scope of youth media. It is a mistake to dismiss popular media cultures as homogeneous, static, or unified in depicting sexual minority youth. Queer youth are increasingly immersed within diverse and niche-oriented media environments and are compelled to struggle over interpretations and stake out pleasures in unpredictable ways. The chapters in this part explore productive tensions between the content and form of mass

157

media texts, local contexts, and queer youth responses. Authors analyze homoerotic subtexts, transgender fictions, schoolgirl crushes, and pornographic fascinations, exploring intriguing spaces between the textual productions of adult media makers and the unruly receptions of young readers.

A growing body of literature examines images of youth across a range of media (Davis and Dickenson 2004; Doherty 2002; Driscoll 2002; Giroux 1996; Shary 2003), connecting a multitude of representations of youth within a postwar era characterized by the proliferation of consumer cultures and specialized media directed toward teens. Analyzing the discursive conditions, visual codes and narrative patterns of texts, adult critics examine how youth are constructed and marketed across varied media formats and genres. Trying to pay more attention to the interpretative creativity of youth, a vein of research has shifted away from detached analysis of texts to consider mobile contexts of reception and the work of resignification undertaken by youth in their daily lives. It is here that theories become woven through ethnographically thick accounts of youth as shrewd and inventive cultural participants (Dimitriadis 2001; Kelly 2004; Kearney 2006; Thornton 1996). While these approaches open up images and stories to the curiosities and emotionally charged investments of youth, the experiences and voices of youth that enter the purview of these texts continue to go unmarked as heterosexual. While the literature available on youth media provides methodological tools that enable youth perspectives to guide a critical heuristic process, the unique and dynamic status of queer youth remains a blind spot.

Although queer influences within popular culture have proliferated over the last decade, youth are often left out of the picture or fetishized as objects of desire. Sexy and sophisticated queer interventions into mass media production and reception rarely take into account the ideas and perceptions of young subjects (Doty 1993; Martindale 1997; Stein). Simultaneously, marketing and research surrounding teen media have reinforced hierarchical ideals of sexual, gender, and generational differences. As part of the general conception of young people as straight consumers and mass cultural participants, most work focused on queer youth tends to ignore or bracket out destabilizing pleasures afforded by TV, films, comics, and music. While there are a few examples of research focused on queer youth and popular cultures (Buckland 2002; Driver 2007; Dennis 2006; Whiteley and Rycenga 2006), these remain exceptions that get crowded out by the saturation of "straight teen" academic discourses. Yet as Rob Linne argues, it is impossible to understand sexual minority youth without taking seriously how queerness emerges in the surprising revelations and confrontations generated in relation to popular fictions. In this view, popular cultures are a formative part of coming of age and shaping queer futures. Linne writes:

> Scratch the surface of most coming out narratives and you'll find a story about literacy, about learning how to read between the lines. Many lesbians and gays tell stories of hearing something in a film or reading something in a book that piqued their early interests in things queer. Such thoughts or ideas tend to set the proto-dyke or fag off on a search for other texts or images that might tell her or him more about what queerness is [. . .]. For many, the first reading of a queer book or film marks a pivotal turning point in their life histories. (201)

The very constitution of identifications and queer rites of passage are inextricable from dynamic uses of popular culture. As sites of intense and contested readings, mass media comprise everyday languages through which youth come to affirm identifications, envision resistance, and question the world around them.

Although studying connections between queer youth and mass media is essential, there is no doubt that relations between them are often troubled and ambivalent. The chapters that follow explore the contradictory ways queer youth are depicted in media, and negotiate with media. Deriving meaning, value, and enjoyment from mass-produced texts becomes a tricky process, compelling youth to embellish, misread, and reimagine established codes and formats. The status of and specific terrain encompassing "popular culture" specific and relevant to queer youth is neither self-evident nor guaranteed. What counts as queer youth–oriented popular cultures is contingent on shifting and intersecting social and semiotic relations that complicate the very boundaries defining minority media. Many ostensibly "positive" and inclusive images also work to reify or normalize particular subjects, and seemingly heterosexual media examples may provoke unexpected and productive queer readings. The point is not to secure and define exactly what constitutes queer youth culture but to spur multiple lines of inquiry across the expansive interpretive spaces and temporalities of queer reception.

Popular cultures matter to all youth, but the stakes are higher for those who struggle against pervasively narrow racist, homophobic, and sexist representations. Growing up within mass media environments that naturalize and celebrate white, middle-class heterosexual teen romance, young people with same-sex desires and gender-variant inclinations learn to read popular texts critically and imaginatively. Reception-oriented approaches tap into creative strategies through which youth negotiate institutional invisibility as well as psychic shame and loneliness. In this way, the vulnerable status of queer youth on the boundaries between mainstream and alternative cultures is framed in terms of active hermeneutic practices. Extending queer reception research to consider the specific conditions and directions of young people, Mark Lipton moves between texts and the emotionally charged insights of young readers in his chapter, "Queer Readings of Popular Culture: Searching [to] Out the Subtext." Exploring how he became aware of his homoerotic attractions as a boy through subtextual readings of Archie comics, Lipton calls for situated analyses that take account of socio-symbolic conditions of erasure and devaluation as a backdrop to personally charged and interactive readings. Interviewing youth who recount pivotal moments of recognition and erotically charged memories, Lipton places emphasis on the deft ways youth maneuver queer meanings out of a range of media sources and personal circumstances. Lipton's work contributes to an empirical reframing of queer youth in relation to practical media engagements and dialogues.

Whereas Lipton focuses on the dynamics of media reception, Melissa Rigney's chapter, "Brandon Goes to Hollywood: *Boys Don't Cry* and the Transgender Body in Film," examines the process of representing transgender youth within Hollywood films, staying close to textual ambiguities and ideological closures of meaning. No longer relegated to subtexts, television and film characters and plots have come to explicitly address lesbian, gay, bisexual, transgender, and questioning subjects. While there is no single or transparent rendering of these identity formations, patterns emerge through which transgender selves and relations are made publicly intelligible. As images of marginalized youth enter fields of popular vision, complex modes of commodification and normalizing work to delimit the very terms through which they are popularized. Rigney demonstrates the importance of intertextual analysis to understand how trans youth are framed according to mainstream assumptions. Rigney maps out constructions of transgender bodies in film in order to position the fictional account of Brandon Teena's life within a broader context of commercial media production. She calls attention to the ways transgender subjects become subsumed within stories centered on essentialized lesbian desires, or heterosexual fascinations with gendered "others," reproducing safe and contained public discourses. At the same time Rigney analyzes ambiguous narrative lines deployed by this Hollywood film, theorizing them as part of a cautionary tale about the threat of violence against those who embody queer differences.

What becomes clear whether critical interest is directed toward the creative tendencies of queer youth reception, the ideological powers of media content, or indirect and elusive signifiers of desire, is that mass media representations are systematically produced by adults and rarely involve the voices of youth as participants in the process of making media. Considering this institutional imbalance, it becomes very important to address those rare instances of queer youth working within mainstream industries. This is especially important when it comes to industries such as pornography that have traditionally exploited youth bodies as spectacles of adult entertainment and voyerism. In his chapter, "Queering Pornography: Desiring Youth, Race, and Fantasy in Gay Porn," Zeb J. Tortorici reflects on his work within the gay male porn movie industry in Los Angeles as a white queer university student, tracing the contours of his own longing and ambivalence toward being a visual and commodified object of desire. He provides room to consider the contradictions of being a porn model and consumer of porn, while also challenging the hegemonic ideologies and structural inequalities entrenched by commercial porn producers. Exploring his sexuality in the context of making money as a porn model, Tortorici overcomes one-sided emphasis on porn as a mode of predatory control over youth bodies. This essay refuses easy answers, combining life writing and critical theory into an essay style that both locates and complicates an individual tale of pornographic adventures. Tortorici engages with historical legacies of racialized, gendered, and age-based fetishization while addressing his specific erotic curiosities about doing and watching porn as a youth. This reflexive attempt to foreground the experiences of a young queer person working within porn industries overcomes tendencies to focus exclusively on the exploitative commercial powers of porn production.

WORKS CITED

Buckland, Fiona. *Impossible Dance: Club Culture and Queer World-Making.* Middletown, CT: Wesleyan, 2002.

Davis and Dickenson, eds. *Teen TV: Genre, Consumption, Identity.* London: British Film Institute, 2004.

Dennis, Jeffery P. *Queering Teen Culture*. New York: Harrington Park Press, 2006.

Dimitriadis, Greg. *Performing Identity/Performing Culture: Hip Hop as Text, Pedagogy and Lived Practice*. New York: Peter Lang, 2001.

Doherty, Thomas. *Teenagers and Teenpics*. Philadelphia: Temple University Press, 2002.

Doty, Alexander. *Making Things Perfectly Queer: Interpreting Mass Culture*. Minneapolis: University of Minnesota Press, 1993.

Driscoll, Catherine. *Girls: Feminine Adolescence in Popular Culture and Cultural Theory*. New York: Columbia University Press, 2002

Driver, Susan. *Queer Girls and Popular Culture*. New York: Peter Lang, 2007.

Giroux, Henry. *Fugitive Cultures: Race, Violence and Youth*. New York: Routledge, 1996.

Kelly, Jennifer. *Borrowed Identities*. New York: Peter Lang, 2004.

Linne, Rob. "Choosing Alternatives to the Well of Loneliness." In *Thinking Queer: Sexuality, Culture and Education*, ed. Susan Talburt and Shirley R. Steinberg. New York: Peter Lang, 2000.

Martindale, Kathleen. *Un/Popular Culture: Lesbian Writing After the Sex Wars*. Albany: State University of New York Press, 1997.

Shary, Timothy. *Generation Multiplex: The Image of Youth in Contemporary American Cinema*. Austin: University of Austin Press, 2003.

Thornton, Sarah. *Club Culture*. Middletown, CT: Wesleyan, 1996.

Whiteley, Sheila, and Jennifer Rycenga. *Queering the Popular Pitch*. New York: Routledge, 2006.

CHAPTER 8

QUEER READINGS OF POPULAR CULTURE

SEARCHING [TO] OUT THE SUBTEXT

Mark Lipton

Queer youth are imaginative and dynamic readers of popular culture. The negotiated meanings queer youth make of these cultural forms reveal a great deal about the queer imagination and its relationships to sexual desire and political resistance. This chapter identifies the reading practices of queer youth to describe the means and motives of their engagement with popular culture. Richard Dyer explains, "Because, as gays, we grew up isolated not only from our heterosexual peers but also from each other, we turned to the mass media for information and ideas about ourselves" (1). As queer youth participate with popular media, they question and investigate the various modes by which desire and identity are produced; queer reading practices help young people explore the links between pleasure and power, between the body and subject, in the formation of a queer identity.

This chapter first tells my story about an emergent queer reading practice. Then, I discuss research I conducted with queer youth about popular media. They had a lot to say. For various reasons, everyone spoke at length about the queer content and context of their quotidian practices with media. Media make up a significant amount of their leisure time that is often spent in pursuit of pleasure and affirmation, and, as such, media function as a tool that gives queer youth agency to construct complicated, non-heteronormative identities. When queer youth actively engage with popular culture, the engagement itself reveals the inner workings of the queer imagination and the process of GLBTTIQQ world-making. I employ the term "queer youth" to highlight the anti-essentialist approach the people I spoke with applied to their own lives. Queer theory challenges and breaks apart conventional categories of male and female and by extension the paradigm of hetero versus homo identities that proliferate in popular culture. Queer youth actively reconstruct the ontology of conventional categories through queer reading practices that are both interactive and resistant, both participatory and distinct.

JUGHEAD WEARS A TIARA: *NON COMPOS MENTIS*

As a teenaged queer, I engaged in a negotiated reading practice with Archie comics. The characters in this comic series are made up of a group of high school students, including one particular character named Jughead. After some consideration, I realized that to me, Jughead—Forsythe "Jughead" P. Jones—is gay. There are so many stories to retell that illuminate my reading of Jughead as queer. His habit of running in terror from big Ethel's advances suggests his distaste for aggressive women. In fact, I took Jughead to avoid sexual innuendo with all women. Despite his close friendship with both Veronica and Betty, he never put the moves on either. Eventually, I was reading comics to see how often Jughead would confess his hatred of girls. In "The Tender Trap" Jughead finds his best friend, Archie, in his bedclothes; Archie is not well and is unable to date Veronica for the next few days. Archie hatches his plan. To prevent his archrival, Reggie, from moving in on his girl, Archie plans to ask someone he trusts "to run interference." Jughead shrugs off the plan, for he can't think of a single trustworthy fellow Archie could ask. Archie winks at Jughead hinting there is one such guy. I know what's coming—as do all regular Archie readers. But what happens in the next few comic frames is worth citing here to make my point:

> Jughead: Boy! What a three-cornered square he must be! He can't be Human! Is he really alive??

> Archie: Sure! It's just that he doesn't flip over the gals!

Jughead: Yuk! Yuk! Besides being *non compos mentis*, this guy must also have holes in his head! Who is he, Arch?

Archie: You!

Jughead: Well, look for someone else to trust! I'm not taking anybody's girl to anyplace for anybody at anytime!

Archie: Jughead! You've got to keep my date with Veronica for me!!

Jughead: No! No! Girls are nothing but trouble.

There are three issues I want to address by referring to "The Tender Trap." First, this is an example of the exact moment that provided me with reading pleasure. It's what I read for, if you will. According to Jughead, "Girls are nothing but trouble." Michel de Certeau's metaphor of reading as "poaching" is particularly apt: my reading "insinuates into another person's text the ruses of pleasure and appropriation" (xxi). I have reclaimed Archie comics for myself, Jughead as my own. And, exactly what is Jughead doing in the bedroom of the nearly naked Archie? My subtext implicitly acknowledges Jughead's love of Archie. Here, my reading satisfies the notion of "queerness," in Alexander Doty's term, "as a mass culture reception practice" (2). Hurray! Finally there was someone like me in my everyday practice of life. He was fictitious, animated, a cartoon—but you can't have everything. The pleasure of Jughead was only the beginning of a queer reception practice that, for decades, has me searching and seeking a subtext.

The second issue is the importance of Jughead's denial. "He can't be Human!" My identification with Jughead's closet provided me with a psychological role model. The queer worldview Jughead taught me about was defined by the closet. Clearly, the Juggie doth protest too much. Knowing that I didn't have a best friend from whom I needed to hide my feelings, I took a somewhat different approach to my denial—I was quiet. I needed to deny my sexuality from the entire world, including myself. My refusal was silence. For Michel Foucault, there is not one but many silences, "and they are an integral part of the strategies that underlie and permeate discourses" (27). My silence was the result of the inner fantasy space created through my lonely readings. Lonely, because as an adolescent I thought I was totally alone—single-handed, if you will, in my desire for same-sex relations. Nonetheless, my silent reading of Jughead, wanting Jughead, made me feel good. But it was a silent practice, the creation not just of a fantasy space, but a safe space—a dark closet. If I identified with Jughead's sexuality because of his repeated refusal, my situated place as an adolescent warned me that others would see through my charade if I were to protest as often, so I learned to hide.

The need for this hiding was emphasized by Jughead's tendency toward self-hating homophobia—*non compos mentis*. This homophobia is my third issue. Jughead's non compos mentis contributed to the intense insecurity I felt about defining my identity in normative terms. Despite finding myself in popular culture, it was still within a homophobic context. I had all the more reason to hide my sexual desires—from others, and myself—for the subtle messages of queerness in Jughead warned me of a mental instability. As Eve Kosofsky Sedgwick articulates, "*Closetedness* itself is a performance initiated as such by the speech act of a silence" (4). Silence hid my insecurity and fear of the antilocutional attacks, discrimination, if not violence I might endure as a result of my desires. Shhh . . . best to be silent. The darker my closet, the more I hid, the more I hated myself. I soon agreed, I believed, I was not mentally competent. De Certeau distinguishes between "believing and making people believe" (177) and his argument posits the dangers of assuming "that the objects believed are the same as the act of believing" (184). As I learned to believe in my poaching practice, that Jughead was queer, the resultant behaviors had me concerned with making other people believe. Negotiating my readings of Archie comics gave me a sense of identity and pleasure, taught me to deny this identity through silence, and exploited my closeted identity in ways that reinforced homophobic discourse. Like Jughead, I had fallen into "The Tender Trap" of queer identity.

HIDE AND SEEK

In hindsight, I recognize the contradictions of how my reading practice gave me a sense of identity and yet the messages in popular culture taught me to deny this identity. Here was my life, a game of hide and seek. Hide my sexuality and seek my sexual identity in my practice of everyday life. Hide and seek was more than a game, it was my closeted survival strategy. Yet, it was also my parlance into homosociality. When I discovered this guy in my class with a Jughead T-shirt, it was my first official opportunity to come out of the closet, to emerge from hiding with Jughead holding my hand. And I was safe. Eventually, Jughead's internalized homophobia was exactly why I read queerness. To combat the darkness of the closet, it was important for me to struggle for power through the practice of "outing" popular culture as queer. My reading practice was a political act, not just a means of reinforcing the closet, but as my way out as I learned to use my voice to demand attention, respect, and equality. Thank you Forsythe "Jughead" P. Jones.

In beginning this study, I hoped to determine if other queer youth read texts in a similar way, and explored the influences of media at individual and collective levels of engagement. In thinking about my experiences, I wanted to generate data about how cultural identities are produced and to hear the stories of other queer youth. My study is ethnographic in nature as I am interested in the specific social contexts and subjective dimensions of queer reading practices. Consequently, I interviewed twenty-four "out individuals between the ages of 18 and 23. The majority of their discussions focused on film and television, yet others discussed poetry, literature, celebrity, gossip, comic books, cartoons, and music. This project recognizes the importance of reading as a complex social event that is interpretive and distinctive. With this in mind, I look at a queer youth culture to see if this social group acquired a set of learned cultural codes that influences reading practices.

I employ a queer youth hermeneutic code as I try to understand this culture's interpretive reading practices. Hermeneutics is the act of and study of interpretation, leading to an understanding of the significance of human actions. Hermeneutics assumes that cultural products are texts (in a broad sense) that must be interpreted; the primary aim of analysis is understanding, not explanation. As such, a hermeneutic approach refers to a relatively open, loose, and often unconscious system of implicit interpretive practices (see, for example, Guiraud). The text is recognized as something woven, and readers join authors as the weavers. That is, the emphasis is on the text as an open and perhaps even unfinished process in which the reader has some (specific) work to do. By asking queer youth to identify the codes and conventions within media representations to which they attend, I was able to describe queer youth reading practices and how these practices help in understanding the formation of identity in queer youth culture.

In this chapter, I rely on the voices of my participants to explain how a queer reading practice works and the pleasure and power of their readings. Following strict research protocols, the names in this chapter have been changed to protect the identity of my participants. The bulk of this research was completed in 1990. Some of the examples, then, should reflect the popular culture of the 1980s and 1990s. I end this chapter with some short reflections in the years since I undertook this research. About ten years later I repeated a less formal study with a younger group of high school students enrolled at Harvey Milk High School in New York City. I am not only interested in how queer youth readers comprehend various texts, but in shifts in the queer imagination that may have resulted in a decade where queer representations have become more commonplace.

THE PRODUCTION OF QUEER IDENTITIES: YOU ARE NOT ALONE

Unequivocally, the queer youth that I interviewed decode texts against the mainstream, heterosexual grain. The practice of queer identity production occurs in three important ways. Some directly sought to alter the intended meaning of a text as a result of their personal agendas—to bend interpretation from a heteronormative reading. These readers could find homosocial/sexual content present in almost any text. A second group of youth engaged in more specific practices of negotiation—with a specific text, a specific character, like my experience with Jughead. It seems these readers use both conscious and unconscious processes to fabricate an imagined text, a queer world, as a result of their (often isolated) sexuality. And a third approach to negotiation placed the reader in the role of detective. These readers insist their queer reading is directly embedded within the text by the author and their job is to find the hidden messages—meant only for them. Certainly many queer youth negotiate meanings in such ways that accommodate all of these approaches. Nonetheless, these differences are significant in determining the particulars of queer reading habits, the queer imagination, and the implications for queer youth culture.

Among the people I interviewed, the degree of involvement with the text is what marked their interpretations.

> If I read a superhero comic, like Spiderman, I would always see him as being a fag. I don't know why. Now I couldn't see Superman, but I could see Spiderman because he was more human than most comic characters. The way he moved, he was quite flexible and I could sort of envision him as real. Yeah, I would eroticize him, in that sense, but I was also a huge fan. (Tom, age 22)

> For example the T-shirt that I am wearing is an example of
> what you're talking about, you know, the "Brady Girls." How
> many girls of my age didn't have a crush on Marsha or Jan
> when they were growing up? And not just thinking that she
> was in love with some guy in high school and just always
> inserting yourself in the role of that guy, imagining that it was
> you. This [T-shirt] is a symbol of the whole process that you're
> talking about. (Christine, age 22)

Christine illustrates her involvement with *The Brady Bunch* by wearing
a T-shirt, and continually discussing her involvement with the show. She
justifies her serious dedication to Marcia and Jan by explaining the
necessity for her interpretation. Tom is a "huge fan" of Spiderman.
These examples describe the imagined text, where Marcia Brady and
Spiderman function as the textual element, if not fetish object, that
initiates a serious commitment to the process of negotiation.

PLEASURE, LEISURE, AND AFFIRMATION

Everyone I interviewed indicated the pleasure they derived from their
interpretations, from their practice of reading—a practice of leisure.
Simply put, most entertainment media texts are written with the
intention of being enjoyed. However that need is perceived, it is
important to acknowledge the experience of pleasure as integral to
the process of reading.

> If I pretend she's a dyke, then I can accept that this character
> might be a real person, instead of just accepting their hetero-
> sexuality and accepting that they're just a character. So I think
> it [my approach to reading] has added a sense of belief in what
> I'm ingesting. It's certainly much more interesting and much
> more entertaining which I think is very important. Like it's
> important to me to have that kind of stimulus in my life.
> Something that's entertaining. Janet or Sabrina as straight was
> less fun than when I believed she was a dyke. So it satisfied that.
> (Gabby, age 18)

For Gabby, the level of delight is increased, not only in the final analysis,
but also in the act of reading. By playing with the text, an individual
can have fun with the end result as well as in the act of creating that

result. In addition, pleasure is not only derived from the actual act of interpretive reading but also from sharing this experience. As Susan (age 22) describes, "I get a real kick out of it, it is real fun and I wish she was gay and I tell other people, and we all get a laugh out of it, and we share bits of information." Pleasure for queer youth is derived in two ways: by playing with the text—the act of negotiation—and by sharing the altered text with others.

Sharing this process of reading has positive implications for the community because it requires interaction as a queer community, exploring shared experiences and potentially forming groups that can support queer youth. Jessica (age 18) demonstrates this affirmation when she said:

> I would think on my own, of my past, of how I would relate to one particular woman in a book or in a TV show. And as I came out and met more queer women, we would talk about Sabrina [Charlie's Angles] and all the other women we believed to be gay. We would compare notes and they loved the fact that I had a crush on Sabrina because they felt the same way. It was something we all had in common and it was something that we ALL know, we all thought that she was a dyke.

As Jessica was coming out of the closet she shared her knowledge of the character Sabrina Duncan on *Charlie's Angels* with other queer women. Her sharing offered a sense of acceptance. This "comparing notes" is a method of breaking out of the isolation that queer youth experience before they come out. Sharing enjoyable experiences is an especially positive and empowering vehicle for change. Unfortunately, not all of the youth engaged in this activity of sharing. Some of them saw their interpretation as something private, for whatever reason, and thought of their reading as a secret. As George (age 23) said, "I never had a real problem with it, except obviously it's a secret. I probably have never told anyone except you, actually." The idea of having a secret is extremely prevalent among queer people. It was "obvious" to this individual that his reading was a secret because he is so easily capable of keeping such queer-related information to himself. It would be helpful for other queer youth to know that it is possible to share this information with others. Both pleasure and group affirmation can empower the individual, to be accepted by others, to end feelings of isolation.

THE DILEMMA OF DESIRE

Desire is a complex and unstable part of queer youth interactions with mass media. Media representations of queer youth are scarce. For the queer youth I spoke with, there were no stable representations of queer sex or queer love to emulate. At least in 1990, there was no gay American idol for us to worship. So, like in the silence of daily life, queer youth engage in the imaginative play of sexual acts with works of fiction. [Imagine Jughead naked.] It is common for an individual to desire a person or character in popular culture. But desire is not just a physical yearning for the unattainable. Frank articulates the dilemma of desire:

> I was 12 and very much in the throes of puberty, and just needed an object, needed something to relate to in that way and since there weren't any other images available it didn't matter that these people were portrayed as straight. All I needed was an object to project desire upon [. . .]. I guess in a sense it's a desire either to be them or be with them.

Because of this dilemma, I classify desire within complex social and psychological relations. I see the physical wanting of others as a social desire. Social because it affects behavior patterns, and sets standards or goals of what individuals find attractive. In discussing Spiderman, Tom articulates his desire, "I always remember sitting around looking at Spiderman's butt. I like Spiderman's butt, I think he has a nice butt. You know what I mean?" Clearly, queer youth are looking for sexual outlets, a desire to be intimate with specific characters/people, or just to be intimate.

As Frank described his desire, he wasn't sure if he wanted to be with his object of desire, or be him. Desire is not just a sexual yearning, but can include other psychological elements as well. An individual may just want to see another character who they believe is queer. Stephen (age 19) describes his desire as a kind of identification, "Well I hoped he was gay because he was really sexy, but whenever some character has some sort of mysterious quality to them, when it is deliberately mysterious, you know, you think that this must be their secret." One method of dealing with the isolation of growing up queer, for these youth, was to create a group of friends from fiction. As Ronald (age 17) says, "I identified with characters around my own age, I was looking for friends who could be gay. Being in school and not having any gay friends, it would make me feel better to have my gay TV friends." Messages in media and popular culture do not inform queer youth about the available choices. By decoding texts in this manner, queer youth can begin to learn how to answer these kinds of questions about desire. By having friends, even fictional ones, queer youth have a type of belonging. There is someone to identify with, giving the individual confidence and assurance.

NEGOTIATING IDENTITIES

I see identity as something constructed for and by queer youth; they reach a point in their lives when they question the significance of their sexuality. When these youth were talking to me in 1990, there were few examples within popular culture to help them make these kinds of identity decisions. Nonetheless, after emerging from the closet, these youth were very articulate about their identification needs.

> Because it's so rare that you can actually identify with someone who actually is a gay character that you kinda make it up or whatever. You know people really need role models, and gay people just don't have any, in TV and stuff, they just are never there. You know for gay men and lesbians, especially lesbians, because they are so invisible already. (Brian, age 22)

> I can identify with their choice and their sexual preference. But it's more like when you have a common link or something it makes you feel strength. Yeah. Someone that reinforces you. Someone that revitalizes you, makes you feel stronger about yourself, or makes you believe in yourself. (Sayeda, age 21)

Queer people have trouble being active participants in mass popular culture because they are not included in society's view of the "mass." Yet, queer reading practices articulate queer positions in and about mass culture that reveal popular culture need not exclusively and inevitably express straightness. The queer imagination helps queer youth find strong moral guidance in a media world where queerness is absent. As Doty writes, "If mass culture remains by, for, and about straight culture, it will be so through our silences" (104). A queer reading practice helps queer youth empower themselves with the necessary tools for constructive living. Queer reading practices provide the conditions for a range of possible identities and subject positions. Since popular cultural production is unable to provide queer youth with sufficient models for behavior, queer reading practices help queer youth negotiate these identity needs.

OCCUPYING THE FANTASY SPACE: QUEER WORLD-MAKING

An alternative worldview, one that is queer, begins with the construction of a safe fantasy space. My findings led me to believe that queer youth have more creative imaginations because they develop a keen ability to fantasize. As Maria (age 22) describes, "Sometimes the fantasy is the only thing you have. It's never bad to use your imagination, it's one of the greatest gifts we have and unfortunately people don't use it enough. Your imagination is a great escape sometimes, especially if the situation you are in doesn't allow for any kind of outlet. It helps you keep your sanity." To examine the implications of a queer imagination is to recognize queer world-making as a talent, honed out of a need to establish a safe space for the individual, but once this talent is developed it can be put to many uses.

> Whenever I was watching television, there was always some fantasy scenario with me in it, in which I would get whatever cute guy I was really attracted to on the show. I fantasized because I think I was still constructing a place for myself. I mean I needed that and I wanted it and I think it was a normal thing to do. Because it wasn't there, I had to make it up. It went into pretty complex narratives, and I'd do this with all kinds of stuff, it would be like, with the *Six Million Dollar Man*, a total babe. My sisters used to really be into teen magazines for girls, you know, they used to have all these teen idol pictures. I used to steal the magazines and read them, but I would always read them in my way, right. I would always read them as appealing to me. My fantasies would sort of be played out, even thought they were always written for girls. (Matthew, age 23)

It is particularly important for queer youth to engage in these fantasies. But what is also important is to let young people know these fantasies are acceptable forms of behavior. Before coming out of the closet, many queer youth experience guilt about their feelings—the beginnings of their queer world-making practice are often silent, hidden private fantasies. By creating a fantasy space, queer youth have an environment where they are free to explore many possibilities. When one emerges from the closet, these feelings are no longer kept secret. Yet this practice continues to be valuable because it reinforces a queer worldview. Even after coming out, it is difficult to feel completely comfortable in a society where you know that a large part of the population wishes you did not exist. If queer youth are unable to express their sexuality on the street, in public, they should have the sense of freedom to do so in a private created space.

It is also important to recognize this is a created space, and not reality. Queer youth do not spend their days in delusion, waiting for Steve Austin (the *Six Million Dollar Man*) to sweep them off their feet. Most individuals engage in this activity fully aware that it is an imaginative engagement and not reality. Yet, this is an important practice because it allows queer youth to know how to make meaning for themselves in a society that holds so many prejudices against them. By creating a queer worldview, a safe fantasy space, queer youth can flee the prejudice surrounding them and feel comfortable. By their own accord, they are included as the "masses" and thus can participate as consumers of popular culture without feeling marginalized.

COMING OUT OF THE CLOSET

Coming out of the closet, this action, is one of the main features of queer youth culture. All my participants talked at length about coming out. And this discourse is not just about an individual declaration, coming out is a complex social process that infuses new meanings with the conventional representations of queerness, like sexual deviance or Jughead's notion of non compos mentis. Of the youth I spoke with, it was clear that the construction of a queer worldview created through a negotiated reading practice supported the construction of identity. For some, negotiated readings helped with the coming out declaration; for others, this process intensified insecurity by defining identity in normative terms. To follow this logic, when I have to imagine a sexuality that isn't on the screen, my discourse reinforces my identity as absent, negative, wrong. But the general consensus was that coming out somehow changed the function of this practice, or the practice itself.

Because I needed it even more before I came out. When you are out you know a lot of gay people, and the more gay people you

but rather, picking up certain clues that are embedded in the text. One of the arguments presented recognizes the infiltration of arts communities by queer people. This belief asserts that these queer authors insert homosexual clues that only queer audience members would recognize.

> I mean simply because so many of the producers are gay themselves. And I think in reality there is a lot of bargaining that goes on. I think a lot of people create these shows, and they know they can't put a gay or lesbian character on a show, especially at the time of *Three's Company*. But—they gave us Janet's short hair. See I think Janet was a dyke. That's why she was always looking for a man and never having a relationship that worked. She was a dyke, no wonder. People who were closeted in their own professions were sending messages to the rest of us that we're here and we're giving you what we can give you. (Sylvie, age 22)

This participant, looking back at the show *Three's Company*, believes that the authors intended the character Janet to be read as a lesbian. Another specific example is with the children's television show *Sesame Street*.

> For me, Ernie and Bert are together. I just think that, only because their creator Jim Henson is a gay man and I'm sure when he created this little world, he must have had the intentions in his head, oh, I'm gonna create these two little cute guys and they're together maybe that reflected his relationship with somebody [. . .]. (Billy, age 19)

This is particularly interesting because the author's sexuality becomes something that is debatable. The notion that these authors intend their work to be recognized by queer audiences further empowers queer youth by placing them in a position of knowing something that mass audiences do not see.

Queer youth often describe their participation with popular culture as a kind of code cracking. The queer imagination shifts from a process of creative construction to an active process of finding the right clues. For many queer youth, the veracity of some popular culture only comes to light when their reading provides some glimpse into a queer world. Hollywood is, after all, full of queers. The youth I spoke with might be right in their assumptions that clues are embedded within the text for

them, as queer, to discover. Nonetheless, the reader as detective still asserts
the importance of negotiated reading practices and the development of
a queer imagination—detectives also rely on an interpretive reading strategy. Whether or not queer subtexts are embedded within texts, what is
important is the notion of interpretive reading. Queer reading practices
resist dominant social and political models of identity and representation
as practiced by American media and popular culture.

WHO DO YOU THINK IS QUEER?

In 1998 I began to volunteer at the Harvey Milk High School in New
York City—the high school celebrated as serving GLBTTIQQ youth.
It had been almost ten years since I began this research and I had
continued to canvass queer youth with the question "Who do you
think is queer?" The proliferation of queer representations in popular
culture today is radically different than those messages in the early
1990s. These students all watched *Will & Grace*. The celluloid closet (and
the 1995 documentary inspired by Russo's work) had been opened,
cleaned out, and aired on public television. Later, *Queer as Folk* and *The
L Word* were in production and these youth had advanced knowledge
of what representations were about to be released into mainstream
media. Popular culture had shifted significantly and I began to wonder
what this meant to my notion of the queer imagination.

First and foremost, what I noticed about these students was that
there was no need to hide. The safe environment, their high school,
supported these youth. Though many of them had compelling stories
to tell about their queer worlds, when I less formally asked these queer
youth about their queer reading practices they were quick to respond
with talk about the current icons of the queer world. We started looking at homo-normative texts, like *Out Magazine* and Rosie O'Donnell.
But these imaginations had not waned from those I had studied a
decade earlier. Here was the queer imagination, still at work. Queer
youth continue to use popular culture to question and investigate the
various modes by which desire and identity are produced.

Most texts produced in popular culture are heteronormative, and
until this changes, queer youth will continue to employ their imaginations and engage in interpretative reading practices. Following Doty,
"Queer readings aren't 'alternative' readings, wishful or willful misreadings,
or 'reading too much into things' readings. They result from the recognition and articulation of the complex range of queerness that has been

in popular culture texts and their audiences all along" (16). Searching
out or searching to out a queer subtext, queer readings have a range of
functions from the personal to the political, from social relations to
psychological desires. My participants and I aren't reading too much
into things. We just read. Thank you for reading.

WORKS CITED

Doty, Alexander. *Making Things Perfectly Queer: Interpreting Mass Culture*. Min-
neapolis and London: University of Minnesota Press, 1993.
Dyer, Richard, ed. *Gays and Film*. New York: Zoetrope, 1984.
Foucault, Michel. *The History of Sexuality, Volume I: An Introduction*. New York:
Pantheon, 1978.
Guiraud, Pierre. *Semiology*. London: Routledge and Kegan Paul, 1975.
Russo, Vito. *The Celluloid Closet*. New York: Harper and Row, 1981.
Sedgwick, Eve Kosofsky. *Epistemology of the Closet*. Berkeley: University of
California Press, 1990.
"The Tender Trap," *Archie Comic Digest*, No. 10, February 1975. Published by
Archie Comic Publications, Inc., 1116 First Avenue, New York, New
York, 10021.

CHAPTER 9

BRANDON GOES TO HOLLYWOOD

BOYS DON'T CRY AND THE
TRANSGENDER BODY IN FILM

Melissa Rigney

Widely publicized and distributed, Kimberley Pierce's[1] *Boys Don't Cry* proved a box-office hit and won a number of awards, including the Best Actress Oscar for Hilary Swank for her portrayal of Brandon Teena. The film brought mainstream media attention to the life and tragic death of Brandon Teena in addition to precipitating extensive academic debate.[2] For the first time, audiences were introduced to a transgender character that was not demonized as either killer, sexual predator, or deranged psychopath. This is no small matter. Within contemporary American culture and film, Brandon Teena[3] has the potential to operate as a force of interruption and disruption putting into "question identities previously conceived as stable, unchallengeable, grounded, and 'known' " (Garber 13). The current fascination with the life and murder of Brandon Teena and the recent release of the film *Boys Don't Cry* suggest a moment when a critical, and potentially transgressive, space might open up within mainstream and popular culture.

Historically, cinematic representations of transgender characters are notorious for their portrayals of the transgendered as psychotic serial killers or as figures of fun and comic relief. Prior to *Boys Don't Cry*, films that included a transgender character often represented that

181

character as abnormal and disturbed, hence dangerous and othered.[4] *The Silence of the Lambs* is an excellent example of the way in which the trans figure is othered and the heteronormative gender and sexual order reinforced and stabilized. In this film, the self-castrated killer murders and skins young women in order to stitch together a female body suit. The motive of the killer is portrayed as stemming from the desire to possess and to become the unattainable, a biological woman. His anger stems from the "illusion" that, born in the wrong body, he is literally cheated out of what is rightfully his.

Almost always, the trans threat is contained via death at the hands of an authority figure, one that represents both order and stability.[5] In the literal case of *The Silence of the Lambs*, the biological (read natural) female triumphs over the unnatural, delegitimized pretender to all that is female and feminine. This film implies that biological sex is fixed at birth, that the desire to change one's biological sex is rooted in abnormality and psychosis, and that the ultimate and unattainable wish to change one's sex leads to both madness and murder.

The Silence of the Lambs is just one example of a number of contemporary films that portray a male-to-female character. In contrast, female-to-male characters, prior to the release of *Boys Don't Cry*, have gone largely unrecognized except in what I would call a heterosexual format. Two contemporary mainstream films with a female-to-male lead are Barbara Streisand's *Yentl* (1983) and the 1980s teen comedy *Just One of the Guys* (1985).[6] Both female leads cross-dress and pass in order to gain access to areas deemed off limits to women. Unhappy with the limits placed on her because she is a woman, and rejecting the role of wife and mother, Yentl disguises herself as a man in order to gain an education typically denied to nineteenth-century Jewish women. A comic and asexual marriage to a woman ensues in which Yentl tries to educate her wife, Hadass, and show her that women do not have to live life in servitude to their husbands. The heterosexual norm is reestablished with the revelation of Yentl's deception and also with the revelation that she has fallen in love with a male friend, firmly securing her as a heterosexual female.

Just One of the Guys is almost identical in plot to *Yentl*. An ambitious high school student applying for a prestigious journalism award decides to enroll in a new high school disguised as a boy. Her goal is to report on the secret life of males and their attitudes toward women. She reveals her disguise only after she falls in love with a male friend and tells him of her feelings. As in *Yentl*, a comic queer scene ensues as the male friend assumes he is listening to a declaration of gay love from his best friend. The only way to prove she is biologically female is to remove her shirt and reveal her breasts. The heterosexual norm is re-established and the two pair up at the end of the film.

As the aforementioned films suggest, the male-to-female and the female-to-male have a somewhat long history in film, but the masculine-identified lesbian woman, however, is somewhat more difficult to find.[7] There are three compelling exceptions to this observation: *The Killing of Sister George* (1968), *Bound* (1997), and *Set It Off* (1996). Each of these films depicts female/lesbian masculinity and, I suggest, creates a tradition of representation for the depiction of female masculinity that *Boys Don't Cry* will emulate. Unlike Brandon, however, the lead characters in each of the aforementioned three films never attempt to pass as male, and all are either coded as or identify as butch lesbians. Beginning with *The Killing of Sister George*, we see female masculinity represented as a corrupt form of masculinity manifested as a sinister desire to exert male authority, power, and control. Female masculinity is never rendered as something separate from male masculinity, but is instead portrayed as a weak copy of a potent original. Furthermore, films such as Altman's *Sister George*[8] suggest that the masculine woman is doomed to enact a destructive desire for a masculinity that can never be fully realized and can only be unsatisfactorily copied.

Recently, the butch has taken center stage in the film noir thriller *Bound* (1997), by the Wachowski Brothers, in which a butch-femme couple outwit the mob and get away with two million dollars. In both *Bound* and *Set It Off*, starring rap star Queen Latifah as a tough butch bank robber eventually killed in a police stand-off, the butch is placed on the fringes of society as an outlaw element enmeshed in a lifestyle of crime and violence. Female masculinity, in both cases, poses both a literal and metaphoric threat to male masculinity and the sex/gender binary. The threat of the masculine woman is linked to her manipulation and co-optation of masculine gender characteristics. Alisa Soloman compares the "passing" butch to Augusto Boal's concept of invisible or guerrilla theater. Like the passing woman, guerrilla theater masks its theatrical/performance status. Ultimately, Soloman argues, butch is the "most dangerous queer image" because it challenges male privilege and points to the constructed nature of masculinity: "butches threaten masculinity more than they imitate it; they colonize it. Making aggression or toughness or chivalry or rebelliousness their histrionic own, butches reveal the arbitrariness with which traits are said to belong to men. Rather than copying some 'original' image of masculinity, butches point to the embarrassing fact that there is no such thing; masculinity is an artifice no matter who performs it" (Soloman 37). To take this one step further, I suggest that the exposure of the construction of gender by the masculine female accounts for the ways in which masculine-identified women are often symbolically castrated in mainstream film.

A patriarchal society can only benefit from constructing women's bodies as weak, fragile, dependent, and physically dissimilar to the male/ masculine body. Cultural definitions of womanhood are not just dependent upon biological sex but upon shaping the body to fit cultural expectations and mandates, explaining Wittig's claim that lesbians are not women, at least not in the heteronormative sense of the word. The construction of a woman's body is related to issues of power and control. Drawing on Foucault, Sandra Bartky argues that the late twentieth century is marked by the increased surveillance of the body. This increased control of the body is overseen by a number of "regimes of power" including work and school. School is primarily structured as a place of preparation: for adulthood, responsibility, and full-time work. School then prepares individuals (bodies) for the surveillance and regulation they can expect to encounter and conform to throughout the lifespan. This manufacture of the "docile body" is crucial to the effective functioning of a "disciplinary society." Bartky goes on to note that the creation of "docile bodies" is especially significant for women because disciplinary practices also engender the body. Women, then, have an additional layer of discipline/docility inscribed upon their bodies that is made visible in the form of femininity and acceptable forms of female behavior.

Following from this, the female body is a site that must be both controlled and tamed. Female masculinity is a sign of a resistant body and is read as both deviant, transgressive, and subject to greater control and censorship. The history of the masculine woman in culture (and in film) is also bound to the history of the female body. The female (and feminized) body must be kept under control, rigidly stylized, and differentiated from that of the male/masculine body. In other words, if women lose (as in old age) or reject their femininity and hence appear "mannish" or masculine, and begin to blur or challenge the clear-cut boundaries between the two genders, then men and male bodies are implicated in cultural definitions and perceptions of the female body as unclean, corrupting, and sinful. The fear is not only will women become more like men but that men will become more like women.

On the surface, *Boys Don't Cry* appears to hold the potential of rendering gender in excess: the figure of Brandon Teena can be read variously as butch, male, lesbian, transgender, transsexual, and heterosexual. He appears to embody a number of contradictory sexual and gender identities, not a small part of which accounts for the ongoing media fascination with his life and his murder. Although female masculinity comes to the forefront in this film, I argue that the film works to subsume the transgressive potential of the gender outlaw within a lesbian framework and narrative, one that reduces and, ultimately, nullifies Brandon's gender and sexual excess.

The destruction of the transgressive power of the female-to-male is enacted through the symbolic castration of Brandon Teena graphically portrayed in two key scenes: the revelation of Brandon's biological sex when his assailants, Tom Nissen and John Lotter, strip him and force his lover, Lana Tisdel, to acknowledge that he is biologically female; and the long (and mostly gratuitous) rape scene that ends with Brandon promising his rapists he will stay silent and not report their "secret." The revelation of Brandon's biological sex through the forced removal of his clothes is a powerful and central scene in this film. Nissen and Lotter's refrain of "Are you a man or a woman?" echoes throughout and forms the core of *Boys Don't Cry* as it, and they, work to untangle fact from fiction regarding their interpretation of Brandon's sex. That there is something or someone to be untangled, that there is actually a moment of fact that can be separated from that of fiction when it comes to the representation of sex and gender is something this film never interrogates.

The repetition of the question "Are you a man or a woman?" signals a breakdown in meaning. The act of asking and answering this question indicates a rupture in the seemingly solid and identifiable categories of sex and gender. The question, through its repetition, is queered, and hence so is the notion of sex, gender, and sexuality. Alexander Doty argues that the "queerness" of any mass culture text is not about identifying any inherent properties that the text might hold or exhibit and that are somehow just waiting to be discovered, but is instead about examining properties that are closely related to "acts of production or reception" of the text (xi). Doty refers to this as "constructing the sexualities of texts." Defining queerness as an "open and flexible space" he describes texts, and moments in texts, that are anti- or contra-straight (xv). I would argue that the repetition of the question "Are you a man or a woman?" is a queer moment in this film. It asserts the transgressive position of the female-to-male transgender body and forces a recognition that sex and gender do not necessarily follow along heteronormative lines of male/masculine and female/feminine. The sexuality of this text, for a while, is decidedly queer.

The repeated refrain of the question and the quest for a knowable and known fact or truth produces an alienation, and a split occurs between language and meaning. We see Brandon hesitating, weighing his options and the two stark choices laid out for him: man or woman. The answer loses any inherent meaning, and the audience is aware that neither choice fits Brandon: that he is neither man nor woman. This queer moment is interrupted with the revelation of Brandon's biological sex and the reassertion of a biological fact, that Brandon is female. This moment, however, leads to further questions: Can this queer moment place Brandon's biological sex in doubt? Can a "woman" appear masculine and pass as a man and still be a woman? Or a man? Is a space opening up for a third term, one that cannot be fully represented by either that of male or female? These questions continue to linger even as the film attempts to secure Brandon's identity as both female and as a confused and/or closeted lesbian.

The rape fixes Brandon's sex as female and operates as a tool in which to control Brandon, forcing upon him the status of object rather than subject, female rather than male. The rape also normalizes Brandon's body and, to a limited extent, realigns categories of sex and gender. It is a graphic visual assertion of who is "male" and who is "female." Through this scene and the violence done to Brandon's body, the threat to masculinity is eliminated and the status quo reestablished. Brandon is no longer the "better boyfriend" or the better man, but is instead a victim forced by his attackers to take responsibility for the crimes committed against him. The securing of Brandon's identity as biologically female is a symptom of a national desire for fidelity, unambiguous identity, and loyalty. Brandon is a marker of difference and of inconstancy, a threat to both individual and national identity and security. He is a marker of split allegiance in a country and an ideology that has little room or patience for anything less than a "whole" or "unified" identity. I suggest that Trans is the marker between difference and hegemony. It can function as resistance to all that is posited as the norm or normative. Despite Brandon's desire for "normality" he comes to stand for an act and an identity (transgender) that represents resistance and a desire to remain separate and "different" rather than seek the obliteration of assimilation.

The violence of rape and murder as a means of engendering the body is significant, especially when seen in connection with the family dynamics that spring up around Brandon in relation to Lana, Nissen, and Lotter. Brandon is taken in by Lana's family and accepted as a family member, a rhetoric that lulls Brandon into a sense of belonging and security. The violence that springs from these relationships is connected to the rhetoric of family violence, especially in terms of the final objectification of Brandon when he is stripped and then eventually raped. Teresa de Lauretis argues that violence itself is "engendered in representation" (266). As an example, de Lauretis examines the creation of the concept and the term "family violence." Although spouse abuse, child abuse, and incest are all acts that have been documented in history, these acts were not seen in relation to the family and as a social problem until the creation of the term "family violence." The term itself brings the concept into existence, and thus a vital connection is made between the semiotic and discursive with the social (266). At the center of the family are gender and power relations. Therefore, gender and power relations are also at the center of violence in the family. De Lauretis argues that the rhetoric of gender and the rhetoric of violence put men and women into opposite and opposing positions. This construction and this opposition engender violence. The masculine and feminine positions, whether in relation to science, myth, or narrative cinema are always constructed as the actor (masculine) and the acted upon (feminine). A rhetoric of violence constructs the "object as female and the female as object" (274). I suggest that the graphic representation of Brandon's rape and murder construct Brandon as the female object of family violence. The violence itself engenders Brandon, reasserting his identity as female.

The censorship of Brandon's body emerges literally in the case of his rape and murder but also figuratively in the film's failure to take Brandon seriously as a man, rewriting his identity as a masculine lesbian. The question of whether or not Brandon's girlfriends knew he was biologically female is explained within the context of the film when Lana accidentally discovers Brandon's "secret." During a long sequence when Lana and Brandon have sex for the first time, Brandon's biological sex is revealed. Shot from Lana's point of view the audience, along with Lana, glimpses cleavage and Brandon's secret quickly unravels. From here the film cuts to a close-up shot of Brandon's clothed genital area as Lana feels around for, ultimately, what is not there: Brandon's male genitalia (that Brandon wears a dildo is not taken into consideration in this shot). Finally, Lana caresses Brandon's chin and neck searching for signs of hair growth. Lana discovers Brandon's "secret" yet consents to sex with him, fully aware, the film suggests, that Brandon is a biological "woman."

Has Lana suspended her disbelief or is she accepting the lie at face value, enabled in her actions and choice to have sex with Brandon because of his masculine appearance and the knowledge that her friends believe Brandon is male? Later, Lana tells two female friends about her night with Brandon, and the film cuts between shots of her having sex with Brandon and shots of her telling her friends about that night. The "truth" lies in between these two scenes: Brandon's secret and Lana's secret knowledge are both revealed and the relationship between Brandon and Lana is written as a consensual lesbian relationship.

This representation of Brandon fits a more mainstream understanding of female masculinity, linked as it is, in the public mind, to lesbian sexuality. Rendering sexuality visible through gender expression eases the anxiety produced by the nonconforming or queer body. Brandon's ability to veil his biological sex, gender and, hence, sexuality, creates panic and fear because the stereotypically identifiable traits of the lesbian (masculinity) are rendered invisible through his ability to pass as male: masculine traits cross the line into "the masculine." According to Butler, "The cultural matrix through which gender identity has become intelligible requires that certain kinds of 'identities' cannot 'exist'—that is, those in which gender does not follow from sex and those in which the practices of desire do not 'follow' from either sex or gender" (17). Hence, the assured destruction of Brandon and the realignment of sex, gender, and sexuality to make Brandon readable on the sex/gender scale.

What happens when the female to male cannot be read as a butch lesbian but instead passes as male? At the center of *Boys Don't Cry* is the ability of Brandon Teena to successfully pass as a man. As a female-to-male, Brandon brings into question all that was once grounded and stable and posits the question who/what is a real man and who/what is a real woman? There is a twofold pleasure/tension to the viewing of Brandon Teena on the cinematic screen: the pleasure derived from his (Hilary Swank/Brandon Teena) ability to pass as male and the pleasure derived from prior knowledge of the secret at the heart of the film and at the heart of Brandon Teena's life, that he is really a she. The audience's attention is riveted upon finding gaps in the performance of gender, comparing their knowledge of masculine gender characteristics with their knowledge of Brandon's biological sex.

In part, this pleasure/tension answers the question as to why the death of Brandon has become such a fascination in this country since his

murder in 1993.[9] It is not the murder per se but instead a rapt enthrall-
ment with Brandon's ability, for a brief time anyway, to get away with the
unthinkable, to cross the seemingly grounded and solid lines of gender,
for a woman to become a man. Brandon's desire for "normality" is itself
a transgressive act. The fulfillment of his fantasy proves that borders are
permeable and can be crossed, that reality and appearance have no substance, and that women can be men and men can be women. The
borders between the "normal" and the "abnormal" have been crossed, a
transgressive act in itself. Not only is Brandon's body censored, therefore,
but so is his desire for "normality." The fascination sparked by Brandon's
story is closely bound to his ability to "fool" an entire community and
the depths of fear and hatred this sparked, not only in his two killers, but
also in the Falls City community. Despite this fascination and the pleasure
derived from it, the dissonance created by the transgender figure of
Brandon Teena is erased. The factors that spark interest and fascination are
resolved within an explanatory narrative that fits within mainstream notions
and definitions of gender and sexuality.

Brandon's desire to pass as a man is wrongfully explained as sexual
confusion, an internalized homophobia that made it preferable for him
to pretend he was really a man rather than face the knowledge he
might be lesbian. This normalizing narrative makes sense to a culture
that is itself homophobic; a culture that in many quarters either believes
homosexuality is a sin that can be "cured" through reparative therapy,
or that no one, if they could, would "choose" to be gay or lesbian. It
makes sense then that a young woman from the rural Midwest would
choose to transform herself into a man in order to escape the reality
of her sexuality. For a while, the film seems to argue, Brandon found
the love and acceptance he seemed to need and want. As long as no
one knew his "secret" Brandon imagined he could be "normal."

The opening scene implies Brandon's cross-dressing is a symptom
of internalized homophobia. Opening shots of *Boys Don't Cry* show
Brandon entering his cousin's trailer in order to escape the angry (male)
relatives of a young woman he is dating. The men call Brandon a
"dyke" and warn him to stay away or they're going to kill him. Brandon's
cousin insists that "Teena" face up to the fact that she is a "dyke" and
stop pretending to be a man because she is going to end up jail if she
isn't careful. It is not clear at this point why the cousin thinks Brandon
will end up in trouble, but the implication is that Brandon's actions will
lead to some form of punishment in the future. The opening chase
scene suggests not only the violence to come but also that violence

seems the inevitable end to someone who so flagrantly violates cultural rules of gender and sexuality. The violence Brandon faces always comes from men: first the male relatives of the unknown young woman and later Tom Nissan and John Lotter, friends of Lana Tisdel. This is a scenario, the film suggests, with which Brandon is both familiar and also finds somewhat exhilarating. He enters his cousin's trailer laughing and elated (rather than in fear of his pursuers), thrilled with the idea that, although biologically female, he is the best "boyfriend" that many of his partners have ever had and that for a while at least the masquerade is successful. Although the film quotes Brandon explaining a desire (need) to cross-dress as the result of a "gender-identity crisis," the film portrays Brandon as someone who cross-dresses for the thrill of the deception and the possibilities this opens up for him in terms of dating and acceptance from the young women he is interested in and later, after he meets Lana, as an expression of his sexuality and internalized homophobia.

It is important to note that while *Boys Don't Cry* acknowledges the homophobia and the violence of Nissen and Lotter, it, like the towns-people of Falls City, places an element of blame for what happened on the shoulders of Brandon. The film suggests that the source of Brandon's demise is his outrageous confidence in his ability to pass as male. His crime is a crime of arrogance: to flagrantly violate gender norms while not expecting punishment. This attitude arises out of a culture that regularly and publicly punishes those that do not fit into the conventional categories of male and female or masculine and feminine. Brandon's failure is tied to his inability to realize the series of mistakes he makes in trusting the people of the town of Falls City and believing the reality of his own lie. His naiveté and his confidence pull him into a situation that proves fatal. It is also this naiveté and confidence that allows the audience both to sympathize and to identify with Brandon.

Despite knowledge of the outcome of Brandon's life, the audience is placed in a position of continually advocating for Brandon, willing him not to make the fateful decisions that he comes to make. Pierce accomplishes this by emphasizing crucial decision making moments that offer Brandon (and the audience) a point of escape from the inevitable end. Early in the film, and just a few days after his arrival in Falls City, Brandon contacts his cousin who persuades him to return to Lincoln. Candace arranges a ride for Brandon and, for a moment, the film offers an instance when Brandon might have escaped Falls City and the approaching violence. While Brandon waits outside for the trucker who is going to give him a ride back to Lincoln, a car pulls up containing Lana, Candace, Nissen, and Lotter. They encourage Brandon to join them and forget the trucker (who, they are quick to point out, looks "psycho" anyway). Brandon, unable to take his eyes off Lana, gets in the car and goes on a joy ride with his new friends. Achieving full acceptance and inclusion for the first time in his life adds to both the excitement and the danger of his position. This moment of choice is crucial and is represented as a turning point for Brandon, a moment that pulls him into the series of events that eventually lead to his rape and murder. The characterization of the trucker as "psycho" by Brandon's new circle of friends suggests the central binaries operating both in this film and in the culture at large: Who is the criminal and who is the victim? Who is friend and who is foe? Who is lying and who is telling the truth? Where is the line between image and identity? Who is a man and who is a woman?

Public reactions to the murder of Brandon are tied to these questions, but especially to the issue of deception. According to Susan Muska and Greta Olafsdottir, makers of the documentary *The Brandon Teena Story*, "residents of Falls City, the site of Brandon's murder, seemed more concerned with the fact that Brandon lied and misrepresented himself to the women he dated: People would say, 'She lied and no one should do that.' The lying was a big thing" (qtd. in Yabroff). In the same interview, Muska notes that "the people involved didn't treat the murders as anything remarkable—it was all rationalized into something they could understand. In their eyes the murderers were nice guys" (qtd. in Yabroff). In addition, the effect of Brandon's misrepresentation on the women he dated is also at stake. Once revealed, Brandon's "secret" leaves these women open to charges of lesbianism. The media and the public were unable to answer the question of how Brandon's girlfriends were fooled. Muska's explanation of the unexplainable probably comes as close to the truth as any: "I think it's fair to say they suspended their disbelief because Brandon was such a great guy" (qtd. in Yabroff). In order to rationalize the murders both the press and the public had to turn "such a great guy" into a monster, albeit a "nice" one: someone who is misguided, psychologically disturbed, a liar, and a thief. These circumstances begin to overwhelm the representation of Brandon and distract from the central issue that one of the fundamental categories of human organization was wholly and successfully violated.

The reaction of the Falls City townspeople, and society in general, to Brandon and the murder comes from a belief in the immutability of gender. Taking a cursory look at mainstream film and television, it becomes evident that when gender lines are crossed they are often crossed in a visible and marked manner. Ultimately, the secret is an open secret. It is a part of the entertainment "image," and as entertainment it remains at a suitable and acceptable distance from "real" life. Mainstream cross-dressers such as RuPaul, an individual who has achieved celebrity status as a "drag queen," never attempt to pass as the opposite sex but instead are recognizably "in drag." Other mainstream cross-dressers include such figures as Annie Lennox and Boy George who, like RuPaul, make no attempt to hide their biological sex beneath their cross-gendered appearance and who include gender markers[1] to indicate their biological status. These individuals represent what it means to cross-dress in mainstream America today. There is no secret beneath the masquerade, for everything is out in the open, so to speak. Inasmuch as the closet purports to hide and protect gays and lesbians, it is the closet, it appears, that ultimately brings about the death of Brandon Teena, the unmarked transgender cross-dresser. The film seems to suggest that perhaps this is the fate of those that can and do "pass."

The mainstreaming of Brandon Teena and his evolution into a marked cross-dresser occurs through the linkage of Brandon with recognizable Hollywood icons such as James Dean and Marlon Brando. The poster art for *Boys Don't Cry* depicts a young man dressed in jeans, belt, and hat, walking down the center of a highway. This image aligns Brandon with the figure of the drifter or the mysterious stranger who wanders into town with no name and no history. This depiction reflects the classic American western of the Eastwood variety: stranger arrives in town, saves townspeople, and leaves just as suddenly and mysteriously as he had arrived. Brandon is depicted as literally saving Lana. It is through him that Lana finds the strength to leave a town in which she is both bored and trapped with little hope of ever getting out. With the arrival of Brandon in her life Lana is literally swept off her feet and given a new sense of optimism and sense of self. For it is Lana (not Brandon) who escapes at the close of the film, free to explore both self and world as she prepares to live out Brandon's dreams, dreams that have now become her own.

Through the manufacture of Brandon's image as a rebel and an outsider his life is made to fit within the lines of the classic American male coming-of-age story, a story that often comes with a tragic ending. Yet, it is the tragedy itself that captures the hearts and minds of any audience. At the center of the Hollywood male image is the lonely drifter in a never-ending pursuit of home and a sense of belonging and acceptance. Described as a "love hungry pretty boy" (Kort), Brandon comes to represent, in the mind of the audience and of the media, such doomed American icons as James Dean and Marlon Brando, figures who portray a masculinity that is wild, excessive, and out of bounds. Signifying unrealized potential (Dean) or loss (Brando) they crash and burn early or fail simply through the inability to retain their youthful image. Brando is a failure because he succumbed to old age, losing both his looks and his lean masculinity, while Dean and Brandon, through their own excessiveness, die tragically and violently.

The significance of Brandon's life and death is given a wider perspective in American culture when Pierce locates him within the image of the male Hollywood hero of a bygone film era: "Brandon actually embodies many traits of the traditional Hollywood hero. He had the innocence and tenderness of Montgomery Clift in *Red River* or a young Henry Fonda, the naive determination of Jimmy Stewart. He was a rebellious outsider like James Dean, a shy and courtly gentleman around women like Gary Cooper." Pierce's comments show how she has worked to combine the erotic wildness of a James Dean with the gentle and nonthreatening persona of a Gary Cooper or even, perhaps, a Leonardo DiCaprio. I believe that Pierce is attempting to locate Brandon's masculinity within a register that is familiar and identifiable to a mainstream audience, an audience that might potentially be repelled by the embodiment of masculinity within a female body.

In contemporary American culture, women who dress in male clothing (without obscuring their sexual or gender identity) are often erotized, perhaps explaining the link Pierce establishes between Brandon and cinema icons like Dean and Brando. The masculinity that Brandon is associated with is an erotic masculinity, one that forms the basis of heterosexual female fantasy. Described as "charismatic" and "courtly," Brandon's rave reviews focus on the impression he left with his various teenage lovers. The issues of sex, gender, and sexuality are erased in favor of love, romance, and the way Brandon treated the women he dated. It appears that Hollywood has found another ladies' man, one who apparently charms young women on the screen as well as in life.

According to Pierce, "younger women have confessed that they loved the sex scenes and that the scenes made them consider crossing over—and that was my intention." Pierce forms an identification between Brandon and a mainstream, and largely heterosexual, audience. Pierce notes that even though "Brandon was in many ways a traditional hero who would do anything to get and keep the girl, we still had our doubts about whether he would be accessible to a mainstream audience. He was, after all, still a biological girl passing as a boy." The identification Pierce creates between Brandon and the audience erases his queer identity and any transgressive potential that a transgender figure might offer in terms of opening up a play of sexual and gender identities. Brandon is made into just another film star, another male hero in a long line of Hollywood stars, each offering up the same version of heterosexual love and romance, sex and desire. How is queer understood in the context of this film? Like Brandon, the notion of queer is also erased. According to Pierce, Brandon is a queer character with the queer erased: "we've gained a wonderful queer character whom most people are able to see as wonderful without having to add 'queer.' " Is it possible to have a "queer" character with the "queer" erased? Perhaps. For a mainstream audience, the concept of queer is compromised yet, at the same time, no matter how Brandon Teena is represented he is still a transgender female-to-male and, for a brief time, passes successfully as a man. Perhaps the power of Brandon, and the cultural fascination with his story, is also linked to the fact that the queerness of Brandon can never be totally erased, that behind all efforts of the filmmakers and the audience to fit Brandon into a recognizable register, he ultimately defies explanation.

Although mainstream cultural texts have no place for the ambiguous or the different, the fact remains that the other is still present, an interrupting (and disruptive) force in the bright realm of the heteronormative. What then is most transgressive, that which passes or that which can be seen and recognized as other? Herein rests the problem: to successfully pass is a transgressive act. Yet, it is an act that goes unrecognized and poses no threat to the heteronormative sex/gender system. On the other hand, that which is recognizable runs the risk of being co-opted by the norm.

It appears that the accessibility of *Boys Don't Cry* is dependent on the audience's ability to identify with Brandon. This leads me to question exactly who mainstream audiences are being led to identify with. According to Pierce, they are identifying with Brandon as an embodiment of Hollywood maleness and masculinity: Brandon as a "new Hollywood movie star." This confusion about how to identify Brandon comes through in several reviews of the film that variously describe it as a "tragic romance with strong Romeo and Juliet connections," an exploration of "the contradictions of American youth and identity," and "Biography, crime, gay, thriller." One reviewer even notes a flaw in the film: "one disadvantage of a film based on a true story, is that many people who know the story therefore know the ending, since stories worthy of being a movie are so often about their resolution."[11] For this person, knowledge of Brandon's death destroys the films entertainment quality and ruins any potential suspense this drama could create for its audience.

The contradiction and the tension created by a queer and a mainstreamed version of Brandon is further exemplified when Pierce merges "Brandon" with actress Hilary Swank. According to Pierce, Hilary Swank is the living representative of Brandon Teena. In an interview, Pierce describes her reaction while watching Swank accept the Golden Globe award: "It suddenly dawned on me that Brandon had seeped into the Hollywood arena and thereby the American main-stream when I saw him walk up on stage—still embodied by the wonderful Hilary Swank—and accept the Golden Globe on national television." This act blurs the identity of Brandon with that of the actress portraying him. What are the consequences of merging the identity of Brandon with that of Hilary Swank? Which "Brandon" is Pierce actually referring to here?

Finally, however, both mainstream and gay/lesbian media, like the film, work to normalize and explain Brandon's life, gender, and sexuality in terms that mainstream culture can recognize and understand. *Boys Don't Cry* rationalizes both Brandon and the murders, explaining Brandon as a confused, closeted lesbian and the murderers as violent and intolerant "white trash." I think it is important to remember, how-ever, that despite these easy stereotypes, Brandon Teena, a transgender character in a contemporary film about sexuality, gender, and a sensa-tional small-town murder, is no cartoon or caricature. Instead, *Boys Don't Cry* offers a warning about the consequences of being different in straight society. Since the 1960s, when society began to recognize the presence of gays and lesbians, mainstream depictions of lesbians took an ominous turn: "the dykes became predatory and dangerous. Lesbians were still creatures to be conquered or defeated, but now viciously so, as though they were other men" (Russo 154). Although Brandon can in no way be called predatory or dangerous, his lying and arrogance are offered and accepted in many quarters as sufficient cause for the fear and anger he produces in the town of Falls City, Nebraska. And, as in prior representations of trans characters in film, Brandon is viciously conquered and defeated. Is *Boys Don't Cry* just another homosexual horror show? Perhaps this answer can be found in Vito Russo's classic study of homosexuality in film. According to Russo, "Mainstream films

about homosexuality are not for gays. They address themselves exclusively to the majority. How should 'we' (society) react to 'them' (me)?"
(325). I think Russo's assessment must be considered when addressing
the representation of what can be broadly labeled "queer" (or identified
as a queer presence) in mainstream film. *Boys Don't Cry* is addressed to
the majority and asks a similar question as that posed by Russo. The
message that comes through for queer viewers is one of increased
caution: pushing the envelope of gender and/or sexuality holds the
possibility of violence, police incompetence and inaction, and media
sensationalism. Lastly, it must be noted that throughout the film, and the
Muska/Olafsdottir documentary *The Brandon Teena Story*, there is a not
so subtle suggestion that indicates a murder such as this could happen
only in a conservative state such as Nebraska. Media accounts of the
film and the events surrounding the murders neither refer to Brandon
as transgendered, nor do they cite the numerous acts of violence committed against transgender and transsexual individuals every year and in
all areas of the United States, including places as diverse as San Francisco and New York.

NOTES

1. See Kimberly Pierce, "Brandon Goes to Hollywood," *Advocate* (28
March 2000).

2. Most notable is the debate that covered three issues of *Screen:* Judith
Halberstam, "The Transgender Gaze in *Boys Don't Cry.*" *Screen* 42, 3 (Autumn
2001): 294–298; Lisa Henderson, "The Class Character of *Boys Don't Cry*,
Screen 42, 3 (Autumn 2001): 299–303; Jennifer DeVere Brody, "Boyz Do Cry:
Screening History's White Lies," *Screen* 43, 1 (Spring 2002): 91–96; Patricia
White, "The Boys Don't Cry Debate: Girls Still Cry," *Screen* 42, 2 (Summer
2001): 217–221.

3. Brandon Teena's birth name was Teena Brandon. Throughout part of
his adult life he chose to go by the name Brandon and lived as a male. In
deference to that choice I will use both the name Brandon Teena and the
masculine pronoun when referring to him.

4. Films that portray the transgender character as disturbed and dangerous include *Psycho*, *Dressed to Kill*, *The Silence of the Lambs*, and *Freebie and
the Bean*.

5. See also *Caprice* (1967) starring Doris Day and Ray Walston, who
plays a murderous cross-dresser who in turn is killed by Doris Day. Vito Russo,
in *The Celluloid Closet*, describes these films as part of the "kill 'em or cure 'em"
climate of the 1960s (162).

6. There are a large number of films that, like *Yentl* and *Just One of the Guys*, create what Chris Straayer, in *Deviant Eyes, Deviant Bodies*, calls the "temporary transvestite." The temporary transvestite film has characters cross-dress usually for purposes of disguise. Since many of these films are also romantic comedies, the cross-dressed character returns to "normal" garb and a heterosexual pairing. Straayer includes such films as *Victor/Victoria*, *Tootsie*, *Some Like It Hot*, *Mrs. Doubtfire*, and *Queen Christina* as just a few examples of the temporary transvestite film.

7. See Judith Halberstam's *Female Masculinity* for an extended discussion of the butch in film.

8. An early example of a butch lesbian appears in Robert Altman's *The Killing of Sister George* (1968). The lead character, June Buckridge (Beryl Reid), loses her part as Sister George on a BBC soap opera. June's crime is that she is a "loud, aggressive, butch lesbian" (Russo 171). June is progressively pushed back into the closet and punished for her overt lesbianism. According to Russo, the "only options are invisibility, assimilation, or ostracism" (173). I would add death to Russo's list of options for butch lesbians. *Bound* is an exception to this rule, but stereotypes also prevail in this film.

9. Listed here are just a few of the newspaper and magazine articles discussing the life and murder of Brandon Teena. In addition to wide media coverage the murder also inspired a true crime thriller by Aphrodite Jones, *All She Wanted: A True Story of Sexual Deception and Murder in America's Heartland*. (New York: Pocket Books, 1996); Austin Bunn, "Fanning the Fame," *Village Voice* (21 July 1998): 33; Jay Carr, "Denial and Death in Falls City," *Boston Globe* (15 January 1999): D7; John Gregory Dunne, "The Humboldt Murders," *New Yorker* (13 January 1997): 45–62; Stephen Holden, "A Rape and Beating, Later 3 Murders and Then the Twist," *New York Times* (23 September 1998): 5; Eric Konigsberg, "Death of a Deceiver," *Playboy* (January 1995): 92–94, 193–199; Donna Minkowitz, "Love Hurts," *Village Voice* (19 April 1994): 24–30; Amy Taubin, "Splitting Image," *Village Voice* (29 September 1998): 128.

10. RuPaul is open about his gay sexuality and his status as a female impersonator. Performers such as Annie Lennox will vary their appearance, sometimes androgynous and sometimes feminine.

11. Reviews quoted from Upcomingmovies.com

WORKS CITED

Bartky, Sandra Lee. "Foucault, Femininity, and the Modernization of Patriarchal Power." In *The Politics of Women's Bodies: Sexuality, Appearance, and Behavior*, ed. Rose Weitz. New York: New York University Press, 1998.

Butler, Judith. *Gender Trouble: Feminism and the Subversion of Identity*. New York: Routledge, 1990.

De Lauretis, Teresa. "The Violence of Rhetoric: On Representation and Gender." In *The Gender Sexuality Reader: Culture, History, Political Economy*, ed. Roger N. Lancaster and Micaela di Leonardo. New York: Routledge, 1997.

Doty, Alexander. *Making Things Perfectly Queer: Interpreting Mass Culture*. Minneapolis: University of Minnesota Press, 1993.

Garber, Marjorie. *Vested Interests: Cross-Dressing and Cultural Anxiety*. New York: Harper Perennial, 1992.

Halberstam, Judith. *Female Masculinity*. Durham: Duke University Press, 1998.

Kort, Michele. "Gone Too Soon: The Brandon Teena Story." *Advocate.com*. 15 March 2000. <http//:www.advocate.com>.

Pierce, Kimberly. "Brandon Goes to Hollywood." *Advocate*. 28 March 2000.

Russo, Vito. *The Celluloid Closet: Homosexuality in the Movies*. New York: Harper and Row, 1987.

Soloman, Alisa. "Not Just a Passing Fancy: Notes on Butch." *Theater* 24, 2 (1993): 35–46.

Straayer, Chris. *Deviant Eyes Deviant Bodies: Sexual Re-Orientation in Film and Video*. New York: Columbia University Press, 1996.

The Brandon Teena Story. Dir. Susan Muska and Greta Olafsdottir. Zeitgeist Films, 1998.

Weiss, Andrea. *Vampires and Violets: Lesbians in Film*. New York: Penguin, 1992.

Yabroff, Jennie. "Documentary Filmmakers Susan Muska and Greta Olafsdottir Talk About the Story Behind 'The Brandon Teena Story.' *Salon.com*. 15 March 2000. <http//: www.salon.com>.

CHAPTER 10

QUEERING PORNOGRAPHY

DESIRING YOUTH, RACE, AND FANTASY IN GAY PORN

Zeb J. Tortorici

Within the genre of gay male porn, young "gay" bodies are both ubiquitous and highly visible. Paradoxically, the voices of youth—gay, straight, and everywhere in between—acting in porn are often left out of the analysis and public discussions on porn. In terms of representing queer youth in relation to pornography, I have over the past few years experimented and interacted with gay porn as an actor, student, and activist. This chapter not only traces my forays as a graduate student into the world of gay porn but also more importantly shows how I have immersed myself in activist cultures through my visual, sexual, intellectual, and political dialogue with pornography. A large part of my experimental porn project deals with the ways that I've sought to expand the audience of my pornographic production from those who anonymously look at my pictures online to include a more politicized audience of students, activists, sex workers, and queer youth. This chapter therefore ultimately demonstrates my attempts at queering pornography from a "queer youth" perspective—a highly personal journey that began a few years back when I was an undergraduate at UCLA.[1]

At least up until recently, there was a long-running ad in the Bruin Classifieds section of UCLA's student newspaper, *The Daily Bruin*, that continuously called out to the university's undergraduate male population: "MALE MODELS. UP TO $1000/day immediate pay. Paid screen test! Must be 18–23. Great face, nice body. Nude magazine/ video work SURFER/JOCK/STUDENT, teen-looking preferred." While my experiences in gay pornography in Los Angeles did not begin until 2002 when I finally responded to the advertisement, I had first seen the ad in 1999. I was then twenty and in my fourth year as an undergraduate at UCLA, and though the first few times that I saw the ad I really didn't know what to make of it, something about that ad definitely caught my eye. In retrospect, I realize that ad made me think, perhaps for the first time, critically about porn and its meanings—a story and process that I relate at length as follows.

Now, writing this in 2005, I better understand that newspaper ad's explicit preference and desire for "teen-looking" models and how it relates intimately to the fetishization of youth within certain genres of gay porn. Age in all genres of porn is arbitrary in the sense that young actresses and actors in their twenties and thirties can and are marketed as "just 18" or "barely legal." The autobiographical analysis of gay porn offered here shows how youth and race, clearly in conjunction with one another, are both deliberately and problematically staged as desirable. While pornography has been endlessly interrogated and criticized, it is rarely done from the perspective of someone with personal experience in the porn industry and, as far as I know, never done from queer youth subjectivity.[2] My ultimate approach to porn therefore has been to fuse my own queer youth identity and my experiences *doing* porn with my academic and political theorization of porn.

Ultimately, this essay literally *queers* gay porn by critically thinking about porn from a "queer youth" perspective. In conceptualizing what it means for me to queer porn, I look to the following working definition of queer theory offered by the editors of *Social Text*'s 1996 issue "Queer Transexions of Nation, Race, and Gender." They write, "*queer theory* is an articulating principle functioning in, across, between, and among various social domains and political experiences, and it is therefore consciously provisional and dynamic, strategic and mobilizing, rather than prescriptive or doctrinal."[3] The queering of gay porn, for me, therefore has less to do with my queer sexuality per se than it does with the ways that I function within those social domains—academia and pornographic mediascapes—to effectuate change through queer personal politics. "Queer" is not a term that I conflate solely with LGBT identities and sexualities, and I experience queerness and identify as queer as much through my experiences with sex work and my politics as I do through sexual desire. Thus, my personal queering of gay porn also comes about through the integration of my sexuality, my age, my identity, and my politics with the discourses of pornography.

In conjunction with age as a sexualized marker come race and ethnicity. Whiteness, as opposed to the explicit preference for youth, was more implicitly encoded in that ad through the racial connotations of "SURFER/JOCK/STUDENT." My earliest experiences as a gay porn model personally demonstrated to me how age and race are fetishized in complementary ways to convey a particular type of desirable masculinity in mainstream gay porn. This genre of gay porn normalizes both whiteness and youth through what are ultimately racist and ageist tropes. In 1999, however, I wasn't thinking quite yet in these terms, and admittedly, the first few times I saw the ad I really didn't know where to start thinking about it. I was in a long-term relationship, and I really couldn't really imagine stripping in front of a camera. I was sort of comfortable with my body, so it wasn't that, but it just didn't seem like something that I'd really want to do for a variety of reasons. But still, something about that ad clearly appealed to me.

Pornography had always held an ambivalent place in my life. I liked porn because it helped me to explore my own desires, but at the same time, I imagined and internalized the stigma attached to looking at it. I felt that it was somehow demeaning and objectifying to look at, but I especially liked Internet porn due to its anonymity: I didn't have to buy anything, present myself as a consumer of porn, or let anyone else know that I was interested in such sexually explicit material. Talking about this now nostalgically reminds me of undergrad days at the UCLA dorms—with my first fast Internet connection at Hedrick Hall—when my roommate was gone. Even while living in the dorms freshman year, I remember when one night a few of my friends went to a movie theater on Sunset Boulevard to watch late-nite, 3-D vintage porn. I also wanted to go, but felt intensely uncomfortable. Up until recently, I guess I'd always justified not going that night by convincing myself that I was making an ethical decision. I did not want to demean women or objectify bodies, and especially *not in front of other people*. Of course I wanted to look at the naked bodies of both women and men (and secretly really wanted to see 3-D porn!), but only in private. In a bout of scopophilic anxiety, I was nervous that others would see me deriving pleasure from the bodies on the screen and was most afraid to have the gaze on me *as a spectator.*

Seeing that ad however eventually got me thinking about the ways that porn was loaded with meanings and subtexts. I thought, at first hypothetically, about the possibilities of answering the ad and doing nude photo/video work, but I was most concerned with issues of safety, comfort, and anonymity. I logically did not want to put myself at risk in terms of sexually transmitted diseases, and reasoned that porn wouldn't endanger me if I stuck to solo work. I figured I could deal with comfort issues as I went along and experimented at my pace. The anonymity/identity issue took a little longer for me to figure out and this is what stalled me from answering the ad for such a long time. To make a long story short however, I thought about the pertinent issues for about three years, and decided during my first year of graduate school in 2002—a decision very much influenced by the fact that I *was* a grad student studying the history of sexuality and queer studies—to go for it. I contacted the director from the UCLA newspaper ad and arranged my first video shoot in September 2002, and have since then done several solo photo and video shoots for both Internet and DVD distribution. Although this chapter offers at best a fragmented discussion of my own history and negotiation with porn, my personal experiences as a performer have demonstrated to me that while pornography is an indispensable cultural text, it is a problematic yet productive space in which to work. Thus, a large part of my own experiments with porn has been to problematize pornography as it relates to the production and consumption of race, youth, masculinity, and, fantasy in sexually explicit imagery. This however, as will be shown, is often done in ambivalent and contradictory ways.

The first real photo/video shoot that I did in 2002 happened also to be the only time I've worked with others during a shoot. As safety has always been a primary concern of mine, after answering the *Daily Bruin* ad and successfully passing the "paid screen test" (me masturbating on video), I decided to perform in a softcore circle-jerk video in which the only sexual contact between the other guys and me was kissing, some touching, and mutual masturbation.[4] Intimately related to the staging of masculinity are the performances of race, youth, and *hetero*sexuality within the context of gay porn. That this short video starred me and three other white boys who were all in their late teens and early twenties becomes central to the ways in which a youthful whiteness was posited as something intrinsically desirable to the hypothetical viewer. In this 4-boy circle-jerk video shoot (where we progressed from washing a car naked in the backyard to the bedroom where we eventually ejaculated onto the stomach of one of the boys), in an attempt to make things feel more real and more erotic for me, I started to kiss the naked boy lying next to me on the bed. I remember the really bad straight porn playing on the TV in the background that was not quite doing it for me. I also remember being really nervous because it was my first real video shoot, and quite frankly, the other boys had really big penises. So, in an effort to make it feel more real, and a little less performed, I kiss the guy next to me. I kiss him to counteract the performance anxiety that stems from me wanting to get erect and wanting to stay hard. And I continue kissing. If I recall correctly, fairly quickly the director tells us to stop. He tells us that there should not be any more kissing in the scene (or that it should be minimal) because, as he basically explains, "gay guys think its hot when straight guys are doing it together." Here, *doing it together* theoretically meant jerking-off, sucking, or fucking, but apparently not kissing.

Ultimately what that off-limits kiss did for me was challenge the rigid masculinity exuding from that bed of four naked boys. That kiss, I think, did somehow expose the theatricality of masculinity and the performativity of the "gay" in gay porn. It showed that I was nervous, and that I might *not* be just another straight guy "doing it" for the camera or for the viewers. That unfeigned kiss, along with my inability to get and remain hard (probably edited out in the final cut that I have yet to see), made visible my highly erotic, nervous, and intimate on-screen body and personality. It is through these "fascinating ethnographic 'quirks' " of porn and through this visibility that the codes of both homosexuality and heterosexuality that so greatly inform all genres of "gay" porn begin to be queered, though sometimes in paradoxically heteronormative ways.[5] Perhaps what bothered me most about that video shoot were the ways that both youth and whiteness became reified through the video's hackneyed portrayal of young white (performed?) desire for other young white boys. This of course happened in ways that are anything but unique for this genre of gay porn. I've since gone on to work with other directors with whom I feel much more comfortable and less restricted to express my desires and explore the boundaries that I want to. That was thus far the only time I've worked with other guys in a porn shoot, and I'm still debating when, with whom, and even if I'd want to work in another non-solo porn project. As for now, I am most happy and comfortable doing solo—and, as I discuss later on, increasingly activist—porn work.

Since having begun experimenting in gay porn, I've been left wondering, in what ways certain acts—the cum-shot, the circle-jerk, an ass being spread, or a kiss between two guys—are relied upon and expected to be queer? Do these acts lose some of their queerness by becoming banal gestures and mundane markers of "gay" that are expected and even counted on? How much queerness do they lose by relying on the overplayed, ageist, and racist tropes of youth and white desirability? Given that many boys who identify as straight participate in gay porn, we also might ask whether these straight guys are queering gay porn or straightening it? Gay pornography is one site in which those supposedly queer gestures like the cum-shot, the circle-jerk, and the kiss have the potential to become dull and interminably mimicked to the point that they perpetually reproduce specific acts so predictable that they are almost meaningless. In his essay "Gesture, Ephemera, and Queer Feeling" José Muñoz discusses certain acts and gestures of queerness and thus opens the door for examining the precision and predictability of queer acts. He defines these acts as "precise and specific physical acts that are conventionally understood as gesture, like the tilt of an ankle in very high heels, the swish of a hand that pats a face with imaginary makeup" (425). While in gay porn the gestures are different from those described by Muñoz, the markers of queerness in gay porn are so relied upon and expected to take place that they become normalized and mundane. The not-so-queer physical acts of "queerness" and markers of the "gay" in gay porn—the cum-shot or the ways in which bodies move (and are suggested to move) in sexually explicit photos and videos—are all there.

In my own experiences with straight porn (as consumer) and gay porn (as consumer/performer), the cum-shot is the most predictable and routine component. There is a constant attempt to define the cum-shot as *the* quintessential component of masculinity and of the male sexual experience. According to Linda Williams's cogent analysis of straight porn, "as the most blatantly phallic of all hard-core film representations, the money shot [cum-shot] can be viewed as the most representative instance of phallic power and pleasure" (*Hardcore* 95). This holds for gay or straight porn. For me personally this is not the case, but in gay porn I sometimes tend to act as if it were (extra breaths, louder breathing, and exaggerated movements for the camera when I come). In a live Internet webcam show I did for Chi-Chi La Rue's "Live and Raw" porn site in 2005, I actually pretended to come five or six times (for different customers in "private chat rooms") within the course of three hours in order to keep the viewers watching and paying for the visual services that I was providing. On another site for which I modeled, a solo masturbation/anal toy gallery of me (inaccurately described as a 20-year-old Skater Boy with Cock Size: 6") is accompanied by the following text: "You have to see ZEB moan as he reaches the point of NO RETURN and starts to pound his cock until he shoots his hot creamy sticky load of cum all over his smooth skater boy 6pack!"[6] Basically, mainstream gay porn is neither consumable nor successful if the penis is not out, erect, and ejaculating as a signifier of masculinity. "Straight" and "gay" subjectivities in the context of porn almost make little difference as both rely on a phallic masculinity to convey the sexual. While my own filmed/photographed cum-shots are, I think, far from queered in the numerous commercial gay porn sites in which I appear, they are queered—as I discuss later in this chapter—when I bring my porn, my photos, my cum-shots, and my queer youth identity into academic settings, queer conferences, and politicized indie porn websites.

In many of the porn shoots I've done, I start out dressed (sometimes with my skateboard or acoustic guitar as a prop), slowly take my clothes off, and end up naked with my mouth a little open, my fingers or my toys entering my ass, penis out, touching myself, and so forth. In a lot of twink gay porn, a youthful and seemingly submissive masculinity is produced as the performer ends up with his ass up and his legs wide open or up in the air. The term "twink"—ubiquitous in gay porn—can best be defined as an attractive, only slightly muscular, clean-shaven, boyish-looking young man. A twink is also usually blonde or light-skinned, often seen as not particularly intelligent, and supposedly derives its name from the Hostess "twinkie" in that it too is soft and filled with cream. That said, following these images, my own instincts, and at times suggestions by the photographer, I will turn myself completely around, ass out, cheeks spread, or laying back with arms raised behind my head, putatively submitting myself to the camera and to the potential viewer. I am positioned as a "bottom" and potentially, at least according to the hegemonic perceptions of gendered roles within gay porn, become gendered as I am simultaneously masculinized (by my erect penis) and feminized (by my receptivity to the camera and by playing with anal toys and tactile penetration) in very specific ways.

According to David Gere, "this is the ecstasy of the submissive 'bottom'—the vulnerability of the open mouth ready to be kissed or to be spat into. The open mouth and the closed eyes might also indicate preparation for that ultimate effeminate performance, man-on-man fellatio, for to submit to male power is to become *effeminated*" (358). I am implicitly told within the context of porn production to code myself as a male who is ready to be fucked and who is "getting into it." Here however, fantasy and reality nicely intertwine through my own expressions of sexual desire and stimulation. While I have been told at least once to look like I am "really getting into it," I really *am* getting into it. To be visually coded as a sexual bottom (the term "bottom" should not be confused with being sexually passive as the disconcerting "active/passive" dichotomy would have it) is not problematic for me because in my own personal sexual relations with other men, I am a bottom. Meanwhile, in terms of consensual BDSM play with men and women, I am both bottom and top, and my partners and I derive pleasure from these acts by playing with and tweaking their corresponding notions of "activity" and "passivity." Ultimately, my own involvement in gay porn, my sexual identity claims, and my adherence to certain gendered roles in this pornographic visual media are both authentic and dissimulating.

In turning more specifically to the fetishized and fantasized representations of youth and race in mainstream gay porn—in my case as a white queer male in my mid-twenties—I sometimes see a deliberate effort on the part of photographers, directors, and producers to convey me as a racially coded, curious straight boy in my late-teens or early twenties. I was described for a few years on a now defunct maxpixels.com website as:

Zeb:
White, young, twink,
lean, defined, smooth,
athletic, toys, penetration,
J/O, cut

I have never done any hardcore (i.e., penetrational oral/anal sex) scenes in any video or photo shoots. There is no penetration by other people, though there has been solo penetration with my toys and my fingers. While the description above does not specify the type of penetration involved, I would argue that this "penetrational ambiguity" is part of the production and performance of a consumable and visually/anally receptive masculinity upon which gay twink porn thrives. This masculinity becomes a site of ocular penetration for the consumers of my images, and a site of fantasized sexual penetration in the minds of the viewers. It is a young, white, and performed masculinity that can be fetishized, consumed, and appropriated by both viewer and performer alike. Most importantly, these images and descriptions are clearly coded in terms of race and age: white, young, twink, et cetera.

On the boyride.com website, the fetishization of youth and race fuse to create the "twink student" and the "white skater boy" fantasy: "Caught in a downpour on his way home from college, Zeb dashes into his apartment and strips off his wet clothes with the intention of tackling his home work [sic]. Once he's naked however, it isn't long before his energies go from his studies to his hard dick."[7] Here I am clearly depicted as a young and horny student. Interestingly, in the aforementioned description, fantasy and reality blend quite well with one another as I actually was a graduate student in my mid-twenties and I really did need to study that day. This particular photo shoot actually was shot at my own apartment in Los Angeles, it really was raining outside that day, and while this description sounds enticing, the pornographic reality temporally coalesces with fantasy as I first suppos-edly dash home, proceed to strip my wet clothes, and *then* start study-ing. To add to the white-skater-boy-student fantasy, I am filmed and photographed with my skateboard (sometimes next to me, other times covering my genitals or nipples) and, at other times, playing my acoustic guitar. For this website I am also described as a "24 Year Old Horny Skater Boy" and as a "Totally sexy skater boy!"[8] In yet another solo masturbation photo shoot I did for a different director in the back trails of the Santa Monica Mountains, my skateboard also became an equally important symbol as I first skate around the paved streets at the foot of the trails, then strip and masturbate on the hiking trails while sitting on the skateboard wearing nothing but socks and tennis shoes.[9] Because the young "white skater boy" fantasy is unambiguously coded in terms of race and age, it thus serves to normalize and reify youth, whiteness, and twinkness in gay porn as the preferred sites of sexual desire.

Whiteness permeates all aspects of porn as white bodies mediate pornoscapes or, in the absence of white bodies, an assumed white male viewer is often centrally positioned and catered to by the producers. In his essay "Looking for My Penis: The Eroticized Asian in Gay Video Porn," Richard Fung asserts that "If we look at commercial gay sexual representation, it appears that the antiracist movements have had little impact: the images of men and male beauty are still of *white* men and *white* male beauty" (118). In my own experience this is clearly true while, simultaneously, much of the pornography coming out of the

United States also upholds fantasies of racialized *others*. Any trip to the porn section of a local Los Angeles video store will likely produce such titles as *Asian Street Hookers #24*, *Hung Black Men*, *Hot Latin Pussy Adventures 39*, and *Anal Specialist: Brazilian She-Males*. Sexual desires in the United States are often dichotomously predicated on white bodies or on the exoticism of a racial, linguistic, cultural, and sexual "Other." According to José Muñoz in *Disidentifications: Queers of Color and the Performance of Politics*, "a subfield such as racially integrated or exclusively nonwhite tapes is roughly equivalent to other modalities of kink such as bondage, sadomasochism, shaving, and so on. The point here is that, because of white normativity of the pornotopic field, race *counts* as a different sexual practice. Thus, race, like sadomasochism, is essentially a performance" (88). Here, Muñoz asserts that race is performed through the production of racialized/racist bodies within any given genre of porn. Thus, race in porn coalesces into kink, fetish, and fantasy. It is equally problematic that "race" itself is defined by anything non-white. This merely serves to centralize and reinforce "whiteness" as a legitimate and indispensable category within pornographic mediums.

In looking at ties between productions of race and youth in mainstream North American gay porn, I cannot overlook the fact that "the mainstream porn image, throughout the late 1980s and early 1990s, continued to evolve into an all-too-familiar clean-shaven Anglo twenty-something clone" (Muñoz, *Disidentifications* 87). In certain respects, I still feel that I am one of those clean-shaven clones. I feel that I problematically perpetuate a particular stereotype of what gay desirability should be and that my "whiteness" and the young age I can pass for are potential signifiers of what gay male culture should be. This in turn forces me to acknowledge the ways in which queer gestures can be imbued with antinormative meanings while also working to inscribe other normative (racist, misogynist, and even nationalistic) meanings. These are issues that I am still struggling with, and up until recently, I didn't really see any plausible satisfactory solution. My more recent desires to operate outside of the rigid boundaries and structural limits of mainstream gay porn have been ambivalent though more productive for me in terms of exploring my desires and political aims.

One of the more recent porn shoots that I did borders on that which might be considered a bit more perverse than mainstream gay porn (though still ultimately falls within this genre). In 2004, I did an auto-fellatio video in which I attempted to contort my body to get my penis as close to my mouth as possible. Not that conventional fellatio with myself is actually possible, but if I bend, twist, and turn a little, it becomes possible to lick the tip of my penis and cum in my mouth. While the auto-fellatio scene I did deviated from other solo masturbation shoots I had done up to that point, I recognize that the desire for self-sucking videos is common and might not deviate much from that which I was trying to get away from in mainstream commercial gay porn. On the other hand, we might consider what Nguyen Tan Hoang, writing about Asian American gay porn star Brandon Lee who swallows his own cum in *Asian Persuasions 2*, concludes: "In the context of the post-AIDS solo-jerk, the eating of [one's own] cum represents a resignification of risk and sexual taboo associated with the exchange of bodily fluids. The scene thematizes the importance of masturbation and the important role of pornography in affirming this sexual practice in the age of AIDS" (255). In light of the fact that I only do solo scenes, my cum–shot as it enters my own mouth passes through a similar process of visual and sexual resignification (is *this* queering the cum–shot?) whereby issues of safer sex are implicitly broached. Despite the fact that I can theorize my auto-fellatio scene in agreeable ways, I find myself increasingly frustrated, tired, and bored with what I see in mainstream gay porn and continue to look for safe and interesting ways to deviate from that.

In terms of truly beginning queer porn, I have found it most productive to work toward shifting the audience of my pornographic efforts to a more politicized and often younger generation of students, activists, sex workers, indie pornographers, and queer kids. The remaining sections of this chapter therefore focus largely on my attempts to get politically involved through porn with a wide variety of queer youth cultures. My most recent endeavor in this camp has been to have two close friends take nude/masturbation photos of me for the unique and unprecedented alternative porn site Veg Porn (www.vegporn.com) that seeks to link vegan politics, sexuality, political essays and interviews, vegan recipes, and other progressive indie porn sites through a pornographic medium. The site describes itself as a "sex–positive porn site made by vegans and vegetarians" and invites viewers and potential members with: "Welcome to the first and only adult site featuring a cast of sexy vegans and vegetarians! Veg Porn is alternative erotica and sex-positive culture for herbivores and those who love them. We think you'll find something here that tickles you fancy—we welcome models of all shapes and sizes."[10]

While race and age still play central roles within the boundaries of this indie porn site, the site itself is not theoretically based on size, weight, color, age, or gender. The site is neither straight, nor lesbian, nor gay, and is always tied to vegan politics, animal rights, and progressive views on sexuality. As an animal rights activist and a politicized vegan myself, this site offers me the space to politically situate myself (in relation to the viewer) both within porn and through it—something that has been far more difficult to do with the online viewers of my mainstream gay porn photos. These recent endeavors at politicizing the audience of my porn however blend quite well with the way that I was described on the Boyride website for about two years:

> Zeb is brite [sic] as he is beautiful. He can win you over in an instant with a flash of his percect [sic] smile and winning personality. He also has a highly charged sexual energy and can tease the camera like a pro. Living as a vegetarian has helped him stay lean and hard from his tight chest to his perky ass. We hope to be seeing more of Zeb in the future!

As a performer in gay cyberporn, I make a definite attempt to portray my own veganism as something that is ethically and philosophically central to me. In 2004 I got a tattoo that bluntly says "vegan" on the inner wrist of my right hand. This, perhaps especially within the realm of video and photo porn, has given me the space to visually portray my own politics and ethics. In the "Live and Raw" Internet webcam shows that I did, the issue of my vegan tattoo was also raised by some viewers who were curious about the word and its meanings. The tattoo becomes an eroticized object of desire and also does certain political work while allowing the viewer to fantasize about where they want the tattoo to go and what they want my hand to do.

Regarding my own relationship and identity with porn, I, as a spectator and consumer, derive pleasure from looking. I find some pornography exciting and other porn tired, mundane, and problematic due to its essentializing and exoticizing tendencies. As a performer and creator of pornographic images, I also derive pleasure by becoming the object of someone's sexual gaze. I derive pleasure from being nonanonymously watched and from being increasingly in control of the pornographic situations that I choose to put myself in. Getting back to one of my initial concerns about getting involved in porn was the persistent question: What if friends or family ever found out? Eventually, I reasoned that it would be best for me to engage in dialogue about porn with those who show a genuine interest. While at first I deliberated over using my real name in my photo/video shoots, I reasoned that part of my political project must be nonanonymity. Using my real first name as my stage name ("Zeb") publicly links my identity to my sexuality, politics, and pornography. If my goals are to assert my sexuality, to redefine porn and its meanings and uses, and to challenge the normalization of heteronormative sexuality, it would be futile to negate my identity in relation to any pornographic pictures, videos, or essays of mine.

I am fully aware of the fact that many viewers who are looking to get off and who stumble across my pics on commercial gay porn sites know little about me, my subjectivity, or my politics (though my vegan tattoo tells at least some of this). However, I found myself wanting to challenge this modus operandi of mainstream and largely anonymous pornographic consumption. This, in turn, led me to seek out audiences with whom I could interact—within a classroom or queer conference setting—in order to actively diminish that gap between the anonymous pornographic viewer and the pornographically viewed. I wanted to publicly question and contest the ways in which the vast panoply of pornographic images informs, reifies, perpetuates, and challenges sexual categories, stereotypes, and desires. I was similarly searching for a setting where I could publicly and autobiographically interrogate the pornographic desires—*my* pornographic desires—and realities that so many people take to be inherently private matters.

I eventually decided to take my stories and my politics to UC Riverside in the summer of 2003 for the UC-LGBTIA Coming Home Queer conference—a conference attended mainly by queer undergrads and graduate students. I presented a paper entitled "Gesture, Performativity, Masculinity, and Race in Mainstream Gay Porn" where I analyzed the exoticism, tropicalization, and fetishization of nonwhite bodies in mainstream gay porn, as well as explore the ways that white bodies get normalized in gay porn. This was of course problematic for me by the fact that I create porn where I am undeniably a young white body—that "clean-shaven clone"—with white-skin and upper-middle-class prerogative. By showing some of my nude photos at the conference, accompanied by my analysis of porn, I sought to assert myself as a sexual being and to critically interrogate the ways in which white bodies mediate the worlds of gay porn. The audience was largely positive and receptive if somewhat shocked at seeing masturbation and anal toy pics of me projected via PowerPoint behind me. This experience discussing my involvement in porn in front of an audience that was largely queer and young forced me to seriously consider how I needed to reconceptualize and reproduce pornography in ways that would be erotically, politically, and theoretically challenging.

Pornography is ultimately an indispensable cultural text that relates intimately to desire, representation, politics, and agency. Popular conceptions and consumption of porn are inextricably related to issues of race, history, imagination, and coloniality. In the words of my friend Tigerlily—a Chinese/Japanese American porn performer—when questioned by me via email about her experiences and perceptions of race in porn, "i understand the asianphiles that i have to deal with . . . 'oriental dolls' 'fantasiany' . . . i also despise the 'i love you long time' phrase . . . but i will and have fucked with people who fuck with me when it comes to [racial] stereotyping because frankly they deserved it!"[11] Ultimately, in any given cultural context, pornography produces a racialized/racist body that performs, perpetuates, and subverts, to varying degrees, masculinity, femininity, and codes of heteronormativity. Tigerlily's comments demonstrate that the porn performer's subjectivity can be mobilized not only to resist patriarchal (pornographic) authority, but to epistemologically challenge, subvert, and simultaneously reinscribe the imagined foundations of pornographic and colonizing authority. At least for some people, porn allows space for the rewriting and reconceptualization of dominant cultural and sexual narratives. While I still remain somewhat ambivalent about my own involvement—and the representations of my whiteness and my age—in mainstream commercial gay porn, it was this ambivalent space that proved productive in terms of critical engagement and negotiation with the dominant discourses of porn and that ultimately led me to seek out more politicized audiences for the reception of my porn.

In his essay "Shortcomings: Questions about Pornography as Pedagogy," Richard Fung asks the very important question "Can the pleasure premise of porn coexist with the pedagogical?" (137). Although Fung is discussing his own involvement as a filmmaker seeking to depict sexually explicit safer-sex videos that overtly challenge the dominant racial tropes of mainstream gay porn, his question is also pertinent to my discussion here. I want my experiences in porn to be pedagogical and informative for myself and for others, but in the genre of mainstream gay porn I still run up against the same problem: the disjuncture between my desires, my political feelings, and what actually happens when I enter the gay pornographic process with all its structural limits and normative discourses on youth and race. This, however, is not a dead end as I am continually searching for ways to make the pleasures of porn coexist and coalesce with the pedagogical and the political.

In terms of other experiences linking porn with education and activism, in 2004 and 2005 I got involved with UCLA's Sex Worker Outreach Project (SWOP-UCLA), which seeks to decriminalize prostitution and provide a safe space for students that work in legal and illegal aspects of the sex industry. SWOP-UCLA's goals also broach pedagogy as the on-campus organization provides a space for those that wish to learn about and from those that work or have worked in sex industries. In March 2005 I took part, along with a group of others who identified as lesbian, gay, bisexual, transsexual, and transgender, in an LGBT panel that was part of UCLA's Sexual Violence Awareness Advocacy (SVAA) Training Program. Here, I was able to speak with other straight and queer identified undergraduate students about my "bisexuality," my involvement with sex work, and my porno-politics. In May 2005, I was also asked with my friend and fellow self-identified sex worker Jenna Jasmine (who started SWOP-UCLA) to run a panel on sex work and violence as part of the UCLA Clothesline Project against sexual violence.[12] These experiences as well as my writing of this chapter ultimately allow me to link the pornographic with the pedagogical.[13]

Images and representations of sex and sexuality, as well as our relationships and interactions with them, can and should be constantly interrogated and problematized. It is important to look at the ways in which the impressive array of pornography perpetuates and challenges conventional notions of youth, race, and fantasy. Pornography is an indispensable cultural and theoretical text that relates intimately to desire, representation, and politics. If certain assumptions exist that porn merely eroticizes an individual's victimization or that its sole purpose is to objectify bodies, then where is the space for resistance? Richard Fung rightly asserts that "the problems in North America's porn conventions are manifold and go beyond the question of race. There is such a limited vision of what constitutes the erotic" (126). While the notion of the erotic in mainstream gay porn is narrow, can pornographic images and stereotypes be appropriated, reinterpreted, and contested within a given—and decidedly more indie and politicized—cultural frame? I argue that they can, but only through the political, activist, pedagogical, and theoretical rewriting of pornography's hegemonic cultural and sexual narratives.

Ultimately this is why I've gotten involved in porn: to fuck with shame, to assert myself as a sexual being, to contest the idea that I have to be either gay or straight, to interrogate and experiment with the pornographic productions of youth and race, and to pedagogically link my sexuality with my activism and personal politics. Albeit, much of this is done in problematic and unresolved ways, it is only through this highly personal engagement with and questioning of pornography that sexualized images, fantasies, and stereotypes can be challenged and reinterpreted. To meaningfully subvert the conventions of mainstream porn however, I must admit that a more radical and independent project would be necessary—a project that I've merely started with my recent involvement with indie porn and with the ways I seek to link pornography with academia, politics, activism, and queer youth cultures. Perhaps my ultimate project is to participate intelligently and critically in the literal production and creation of queer cultures through pornography. Most importantly—as evidenced by the ways that I have been able to expand the audience of my pornographic experiments to include students, other sex workers, queer kids, and animal rights activists—I have begun to play with the gazes of others in ways that are sexually, intellectually, and politically stimulating and challenging. As I shift this audience, I am in effect creating yet another cultural niche where queer youth cultures can thrive. While this unfinished experiment has been both safe and personally rewarding for me, I still have a lot of questions to work through. In the meantime however, pornography keeps me thinking and engaging critically while it also allows me to continually push the boundaries of acceptability, visibility, intimacy, youth, and queerness.

NOTES

1. I especially wish to thank Richard Fung and Pete Sigal for their incisive questions, comments, and help with this chapter. This chapter never would have been written were it not for the creative space provided by David Gere and the other graduate students in his "Queer Choreographies" course in the UCLA World Arts and Cultures Department. Thanks also to Phuong Vu for taking the vegporn.com photos. I owe most of course to the open-mindedness, support, and questions of my family and friends. To my parents and sister Lisa, Jennifer Palecki, Osvaldo Gómez, Joanne Lin, Lorena Soto, Elza Wang, Grant Tyler Peterson, Yukiteru Maeda, Scott Lucas, Su Anne Takeda, Phuong Vu, and Jen Ly: my gratitude is more than I can ever hope to express.

2. For a unique essay that does speak from personal pornographic experience, see Scott Tucker (1990).

3. See the introduction to the 1996 special issue of *Social Text* 52–53, "Queer Transexions of Race, Nation, and Gender," edited by Phillip Brian Harper, Anne McClintock, José Esteban Muñoz, and Trish Rosen.

4. The video referred to here is Brad Posey's "Young, Hard, and Solo #18," and the arbitrary pseudonym under which I can be found is "Lance." This was the first and only time that I used a pseudonym in my porn work.

5. See Cante and Restivo, 148.

6. See <http://www.boyweb.com/free/skater_boy/boys/gallery2.htm>.

7. See <http://www.boyride.com/freetrial/samplezeb.html>.

8. See <http://www.boyride.com/freetrial/videoyngriders1.html>.

9. These pics were takes for globalmalepass.com and at least two photos can be seen at <http://www.kevscave.com/gmpboysbillryanandzeb/>. I am described on the globalmalepass.com site for the same photo shoot by the following: "Gmp Zeb: Zeb is one of many global male model you'll love to fuck." Another one of their pages asserts: "He Was A Skater Boy: Skater Boy Zeb stripped and ready to blow."

10 See <http://www.vegporn.com/>.

11 Personal communication with Tigerlily <http://www.thetigersden.net/>.

12 See <http://www.thecenter.ucla.edu/clothesmid.html>. See Jenna Jasmine's site at <http://www.asianprincessartifacts.com/>.

13 One other way that I have brought the politics of pornography into the classroom is by being publicly out (and outed) about my sex-work on campus. My involvement with on-campus organizations involved with sexuality and LGBT/queer issues has brought student and faculty attention to the fact that I work in pornography while simultaneously teaching undergraduates in the UCLA Department of History and working toward my doctoral degree.

WORKS CITED

Cante, Rich, and Angelo Restivo. "The Cultural-Aesthetic Specificities of All-Male Moving-Image Pornography." In *Porn Studies*, ed. Linda Williams. Durham: Duke University Press, 2004.

Fung, Richard. "Shortcomings: Questions about Pornography as Pedagogy." In *Queer Looks: Perspectives on Lesbian and Gay Film and Video*, ed. Martha Gever, John Greyson, and Pratibha Parmar. New York: Routledge, 1993.

———. "Looking for My Penis: The Eroticized Asian in Gay Video Porn." In *Q&A: Queer in Asian America*, ed. David L. Eng and Alice Y. Hom. Philadelphia: Temple University Press, 1998.

Gere, David. "29 Effeminate Gestures." In *Dancing Desires*, ed. Jane C. Desmond. Madison: University of Wisconsin Press, 2001.

Harper, Phillip Brian, Anne McClintock, José Esteban Muñoz, and Trish Rosen, eds. "Queer Transexions of Race, Nation, and Gender." *Social Text* (1996): 52–53.

Hoang, Nguyen Tan. "The Resurrection of Brandon Lee: The Making of a Gay Asian American Porn Star." In *Porn Studies*, ed. Linda Williams. Durham: Duke University Press, 2004.

Muñoz, José Esteban. *Disidentifications: Queers of Color and the Performance of Politics*. Minneapolis: University of Minnesota Press, 1999.

———. "Gesture, Ephemera, and Queer Feeling: Approaching Kevin Aviance." In *Dancing Desires*, ed. Jane C. Desmond. Madison: University of Wisconsin Press, 2001.

Tucker, Scott. "Gender, Fucking, and Utopia: An Essay Response to John Stoltenberg's *Refusing to Be a Man*." *Social Text* 27 (1990): 3–34.

Williams, Linda. *Hardcore: Power, Pleasure, and the "Frenzy of the Invisible."* Berkeley and Los Angeles: University of California Press, 1989.

———, ed. *Porn Studies*. Durham: Duke University Press, 2004.

PART THREE

TRANSFORMING POLITICAL ACTIVISM

So far, this book has focused on the representational dimensions of queer youth cultures, starting with subcultural fervor and performative artistry of youth and then turning to consider mass mediated texts and receptions. Authors have investigated how queer youth express identities and desires with a passionate refusal to be ignored or labeled against the tide of prescriptive and normalizing discursive conventions. What becomes clear in the chapters that follow is that it is impossible to separate representational and political aspects of queer youth cultures as youth grapple with institutional effects of heteronormalization while forging bonds of love, friendship, and community despite systematic denials and exclusions. The final part, "Transforming Political Activism," pays closer attention to political activist modes of collaboration taking place within the everyday lives of queer youth. Reworking notions of citizenship and social change through their practical engagements, youth endeavor to empower themselves in the face of pervasive social exclusions and hierarchical divisions. Experiences of discrimination, symbolic erasure, and material conditions of inequality are intimately interwoven into lifeworlds of gender and sexual minority youth. While they are never completely defined by oppressive forces, even the most whimsical and singular features of queer youth cultural involvement produce complex if sometimes oblique and contingent political effects. In this sense the cultural parameters of queer youth and their political movements are mutually connected and call for new ways of understanding their combinations and transformations.

Learning from the legacies of queer political groups including Queer Nation, Act Up, and the Lesbian Avengers (Crimp 1988; Epstein

217

1996; Gamson 1991; Schulman 2004), youth draw upon a diverse range of protest styles and tactics from street theater and drag performances to zine production, online mobilization, and visual art. Queer activism over the past two decades has expanded protest to include an expansive array of tools and technologies through which to signify political critique and enact public dissent with unruly flair. Re-animating the visual power of media spectacles for the purpose of disrupting social spaces and interrogating hegemonic discourses, queer activists crisscross boundaries inside/outside mainstream political and cultural fields. Speaking about the unique strategies of queer political artists, Amy Villarejo writes that they

> Are working in a tension between a politics of representation concerned with identity, signification, desire and ideology critique and a politics of affect, which emphasizes the capacity to affect bodies directly in their capacity to mutate, shift focus, attend and display interest, follow flows, coalesce in assemblages. (133)

Villarejo captures the ways queer politics navigates in between corporeal mobility, representational formations, and social systems. Playful and emotionally charged acts of resistance are integrated within the political landscapes of queer youth, fleshing out disembodied human rights rhetorics to dramatize spontaneous enactments of desire and rebellion.

Several recent anthologies (Kumashiro 2002; McNinch and Cronin 2004; Shepard and Hayduk 2002; Sycamore 2004) demonstrate the inventive and contingent political maneuvers of queer youth activism, elaborating new languages and collective rituals of resistance. Queer youth cultures are political in ways that challenge us to think beyond boundaries separating personal and political languages, sexuality and activism, material and symbolic inequalities, citizenship and queerness, creativity and practical engagement. The politics of gender and sexuality reverberate into multiple social and subjective realms, calling attention to the importance of intersectional modes of thinking and practice, and overcoming dichotomous tendencies within mainstream politics. This makes the construction of a separate section on political transformations seem arbitrary, perpetuating divisions between subcultures, popular culture, and politics. Yet the purpose of highlighting politics is not to fixate on an isolated category, but to propel inquiry and explore possibilities through a diversified realm of political discourses integrated with many other aspects of queer youth interests and experiences that include issues of poverty, racism, homelessness, homo/transphobia, violence, and globalization. Framing politics through the lens of queer youth needs and interests, several difficult questions emerge: What exactly comprises queer youth politics? Who is involved in shaping critique, mobilizing dissent, and envisioning alternatives? How are relations of power integrated into political strategies? What social systems are a locus of confrontation and change? Which styles and tactics are used at the ground level of activism? What conditions enable or thwart queer youth political participation? These questions remain open as authors elaborate the tenacious work of queer youth returning the gaze, speaking up, and acting out.

The following chapters explore innovative political interventions by, for, and about queer youth as they refuse to detach humorous displays and volatile bodies from political claims to economic, social, legal, and cultural rights and access. Within this section, the very definition of political action is up for grabs as queer youth resist hegemonic controls over their bodies, words, and associations across several institutional domains. The activities of queer youth are theorized beyond narrow identity politics or individualistic models of expression by contextualizing subcultural practices in relation to historical dynamics of global capitalism, citizenship, nationalism, racism, classism, and heterosexism. Specific political events and representations enacted by queer youth take on their full significance as youth put their bodies on the line to publicly demonstrate against injustice. The chapters go beyond a minoritizing discourse about discrete gay and lesbian identities, demonstrating how important it is to situate and interrogate the ways in which queer youth cultures are implicated in overlapping and hierarchical gender, sexual, national, race, class, and generational relations.

Andil Gosine's chapter "FOBs, Banana Boy, and the Gay Pretenders," provides a critical link between self-representational texts by, for, and about queer youth and nation-state ideologies that both celebrate liberal ideals of tolerance and perpetuate codes of difference erasing or assimilating young queer immigrants. His essay takes seriously the intimate words of youth in zines and video art, against the backdrop of racialized and colonial formations that construct and privilege exclusionary notions of citizenship. Gosine complicates dominant modernist rhetorics that celebrate Canada as a land of freedom, as a nation that welcomes sexual minorities from non-Western countries marked out and belittled as traditional and intolerant, asking difficult questions about the very status of this inclusion. His essay hones in on how queer youth respond to the normalizing pressures of nationalist discourses, detailing the ways they become implicated in liberal ideals that obscure daily economic, social, and emotional experiences of racial injustice. At the same time, Gosine opens up spaces in which to listen and look closely at narratives and images youth use to express discontent and elaborate resistance. In this way, queer youth participation in community-based artistic projects spurs counter-discourses relaying the struggles and contradictory perceptions of young diasporic queers.

Whereas Gosine uses textual analysis to unfold personalized stories of immigrant youth in relation to citizenship discourses, Megan Davidson's essay provides close-up ethnographic accounts of trans youth activism happening on the streets of New York City. Drawing upon extensive qualititative fieldwork with inner-city trans and queer youth of color, the chapter "Rethinking the Movement" addresses the ways in which local communities mobilize themselves. Davidson analyzes the tensions between liberal gay and lesbian politics focused on mainstream acceptance and the unique predicaments of poor urban queer youth. Focusing on the group FIERCE! (Fabulous Independent Educated Radicals for Community Empowerment), Davidson discusses their campaign, Save Our Space, which confronts forces of urban gentrification pushing poor and homeless queer youth of color out of neighborhoods. She argues for an interpretive framework attentive to the local needs of economically and socially marginalized young people along with the coalition building practices exemplified by FIERCE! as a way to mobilize youth as political agents working with youth advocates. City politics are framed through imbrications of class, race, gender, and sexual hierarchies that work to prevent queer youth from gaining access to community resources and space. FIERCE! offers an alternative approach to the white-centered and rights-oriented focus of national gay and lesbian organizations, encouraging diverse youth to get involved in decision making and leadership on the front lines of political action. Davidson approaches queer youth as an invested and committed researcher, suggesting the importance of including youth as agents and experts within an ethically oriented, action-oriented research and political process.

Continuing with a focus on participatory modes of community organizing, Neal Ritchie's chapter, "Principles of Engagement," turns attention directly onto the grassroots contours of youth activism recounted by a self-defined queer youth anarchist. From his location in Asheville, North Carolina, Ritchie sketches out queer youth interventions that contest capitalist and state legitimacy. Resistance is dynamically forged in the back allies and warehouse spaces inhabited by youth living on the economic margins of an affluent tourist city. Theorizing connections between queer youth poverty, gender discrimination, racialized inequalities, and multinational corporate hegemony, Ritchie stretches his interpretive focus to consider multiple and intersecting axes through which queer youth are oppressed and driven to forge global alliances as they fight against the status quo and build social justice networks. Ritchie refuses to limit queer youth politics to narrow issues of state rights and media visibility, expanding the terms through which queer youth politics become intelligible and viable within an expansive context of transnational relations of domination and resistance. Neal Ritchie situates the local activism of queer youth in Ashville in relation to antiglobalization movements, questioning the ways poststructural queer theories and liberal politics separate issues of sexual diversity from analysis of global capitalist systems of power. Ritchie draws upon his own experience as a queer youth working to radically transform, rather than merely be integrated within, the dominant social order.

What connects many of these essays together are affirmations of the creative, performative, and spontaneous facets of queer youth political participation that goes beyond formal protocols and principles of adult-centered gay and lesbian movements. Ritchie demonstrates how community based theater, culture jamming, drag shows, and zine-making combine with more traditional forms of organizing in hybrid ways. Similarly, Ziysah D. Markson argues that local youth-run drag events have the potential to disrupt normalizing tendencies and enact participatory modes of queer citizenship. Writing from the perspective of being a queer youth activist and academic, Markson writes about the public tensions of queer visibility in Peterborough, Ontario, in the final chapter of this book called "Drag it Out!" Markson's essay traces the unique possibilities for queer citizenship at a local drag event. The interactive features of this event inspire queer youth to redefine public space beyond static gender and sexual dichotomies, experimenting with queer embodiment and speech in a collective environment where the lines between performers and viewers become blurred. Those who attend the local event *Drag It Out!* are implicated in a queering of social identities as part of the process of enjoyment and learning within a neighborhood project that defies commodified divisions between queer entertainment and heterosexual spectatorship. Such alternatives are contrasted with the local pride event and media coverage that worked to other and demonize queers who are deemed a threat to the "straight" social majority. Markson develops a vision of queer citizenship drawing upon the practical experiences of youth while also raising critical questions about their limitations and blind spots. It is precisely Markson's reflexive and participatory approach as a queer youth engaged in community projects that points to an exciting future of queer youth political dialogues. The final chapters connect the spontaneous desires, actions, and thoughts of young people with new forms of queer politics and social justice movements.

WORKS CITED

Crimp. Douglas, ed. *AIDS: Cultural Analysis/Cultural Activism.* Cambridge: MIT Press, 1988.

Epstein, Steven. *Impure Science: AIDS, Activism, and the Politics of Knowledge.* Berkeley: University of California Press, 1996.

Gamson, Joshua. "Silence, Death, and the Invisible Enemy: AIDS Activism and Social Movement Newness." In *Ethnography Unbound*, ed. Michael Burawoy et al. Berkeley: University of California Press, 1991.

Kumashiro, Kevin K. *Troubling Education: Queer Activism and Antioppressive Education.* New York: RoutledgeFalmer, 2002.

McNinch, James, and Mary Cronin. I Could Not Speak My Heart: Education and Social Justice for Gay Lesbian Youth. Regina: Canadian Plains Research Centre, 2004.

Schulman, Sarah. *My American History.* New York: Routledge, 2004.

Shepard, Benjamin, and Ronald Hayduk. *From ACT UP to the WTO: Urban Protest and Community Building in the Era of Globalization.* Verso, 2002.

Sycamore, Matt Bernstein. *That's Revolting: Queer Strategies for Resisting Assimilation.* Soft Skull Press, 2004.

Villarejo, Amy. "Activist Technologies THINK AGAIN!" *Social Text* 80 22, 3 (Fall 2004).

CHAPTER 11

FOBS, BANANA BOY, AND THE GAY PRETENDERS

QUEER YOUTH NAVIGATE SEX, "RACE," AND NATION IN TORONTO, CANADA

Andil Gosine

Queer youth are strangely configured in nations, placed somewhere between nationalist proclamations that celebrate young people as (or burden them with responsibility for) "the future of the nation" and discourses framing queer sex as an urgent threat to nations' sustainability. These positions are woven around, into, and from discourses of gender, "race," class, and (dis)ability—and the material conditions they pro-duce—through which queer youth navigate senses of and sensibilities about themselves and the spaces they occupy and cross. Recently, queer and feminist scholars have argued that desires expressed for or partici-pation in homosexual acts would necessarily place queer youth outside their "home" nations. M. Jacqui Alexander innovated this position in her essays on the criminalization of homosexuality in the Caribbean. She suggests:

> The state has always conceived of the nation as heterosexual in that it places reproduction at the heart of its impulse. The citizenship machinery is also located here, for the prerequisites

of good citizenship and loyalty to the nation are simultaneously housed within the state apparatus. They are sexualized and ranked into a class of good, loyal, reproducing heterosexual citizens, and a subordinated, marginalized class of non-citizens, who by virtue of choice and perversion, choose not to do so. (46)

Legal codes and social-cultural norms across contemporary geographies compel heterosexual citizenship, denying, denunciating, and/or punishing any expressions of nonheterosexual desire. Gayatri Gopinath characterizes queers as "impossible subjects" in national imaginaries. Writing about South Asian lesbians living in the United States, Gopinath observes:

Within patriarchal diasporic logic, the "lesbian" can only exist outside the "home" (as household, community, and nation of origin) [. . .] the "lesbian" is seen as "foreign," as a product of "being too long in the West," and is therefore annexed to the "host" nation where she is further elided—particularly if undocumented—as a nonwhite immigrant within both a mainstream (white) lesbian and gay movement and the larger body of the nation-state. (263)

The situation of the *young* diasporic queer is further complicated: an outsider to her "home" ethnicized/racialized nation, and a marginal, racialized figure in the white-centered gay and lesbian community and heterosexual public space of her adopted "host" nation, her "youthfulness" offers the possibility of being shaped to fit nationalist objectives of either (or both). She is recognized as a subject still in formation; her ills may yet be remedied, her outsider status, revised. A young queer is a deviant body but, still, a recuperable citizen.

This essay engages transnational feminist analysis to explore the configuration(s) of immigrant queer youth in and across nations. I read two cultural works produced by queer youth to discern some of the appeals made to and negotiations undertaken by them in their encounters with nationalism(s), in Western metropoles: *Fresh Off the Boat* (*FOB*) (2004), a deliberately named zine that collects stories, poems, and images created by queer-identified, young immigrants working with the social support group Supporting Our Youth-EXPRESS (SOY-EXPRESS) in Toronto, Canada,[1] and *Banana Boy* (2003), a digital video made by (then) twenty-three-year-old filmmaker Samuel Chow about his experience of migrating from Hong Kong to Toronto. As anticipated in feminist literature, both texts demonstrate the incompatibility of queer sexual desire with "good citizenship," and their creators' struggles against marginalization in "home" and "host" nations. But the texts also present challenges to this analysis, and suggest a more complex operation of sexuality in some nation-building projects. They provide evidence of ways in which nonheterosexual desires are being racially maneuvered as cultural capital, presenting some nonwhite queer youth with a strange proposition, among others: of *potentially* crossing "nation" through queer sexual identification and simultaneous invocations of colonial-imperialist narratives about "race." The contemporary resonance of this logic, I suggest, is exemplified in the emergence of, and expression of anxieties about, "gay pretenders"—would-be migrants who adopt "queer" sexual identities as a strategy to access residency and citizenship in Western metropoles.

IN THE SPACE OF IMPOSSIBILITY

Queer, immigrant youth, it appears, occupy—to borrow Gopinath's expression—"a space of impossibility" (265). They are perpetually cast outside the nations they cross: bad ethnic citizens who betray the reproductive prerogatives of the "home," and racialized bodies read as abnormal, incompetent, and/or inferior in the "host," including in its principal gay and lesbian venues. *FOB* and *Banana Boy* provide several examples of the disavowal and derision of queer sexuality in some nation-building spaces, including the family, and the perseverance of racism and/or homophobia in others.

Banana Boy puts pictures to the "space of impossibility." In the video, images of Toronto and China are interspersed with those of Chow submerged underwater, as the filmmaker describes several tensions that shape his experiences of moving from Hong Kong to Canada in 1989. He discusses his parents' active refusal of Chinese culture ("the first thing my mother decided to do [. . .] was to move as far away from Chinatown as possible," he reports, "my mother didn't want me watching Chinese television"), and his confrontations with racism within Canada ("I got teased at school [. . .] I didn't do things the Canadian way") even as he yearned to "fit in [. . .] to be Canadian." Chow tells about his longing to belong and his attempts to move between or in opposition to competing cultural hegemonies. The video's title references his experience of struggling against being read as a banana boy, "white on the inside, yellow on the outside," even as he feels compelled to assimilate into whiteness, to assume rights as a Canadian. Near the close of the story, Chow emerges out of the water as he turns his attention to how his homosexual desires impact these negotiations. He reports encountering resistance from his mother after he comes out as gay, and uncomfortable silence from his father. "Every time the topic came up over dinner," Chow says, his father remarked "it's unnatural." In gay spaces, readings of his body oscillate between racialized exoticism and rejection, recalling one "cute boy who looked at me and ran off screaming, 'Chinese boys are supposed to be smooth!' " and another "who never looked at me because I am Chinese." By the time the video's closing credits appear, audiences have been exposed to multiple ways in which gendered, racialized, and sexualized inscriptions of Chow's body have aggressively situated him outside the territories to which he is attached, and a persuasive case has been made for characterizing Chow as "an impossible subject."

Similar practices of exclusion are described in *FOB*. In the zine's longest and most prominently featured essay, "personal story," a young lesbian recalls how her subversion of prescribed gender roles and expression of queer desires exposed her to various forms of violence in her country of birth, Iran. As a young girl, she remembers being so uncomfortable "acting like a girl" that she hoped divine intervention would change her sex:

> Every night before I go to bed I was praying to my god "God everybody saying that your powerful and generous . . . Can you look at this human of yours down here and grant her wish?? I wish that tomorrow morning when I wake up I won't be a girl anymore. Thank you god, amen" next [day] as soon as I wake up the first thing I would check was if I am still a girl!!! Well god disappointed me every single time I asked him. (6)

She says she longed "to become free, to tell my parents that I like girls," but "That was not a good idea, they would kill me if they would know I am gay." "Thinking about it," years later, in Toronto, still makes her "shiver from my head to toe. Stoning you, dying alive under stones," she says, "that is scary" (6).

When she is found out to be involved with another girl—after police uncover love letters at her lover's house—she is forced to flee to another country, with her family, to escape a possible death sentence. In Canada, she finds some respite from forms of extreme violence, but the young woman still remains excluded from her new, adopted nation. Describing her family's first experiences of the Canadian state, she recalls:

> The immigration people were very rude and impolite. They asked us where are we from and with the little English I learnt in school I told them Iran and the guy started swearing at us "fucking Iranians why you come to Canada?" he was saying stuff but I couldn't understand only from the way of his language I knew he is not saying good stuff. They told us we have to wait until morning till they get somebody to translate to us.

> After the interview and making papers and stuff they told us to go, but where???? We didn't have anybody here, didn't know anywhere. (8).

Eventually, the family moves into a shelter, and, two months later, a more permanent home. But when she later comes out as lesbian to her mother, she is expelled from her family. "My mom couldn't stand me being gay and all the things that she went through because of me so she kicked me out of the house," she says, "I didn't have anywhere."

No mention is made by this writer or by any of the other contributors to *FOB* of the persistence of racism in Toronto's gay and lesbian public spaces, but SOY-EXPRESS staff coordinator Suhail AbualSameed suggests that this is a chief concern among participants. He recalls one example of an experience shared by many of them:

> This young guy went to a queer youth group in the community and [. . .] he went a couple of times there and said it was the worst experience of his life, because everybody was making fun of him. He couldn't speak English very well. He dressed modestly [. . .]. Nobody would engage him in the conversation [. . .]. He felt totally alienated. He didn't go back. (personal interview 2005)[2]

Asked to identify the main problems faced by SOY-EXPRESS clients, AbualSameed also easily references a list of priorities, which include: "isolation, language and communication challenges, unemployment, legal issues, and racism," he says, "especially in the gay community."

The very existence of SOY-EXPRESS provides evidence of the per-
petuation of hetero-racism in Canada, since the organization was conceived as a response to state deficiencies in attending to the welfare of
young, immigrant queers. However, criticism of the Canadian state's
failings is framed in an important and telling way in the introduction
to *FOB*, written by AbualSameed. "Young queer people who move into
this city from other parts of the world," his note reads, "*seeking freedom
and acceptance in a more open and tolerant environment* find no guidance or
support from any of the existing institutions in Canada" (my emphasis,
1). It is not just that young queer immigrants "find no guidance or
support" from the Canadian state, but that there is an expectation that
they would.

In the *FOB* scripts, Canada plays the part of invitational "host" to
sexual outsiders expelled from their "home" nations. The young men
and women writing in the zine describe their experiences of migration
to Canada as flights to freedom; one participant writes:

> i always wanted to fly out of the country where every day
>   was night
> i wanted freedom . . .
> respect for who I am
> YES I AM GAY
> i wanted to say it loud without any fear of getting stoned
>   for who I was
> Travelling
> from THERE to HERE
> from NIGHT to SUNRISE was hard
> i can taste f r e e d o m
> i can be myself and enjoy being myself . . .
> all i want is happiness to come to me. (Anonymous 11)

Echoing this perspective, the poem "There is a place for me and my
friends" describes the author's "trip" from a place of oppression to one
of liberation:

> It's been a trip
> A trip with no ending
> A trip with no wishes

A way to dream and wake
Far away from my place

[to a]

A place of freedom
A place of wishes
A place to find myself
In the way I never found before . . .
And before . . . (Gotz *FOB* 7)

A similarly themed testimonial written by Morlon appears at rocktheboat.ca, a companion website to *FOB*. Morlon migrated to Toronto from Jamaica, Canada in December of 2002, "seeking a better life as a young gay male from the Caribbean." Of his experiences in Canada, Marlon says, "I love living and working in Toronto as I can be myself and enjoy my life without having to hide who I am and lying to myself."

These affirmative celebrations of Canada as "a place of freedom," "a place of wishes," and a place that allows gay and lesbian men and women to "find" and "be" themselves reveal much more than the optimism of their authors; they also suggest the tenacity of nationalist narratives celebrating Canada as a queer or "queer-friendly" state. The introduction of a Multiculturalism Policy in 1971, a Human Rights Act in 1977, and Charter of Rights and Freedoms in 1982, and former prime minister Pierre Trudeau's widely circulated, public assertion that "the state has no business in the bedrooms of the nation" have driven local and global imaginations of Canada as a welcoming place, more respectful of individual choices and cultural and sexual diversity than other countries. More recently, necessary comparisons with our closest neighbor have reinforced the notion that Canada is a site of liberation, especially for gays and lesbians. In the United States, social conservatives seized upon political opportunities made available to them post 9/11, to pursue an agenda that includes new controls on civil liberties, tightened censorship regulations, aggressive militarism and the repudiation of gay rights advances, including legislated prohibition of same-sex marriage in several states. Over the same period in Canada (1999–2006), successful court challenges resulting in the revision of immigration, labor, and pension laws to accommodate same-sex relationships, gestures toward the legalization of marijuana and the refusal of the

Canadian government to join the U.S.-British invasion of Iraq earned its celebration or condemnation as "Hippie Nation" or "Soviet Canuckistan" (Klein).[3]

Consequently, Canada has been declared, as American syndicated columnist Dan Savage put it, a "morally superior" destination for gays and lesbians fleeing repressive regimes (2). In the days following George W. Bush's election to a second term in office, the website marryanamerican.ca elicited thousands of personal ads from Americans looking for Canadian partners (and, through marriage, citizenship). "Forget the brain drain," announced one headline in Canada's most widely circulated gay publication, *Xtra*, "it's all about the gay gain" (Gnutel). Canada has fast become "a country to call homo," declared another (Garro). Since the mid-1990s, in fact, over three thousand immigration permits have been issued to self-identified gays and lesbians seeking refugee status in Canada, more than any other market in the world, including the United States (Jiminez A3). Claimants' successes in immigration and refugee tribunals have permitted such self-adulatory pronouncements as the *Globe and Mail* headline for a story about Al-Hussein, a forty-seven-year-old man who successfully applied for refugee status: "Gay Jordanian Now Gloriously Free in Canada" (Jiminez A3). The title also references Al-Hussein's participation in *Gloriously Free*, a documentary about the experiences of queer men who sought refuge in Canada. The publicity brief for *Gloriously* describes it as: "the first documentary ever to explore the world of gay immigration and the desperate search of five young men to find welcoming arms outside their countries of birth, where persecution and hatred of alternative lifestyles may lead to torture or death." It goes on to praise Canada as "a vast country that now leads the world as the safest haven for persecuted international gays and lesbians" and that "is fast becoming the world's unspoken symbol of sexual freedom."

For many who have taken these flights to freedom, immigration to Canada has been a much more ambivalent experience than the promotional rhetoric suggests. Against depictions of Canada as an egalitarian, multicultural Mecca are its historical truths: the origins of the Canadian state in colonialism, the violent displacement and systemic oppression of Aboriginal peoples, internment of its ethnicized Japanese nationals during wartime, and immigration, education, and housing policies that at various times included legislated discrimination against African, Afro-American/black, Chinese, South Asian, and Jewish peoples. Contemporary scholarship by Himani Bannerji, Frances Henry, Rinaldo Walcott, and Sherene Razack details the multiple ways in which racism, patriarchy, and heterosexism shape Canada's economy and its social, cultural, and legal codes; and novels, films, and music by Dionne Brand, Richard Fung, Faith Nolan, and many others, expose the work of "race," gender, class, and sexuality in determining accessibility to the full privileges of Canadian citizenship and to resources of the Canadian state. Nevertheless, characterization of Canada as a liberating space has persisted.

This mythology is so powerfully wielded that it tends to subsume any potentially oppositional or challenging narratives. In the *FOB* texts, for instance, few examples of the situations that AbualSameed describes of young queer immigrants not being able to access work, encountering hostility and/or indifference in the gay community, and being ridiculed or humiliated for their aesthetic choices are represented. Most often, despite their own struggles finding jobs and homes, accessing comfortable social space, and developing connections within various communities, the works' creators consistently characterize Canada as a refuge. Even the young Iranian-born woman whose essay is quoted at length in the preceding section counters her criticism of racist practices at immigration with positive affirmations about Toronto and Canada, characterizing her and her family's experiences as exceptional situations, not the rule. Following elaboration about one difficult experience in Toronto that brings her to the conclusion that "Coming to Canada was the worst experience of my life," she adds the caveat, "Not that it's a bad city no." She also concludes her essay with another statement professing her loyalty to Canada: "Nowhere is like home but I am trying to make Canada my home, the land that I can be who I and I can live as who I am and I don't have to pretend being somebody else, lots of freedom. Great country a little cold but that's ok!" (8).

Her and other *FOB* contributors' adoption of the rhetoric of state multiculturalism also demonstrates how marginalization comes to be explained in the context of "Queer Canada" narratives. As expressed in their artwork, young queer immigrants appear to feel compelled to explain their experiences of isolation and marginalization as a consequence of their "freshness" to Canadian society (and not of socioeconomic relations in Canada) and, furthermore, to couch their reflections and analysis within a nationalist framework that maintains its celebratory demeanor—to insist that they *will be* "gloriously free" even as *they are not*. This position is reinforced by the organization of SOY-EXPRESS as a response to the "difficulties" faced by "newcomer" immigrant youth, which focuses attention on young queers' "inexperience in

Canada" and not on the country's social and economic policies or its investments in racism or hetero-patriarchy.

"RACE," SEX, AND NATION-CROSSING

The persistence of "Queer Canada" mythologies troubles queer and feminist approaches that emphasize the heterosexual basis of nation-building; it forces us to ask, for example: what to make of nationalisms that are, at least partly and in theory, premised on the inclusion of and recognition of rights for homosexuals? How do we understand emerging situations where expression of queer desires do not simply dictate the exclusion of their holders but may in fact function to include them, in certain ways, in particular national imaginaries (e.g., in Toronto, Canada)? What is being negotiated when queers' admission into "host" nations is premised on sexual deviance in their "home" nations—and what is being said about "race," culture, sex, and difference in the execution of these negotiations? How do we understand *homosexual* "race"-crossing through sex, when racial anxieties about sex (e.g., about interracial sex) obsessively privilege reproduction?

Transnational feminist and queer scholarship about the relationships between heterosexual and gay capital (e.g., Alexander 2005), the sexualized, racialized, and gendered imperatives of colonization and nation-building projects (e.g., McClintock, Stoler, Gopinath, Bhaskaran) and which problematize the universal-imperialist production of sexual identities (e.g., Manalansan, Sinfield, Patton) have laid the groundwork for fuller pursuit of these interrogations. Here, I draw upon some insights expressed in this work to call attention to some of the ways in which strategic wielding of sexual identities in the particular production of (metropolitan) Canadian nationalism, as represented in *FOB* and *Banana Boy*, are articulated through colonial-imperialist narratives about "race."

In the opening sequence of *Banana Boy*, three images locate Chow in a "space of impossibility." The second of these images is of the narrator himself, unclothed and submerged, face up, underwater. His eyes are closed, his expression, tense. This image is sandwiched by two others: that of a fisherman, standing and gently rowing what appears to be a small, wooden boat, his head covered by a round, broad "peasant" straw hat—a familiar, iconic figure that has often stood in for East Asia or "Asian-ness" in many Orientalist texts. The third image is of Toronto's landscape marker, the CN tower. It is an unstable image, likely filmed by a handheld camera, by someone passing over the city on an airplane.

Both images reference the points of departure and arrival for Chow—Hong Kong/China and Toronto/Canada. Chow's use of these two images in this sequence seems to play into and reproduce a racializing developmental narrative that characterizes non-Western countries as primitive/premodern (the "traditional" fisher representing Hong Kong/China) and Western countries as progressive/modern (a tower—"the World's tallest tower" representing Toronto/Canada). As Chow's story unfolds, this juxtaposition of primitive/premodern Hong Kong/China against modern Toronto/Canada is reinforced in visuals and his narration. For example, even though his family is from Hong Kong, not the Chinese mainland, images from the 1989 Tiananmen Square prodemocracy protests form the backdrop of Chow's discussion of their departure to Canada. When the next scene cuts to his arrival in Toronto, the image of the CN tower gives way to a bird flying—perhaps, like the *FOB* contributors, to freedom.

Queer sexuality, in Chow's narrative as well as in many of the *FOB* texts, is the trope that enables his transition from a premodern/primitive Chinese to the modern/progressive Canadian nation. In the third act of *Banana Boy*, Chow emerges from underwater as he explains, "I came out a few years ago. One night, my mum asked me straight out if I was gay. I told her the truth [. . .]." Images of the army tanks that attacked protestors at Tiananmen Square appear next on screen, as Chow completes the description of his "coming out" to his mother: "[. . .] there was no turning back." The appearance of the tank at the moment of this announcement collapses Hong Kong/China with Chow's own "pre-outed," premodern past—the corollary being that Toronto/Canada is his "liberated," modern, gay future. The Tiananmen massacre tanks appear again, when Chow announces, "she still thinks my being gay is a phase." After his emergence from the water—at which point audiences see that he was lying in a bathtub—Chow gets up and moves to the bedroom, where he joins a young, white man in bed. Chow embraces and kisses him. "Now that I'm out," he says, "the banana boy phrase has taken on a whole new meaning."

Chow doesn't develop this idea except in the statements that next follow it with which the story closes: "My father never spoke about my sexuality ever since I came out. He went on his usual ways. Sometimes, I wonder if he is proud of me. Is he proud of his *banana boy?*"

The question is gently posed, but given Chow's earlier references to his parents' determined efforts to put distance between their new lives in Canada and their experiences of "Chinese-ness" in Hong Kong, and to rid Chow of his Chinese accent and consumption of Chinese culture, one wonders whether it is meant as a provocation; is his father "proud" of him becoming such a model "banana boy," of "betraying" his "home" nation so profoundly that he has also become gay—a possibility not available to a "real" Chinese boy? When Chow says "the banana boy phrase has taken on a whole new meaning" since he has come out, does he mean that his adoption of a "gay" identity has provided a final rupture from his Chinese-ness, whereby though he looks "yellow on the outside," he has become "white on the inside" through his declaration of homosexuality? Since this comment comes after we see Chow in bed with a young, white male, is "the whole new meaning" of "banana boy" that his assimilation into white Canadian culture now includes a sexual valorization of white bodies? Does he offer the term as a partner to "Rice Queen" (reserved for white men sexually attracted to East Asian men) to suggest that a "banana boy" seeks white men for sex? Does he mean that he has become a more palatable object in white culture?

Whatever the explanation inferred from his comment, it is always inscribed in "race." Colonial-imperialist narratives of "race" underlie not just Chow's representation of his navigation through competing and/or collaborating discourses of nation in *Banana Boy*, but also those of the *FOB* contributors, through the framing of their experiences of migration that privileges characterization of Canada as a site of liberation. There are four collaborating strategies through which nation-crossing into "Queer Canada" is configured around "race": through (1) the conflation of varied sets of cultural and sexual practices with instruments of the state and results in the racialized characterization of non-white people as "natural" homophobes; (2) the invocation and affirmation of modernist discourses predicated on racial hierarchy; (3) the privileging of white Western ways of knowing and speaking about sex and sexuality; and (4) the neutering of colonial anxieties about the reproductive potential of nonwhite peoples.

In the production of "Queer Canada" narratives, legislated protections for sexuality rights in Canada have come to be understood as the cultural beliefs of the whole nation, which is certainly not the case—even the current prime minister of Canada, Stephen Harper, has declared his opposition to same-sex marriage and other queer sexuality rights. The corollary to this is that the repressive laws of states with punitive consequences for homosexuals also cast whole cultures as homophobic. Thus, Jamaican criminal codes that define imprisonment terms for acts of sodomy become racially reinterpreted as: "Jamaicans are homophobic" or "Jamaican culture is homophobic." In the case of Jamaica, these laws do not merely stand in for public opinion, and emerge out of a particular history of colonialism and directly out of colonial texts. This collapsing of culture with legislative codes also makes little or no accommodation for the ambivalent ways in which they are experienced, including by those who are marginalized and who consequently resist them. In this gesture, no recognition is made of nonwhite peoples' subjectivities.

As so clearly demonstrated in *Banana Boy*'s and *FOB*'s stories of young queers leaving oppressive pasts for freer futures, the "Queer Canada" narrative is a modernization discourse. Alexander points out:

> Modernization discourses and practices it infuses . . . collapse divergent histories and temporalities into these apparently irreconcilable binaries of tradition and modernity [. . .]. In doing so, they also territorialize their own difference, ultimately placing their claims within an ideological universe, whose analytic and material boundaries dovetail with imperatives that are most closely aligned with those of colonization. (189)

The comparisons of cultures and nations articulated in the characterization of Canada as a site of liberation—and those of Third World nations as sites of repression—work to reify perceived ideological differences generated out of this tradition-modernity binary. They necessarily invoke a racial hierarchy that privileges and valorizes whiteness as a marker of progress, civility, and authority and that works to colonize the articulation of sexual identities and practices.

FOB and *Banana Boy* represent nation-crossing into "Queer Canada" as a teleological transition, moving from a regressive to a progressive site of sexual politics, but the experience might be better characterized as becoming familiar with a different set of cultural codes. Sometimes, young, queer immigrants do not experience "Queer Canada" as a "freeing" experience. For example, "Rolondo," an eighteen-year-old Jamaican, bisexual–identified immigrant, found that he encountered less rigid demands made about gender roles in his home country than in Canada:

> In Jamaica [I'm] living with people who were used to me acting like this, so it was not a big deal for them—from the day

that I was born, so it was not a big deal for them. They understood "that's just the type of person [I am]." My mom was the coolest person about it, because I can remember, from age nine or ten, I was washing dishes and cleaning the house and doing stuff that you see mostly women doing. You know, sweeping the room, mopping stuff. (qtd. in Lord 42)

Similarly, "Ahmed," a twenty-three-year-old Somali man who migrated to Toronto with his family, also found that he had to adapt to more strict gender behaviors:

I remember being in grade 6 and being all effeminate, being told "you walk like a girl" . . . it didn't make any sense to me . . . [I had] to learn to walk like a guy by using the cracks in the sidewalk to measure how far my feet were apart . . . I'd walk with my wrists held all high and my hand all dangling and people would smack it like, "Put that down. Don't do that all the time." I always knew that it showed a bit and I didn't like that either. I tried to hide it myself and the whole thing was to hide it from other people. (qtd. in Lord 43)

Twenty-year-old "Nellie," whose family emigrated from Nigeria, also found that even queer traditions that are normalized in Canada presented new difficulties:

That's another big difference between Nigeria and here [Canada]; it was like you had a duty—it was necessary to come out—but back home it was like they knew what you were, it was known . . . and it was hidden so there was no need to come out. Like it wasn't assumed that I was only attracted to men in the first place. That's what having to come out does—I'm not coming out, cause don't assume I am straight in the first place. (qtd. in Lord 42)

Citation of these passages is not meant to suggest that Canada is a more repressive place for queers than the home countries of Nellie, Ahmed, and Rolondo. Instead, it compels reconsideration of assumptions about the easy "welcome" Canada is said to offer queers, and it also calls for more critical appreciation of the complex cultural contexts in countries that are generally dismissed as inferior—including ones that may well

offer more affirmative views of same-sex sexual practices; Nellie's grandmother, for example, used to tell her stories with "goddesses" who were
"pure lesbians," including narratives about women who rescued their
daughters from marriages to men (44). They also challenge the insis-
tence that non-Euro-American queerness be articulated through frameworks of sexuality generated in white-Western/metropolitan culture to
access political consciousness, subjectivity, and liberation.

Nation-crossing into "Queer Canada," finally, also raises the ugly
proposition that queer sexual identification by nonwhite youth may work
to allay white racial anxieties about the reproductive potential of nonwhite people that have circulated since the dawn of European colonization. Nineteenth-century theories of "race," like those posited by Count
Gobineau in *Essay on the Equality of Races*, focused on reproductive sex,
"or rather its consequence, namely the degree of fertility of the union
between the different races" (Young 101). Such racial theory, Robert
Young argues, "projected a phantasmagoria of the desiring machine [of
colonialism] as a people factory." There were great fears about "uncon-
trollable, frenetic fornication producing the countless motley varieties of
interbreeding, with the miscegenated offspring themselves then generating an ever increasing melange, 'mongrelity,' of self-propagating endlessly
diversifying hybrid progeny [. . .]" (181). Although all kinds of "illicit"
sexual practices disturbed colonial officials, anxieties about *reproductive* sex
have been consistently reiterated in contemporary sites, such as the fears
about burgeoning Third World populations that guide family planning
and environmental policies of global institutions (cf. Bookchin; Hartmann;
Gosine, "Dying Planet"). Even responses to the global AIDS crisis appear
most anxious about reproductive sex; homosexual sex might have "caused"
the disease, in their analysis, but it is heterosexual sex between MSM
(men who have sex with men) and their female partners that has gotten
the bulk of attention from global institutions, nongovernmental organizations, and aid agencies (cf. Gosine, "Sex for Pleasure"). Queer identification by Third World youth would, in this context, appear to neuter
worries about the threat posed by nonwhites' reproductive sex to the
"purity" and cultural dominance of the white race.

CONCLUSION: THE GAY PRETENDERS

By way of conclusion to the discussion introduced here, I want to leap
from the cultural texts to briefly bring attention to a curious contemporary phenomenon that demonstrates the analysis of "race," sex, and

nation laid out in this chapter. In 2006, stories about "gay pretenders" seeking refuge in Western states started to circulate in national and community newspapers. On May 6, the *Hindustan Times* ran a story entitled "For Greener Pastures—Turning Gay to Chase British Dream" about "people of Punjab aspiring to immigrate to the United Kingdom [who] have found a new alibi—that of being homosexuals" (Jalandhar). According to the article, legalization of same-sex marriages in the UK last year has resulted in immigration consultancy offices in India "being flooded with queries from youths in search of a greener pasture." Immigration consultant Kamal Bhumbla reported that he has received "at least 15 to 20 queries in the recent times inquiring about the UK law. A number of Punjabi youths are willing to pose as homosexuals, if that helps in moving to the UK." Among the young "pretenders" vying for status was twenty-two-year-old Sukhwinder Singh (alias) of Noormahal, who admitted that he wished to apply for a visa under this category. In the article, Singh explains: "I got hold of one of my friends after I came to know about this law. He too was desperate to go abroad and readily agreed to the plan. My girlfriend knows about it. I have assured her that once I immigrate, I will marry her in the UK." Another hopeful emigrant said it was his father who gave him the idea. "I have been trying to go abroad for the last many years but nothing clicked," says Vikas Dhir, "I know it is simply not acceptable in Punjab, but I don't have any other option to achieve prosperity in life."

Representation of this event in the *Times* (and its similarly framed repetition in other diasporic presses) affirms feminist readings of nation and nationalism that mark homosexuality as threatening. The story reassures Indian nationalist anxieties about homosexuality by suggesting that young men "claiming" to be "gay" really are *not* homosexual, and are even attached to heterosexual partners; queer identification is merely a strategy toward a loftier, and respectable, goal. (In this analysis, physically *leaving* the nation through migration is seen to be less threatening than declaring a public homosexual identity). The act of "turning gay" as a means to access more desirable citizenships, on the other hand, reconfigures the space occupied by young diasporic queers as one of possibilities; queer identification offers new residences, new citizenship, "prosperity." As I have argued here, these offers are mired in racial discourse, but they are nevertheless meaningful to and valued by subjects who pursue their realization.

The article's observation that it is "young" Indian nationals who are willing to "turn gay" in their efforts to migrate to the UK, furthermore, reveals how "youth" is specially rendered in national contestations—as both an object to be regulated and a source of disruption. The figure of the "gay pretender" is a strategic response to the ideological xenophobic and homophobic anxieties of "home" and "host" nations that strives to undermine their material objectives. It speaks not only about the tightly reined and powerfully wielded narratives of "race," sex, and gender through which queer-identified diasporic youth must navigate their futures but also to young people's creative potential to subvert their intentions.

NOTES

Special thanks to the Social Sciences and Humanities Research Council of Canada and to Alexandre Beliaev and Suhail AbualSameed.
    1. As explained on the group's website, SOY-EXPRESS works to:

> provide newcomer and immigrant queer youth with a safer space where they can meet others who share there experiences and feel comfortable expressing themselves and making friends, as well as gain more knowledge about Canada and Toronto that will help them build their life in the city. (http://www.soytoronto.org/current/express.html)

Around sixty people participated in the program from the start. Weekly drop-in meetings have regularly attracted eight to twelve young men and women aged between sixteen and twenty-seven, while many youth keep in touch or request services by telephone and/or email. Most participants have been young men from South America and South Asia, with some participants from Africa, the Middle East, and East Asia. Cultural production has been a major feature of SOY-EXPRESS since its inception. *FOB* was its first group project. The group's coordinator, Suhail AbualSameed, explains the title of the zine:

> The members wanted to reclaim a term that was often used against immigrants in a derogatory way, in rejection and humiliation. They wanted to say "yes we ARE newcomers . . . we ARE immigrants . . . we ARE "fresh off the boat," and it doesn't take any of our humanity or pride away from us. (AbualSameed)

Other cultural production projects followed the publication of *FOB*. In 2003, one of the project's participants proposed production of a video and, with the group and the assistance of a local filmmaker, created a short video, *My Name Is Javier*, and a website, rocktheboat.ca.
    2. In Ruthann Lee's " 'Coming Out' as Queer Asian Youth in Canada: Examining Cultural Narratives of Identity and Community," interviewee Mark describes his experience at the largest youth organization in the city in similar terms:

The first organization that I connected with—I went to LGBYT [Lesbian Gay, Bisexual Youth of Toronto] which is very clique-y, mostly white males, but some people of colour [. . .] and they all fitted stereotypes, I think, when I was there. Some of them didn't but those who didn't weren't there for very long. And stereotypes of flaming gay male or the preppy white boy who's into the gay community type thing. It was very clique-y and they were already friends so it was really a horrible space. (67)

Mark added, "If I am around a lot of white gay males, for example, who are very 'in' with the community, I just feel like I'm not even there" (69).

   3. All of these measures are under review by the Conservative minority federal government elected in 2006.

WORKS CITED

AbualSameed, Suhail. Personal Interview. Toronto: May 2005.
———. "Introduction." *Fresh Off the Boat*. Toronto: Supporting Our Youth, 2004. Alexander, M. Jacqui. *Pedagogies of Crossing*. Durham: Duke University Press, 2005.
Anonymous. "Personal Story." *Fresh Off the Boat*. Toronto: Supporting Our Youth, 2004.
Banana Boy. Dir. Samuel Chow. Inside Out Video, 2003.
Bannerji, Himani. *The Dark Side of the Nation: Essays on Multiculturalism, Nationalism and Gender*. Toronto: Canadian Scholars' Press, 2000.
Bhaskaran, Suparna. *Made in India: Decolonizations, Queer Sexualities, Trans/National Projects*. New York: Palgrave Macmillan, 2004.
Bookchin, M. *Which Way for the Ecology Movement?* San Francisco: AK Press, 1994.
Brand, Dionne. "A Working Paper on Black Women in Toronto: Gender, Race, and Class." In *Returning the Gaze: Essays on Racism, Feminism and Politics*, ed. Himani Bannerji. Toronto, ON: Sister Vision Press, 1993.
———. *In Another Place, Not Here*. Toronto, ON: Vintage Canada, 1997.
———. *A Map to the Door of No Return: Notes to Belonging*. Toronto: Doubleday Canada, 2001.
Dirty Laundry. Dir. Richard Fung. Toronto: V Tape, 1996.
Fresh Off the Boat. Toronto: Supporting Our Youth, 2004.
Garro, Julia. "A Country to Call Homo: How Welcoming Is Canada of Queer Immigrants and Refugees?" *Xtra!* (Toronto) 10 June 2004.
Gloriously Free. Dir. Naomi Weis. OMNITV. 10 June 2005.
Gnutel, Shawna. "Forget the Brain Drain, It's all About the Gay Gain." *Xtra!* (Toronto) 22 July 2004.

Gopinath, Gayatri. "Nostalgia, Desire, Diaspora: South Asian Sexualities in Motion." In *Theorizing Diaspora: A Reader*. New York: Blackwell, 2003.

Gosine, Andil. "Sex for Pleasure, Rights to Participation and Alternatives to AIDS: Placing Sexual Dissidents/Minorities in International Development." *IDS Working Paper #228*. Brighton: Institute of Development Studies, 2004.

————. "Dying Planet, Deadly People: 'Race'-Sex Anxieties and Alternative Globalizations." *Social Justice*. 2006. (Forthcoming—citation info to follow).

Gotz, Andre. "There Is a Place for Me and My Friends." *Fresh Off the Boat*. Toronto: Supporting Our Youth, 2004.

Hartmann, B. *Reproductive Rights and Wrong*. Boston: South End Press, 1995.

Henry, Frances, and Carol Tator, eds. *The Colour of Democracy: Racism in Canadian Society*. 3rd ed. Toronto: Harcourt Brace Canada, 2006.

Jalandhar, Manpreet Ranshawa. "For Greener Pastures—Turning Gay to Chase British Dream." *Hindustan Times* 6 May 2006.

Jimenez, Maria. "Gay Jordanian Now 'Gloriously Free' in Canada." *Globe and Mail* 20 May 2004, A3.

Klein, Naomi. "Canada: Hippie Nation?" *The Nation*. 21 July 2003.

Lee, Ruthann. " 'Coming Out" as Queer Asian Youth in Canada: Examining Cultural Narratives of Identity and Community." Master thesis, University of Toronto, 2003. *ProQuest Digital Dissertations*. 1 June 2005.

Lord, Cassandra. "Making the Invisible / Visible: Creating a Discourse on Black Queer Youth." Master's thesis. Ontario Institute for the Studies in Education, University of Toronto, 2005.

Manalansan IV, Martin F. "In the Shadows of Stonewall: Examining Gay Transnational Politics and the Diasporic Dilemma." In *Theorizing Diaspora: A Reader*. New York: Blackwell, 2003.

McClintock, A. *Imperial Leather: Race, Gender and Sexuality in Colonial Context*. New York: Routledge, 1995.

Nolan, Faith. "Long Time Comin'." Faith Nolan, 1993.

Out of the Blue. Dir. Richard Fung. Toronto: Fungus Productions, 1991.

Patton, Cindy. "Stealth Bombers of Desire: The Globalization of 'Alterity' in Emerging Democracies." In *Queer Globalizations*, ed. Arnaldo Cruz-Malave and Martin F. Manalansan. New York: New York University Press, 2002.

Razack, Sherene. *Race, Space, and the Law: Unmapping a White Settler Society*. Toronto: Between the Lines, 2002.

Savage, Dan. " 'Oh Canada!' " *The Stranger* 21 October 2004, 2.

Sea in the Blood. Dir. Richard Fung. Toronto: Fungus Productions, 2000.

Sinfield, Alan. "The Production of Gay and the Return to Power." In *Decentering Sexualities: Politics and Representations beyond the Metropolis*, ed. Richard Phillips, David E Shuttleton, and Diane Watt. London: Routledge, 2000.

Stoler, Ann Laura. *Race and the Education of the Desire.*

Stychin, Carl F. *Law's Desire: Sexuality and the Limits of Justice.* London, New York: Routledge, 1995.

Walcott, Rinaldo. *Black Like Who? Writing Black Canada.* 2nd rev. ed. Toronto: Insomniac Press, 2003.

Waldner, L. K., and B. Magruder. "Coming Out to Parents: Perceptions of Family Relations, Perceived Resources, and Identity Expression as Predictors of Identity Disclosure for Gay and Lesbian Adolescents." *Journal of Homosexuality* 27, 2 (1999): 83–100.

West, Emily. "Selling Canada to Canadians: Collective Memory, National Identity and Popular Culture." London: Routledge, 2002.

Websites

http://rocktheboat.ca

http://www.soytoronto.org/fob/

CHAPTER 12

RETHINKING THE MOVEMENT

TRANS YOUTH ACTIVISM IN
NEW YORK CITY AND BEYOND

Megan Davidson

When I began my fieldwork on trans activism in the United States, I was questioned repeatedly about my choice of New York City as a field site and told there was no organized transgender activism in New York City. In my first months of fieldwork several activists both in New York and elsewhere explained to me that in-fighting had destroyed the activist networks here and that my work would be uneventful. The construction of "trans activism" was being limited to legislative and lobby organizations, which have struggled in New York. Yet, this circumscribed view of what counts as activism neglects some of the most dynamic, creative, powerful activists pushing for change: queer and trans youth activists of color. In this chapter I detail the efforts of one such group, FIERCE!, taking as a starting point a protest I attended in Sheridan Square. Using this event, and over a year of fieldwork with trans activisms around the country, I offer an analysis of what this struggle in the West Village points to in terms of both the tensions within the national LGBTQ movement and the possible solutions regarding assimilation, inclusion, and a rethinking of the LGBTQ movement found in the activist principles and practices of these youth activists.

FIERCE! RESISTANCE

Hundreds of trans and queer youth of color and their allies gathered
on October 16, 2004, in the West Village's Sheridan Square for an
awards ceremony where members of FIERCE! (Fabulous Independent
Educated Radicals for Community Empowerment) presented mock
awards to West Village residents and business owners, and the New York
Police Department, and the "Powerful Few" who have been involved
in the displacement and criminalization of trans and queer youth of
color in this neighborhood. An hour later, marching down Christopher
Street carrying banners and wearing shirts that read "The Rebellion Is
Not Over: 35 Years After Stonewall Queer Youth of Color Still Fight
Police Brutality," they chanted "Whose Streets, Our Streets" and "We're
Here, We're Queer, Give Us Back Our Fucking Pier."

In a campaign called Save Our Space, FIERCE! is organizing to
reclaim and maintain access to the Christopher Street Pier, a queer and
trans public gathering area for decades. A recent city and state collaborative renovation project aimed at turning a huge section of Manhattan's
waterfront into a park has placed the piers under the supervision of the
Hudson River Park Trust. The piers, now heavily policed with curfews
and extensive rules about public gatherings, are no longer as safe a place
for queer and trans youth to gather. They have been pushed onto the
streets by the curfew, angering local residents and business owners who
were already complaining about an increase in displaced sex workers in
the West Village after gentrification in bordering neighborhoods. These
residents and business owners have responded by organizing to "rid the
streets" of sex workers and youth through both increased police patrol-
ling and vigilante tactics.

The significance of this conflict that lead FIERCE! to organize a
protest in Sheridan Square is even greater because it takes place in a
national atmosphere of similar tensions within the LGBTQ movement.
The transformation of the West Village in the years since Stonewall—
with the closing of sex stores and neighborhood organizing against sex
workers and queer and trans youth of color—is part of the larger
project of mainstreaming gay/lesbian people and the movement (Warner
149–193). The gay/lesbian movement has adopted a civil rights, identity
politics model (Highleyman 109), with "integration into the status quo,
or mainstreaming" as "the guiding principle" and "most widely shared
ideal" of the movement, and this is a strategy that will not "deliver
genuine freedom or full equality" because the goal of winning "main-

stream tolerance [. . .] differs from the goal of winning liberation or changing social institutions in lasting, long-term ways" (Vaid 3).

Based on over a year of participant-observation fieldwork with transgender activists in New York City and around the country, I argue that the conflict between the largely white, middle-class, and often gay or lesbian residents of NYC's West Village and the queer and trans youth of color organizing to reclaim the pier points to both challenges and possible solutions regarding assimilation, inclusion, and rethinking the future of a LGBTQ movement. With transgender activists citing examples such as the Human Rights Campaign, the most powerful LGBTQ organization in the United States, supporting non-trans inclusive legislation; large LGBTQ organizations lacking any trans-identified employees and insufficiently dedicating resources to fight for transgender rights; or the prioritizing of "gay marriage" at the expense of nearly all other organizing in 2004, it seems clear that the LGBTQ movement faces serious challenges.

These examples of a more "mainstreamed gay agenda" (Highleyman 108–109; Warner 61–80; Vaid) contrast sharply with the radical multi-issue politics of trans and queer youth of color in the West Village and elsewhere. Burdick has argued that ethnography that strives to represent the movement can help activists "refine debates and self-critiques," bridge ideological differences within the movement, and reach out to "people in targeted constituencies who continue to remain indifferent" (182). Following Burdick, in this chapter I not only evidence challenges faced by the LGBTQ movement, but also draw on the organizing ethics and principles of FIERCE! to articulate models for LGBTQ activist communities to create a more inclusive social justice movement and actualize collective visions of much-needed social change.

Before turning to these models for building a more inclusive and effective LGBTQ movement, I want to first describe in more detail the events that led to the protest in Sheridan Square and then illustrate how this local conflict reflects larger conflicts between trans activists and "mainstreamed" gay/lesbian political organizing.

THIRTY YEARS AFTER STONEWALL: THE REBELLION IS NOT OVER

Founded in March of 2000, FIERCE! describes itself as a community organizing project for transgender, lesbian, gay, bisexual, two spirit, queer, and questioning (TLGBTSQQ) youth of color in New York City who are dedicated to building power in their communities through a mix of leadership development, artistic and cultural activism, political education, and campaign development. According to their literature, members of FIERCE! "fueled by direct experiences of racial, economic, sexual, gender and age oppression [. . .] have been working to build bridges between movements for justice." Their organizing efforts include work "to turn police violence against TLGBTSQQ youth into a public issue" and advocacy "for alternatives to incarceration that don't subject TLGBTSQQ youth of color to the homophobia, transphobia and racism of prisons and juvenile detention centers."

Their commitments to fighting police brutality and finding alternatives to incarceration came together in the Save Our Space campaign when their members began witnessing increased police harassment and arrests. According to FIERCE!, Christopher Street Pier "has historically been the only safe public space for many homeless and low-income LGBTSTQQ youth of color to find each other and build community," and they founded the Save Our Space campaign "to counter the displacement and criminalization of LGBTSTQQ youth of color and homeless youth at the Christopher Street Pier and in Manhattan's West Village."

A trans activist not associated with FIERCE!, who works with trans and queer youth of color in Brooklyn, told me: "sometimes when you are oppressed and you don't feel comfortable in areas, you tend to go to the piers. Look at the piers, there's a lot of trans people there because they feel safe there, they feel like, 'this is my community,' and now the cops are messing with them because of this multi-million dollar renovation." She told me the piers had been the primary gathering area for youth who felt oppressed in their own communities or were closeted in their family and neighborhood. Youth who spoke at the protest in Sheridan Square similarly argued, "this is our only safe space—we have been coming here for more than 30 years and seeking support when our families, schools, and our lives are not friendly and welcoming." They characterized the pier as "a place to get away from the violence that we face—to dance away the discrimination that we face every day" and called it a place where "we find our community."

What began as an effort to fight gentrification and the loss of the pier as a public gathering space became an even larger effort to organize for the rights of trans and queer youth of color in the West Village when the city and state officially closed the pier for construction in 2001, fencing the youth out and pushing them onto the streets in the village. One speaker told the audience in Sheridan Square, "many of us cannot return to our houses or families," and he asked the very important question, "where we are supposed to go when they close the pier? It is not safe for us to go out into the streets." Bran Fenner of FIERCE!, speaking at a panel hosted by the Center for Lesbian and Gay Studies, said, "In NYC the homeless youth are about 35% queer and trans—they are kicked out, abused, they run away." With more than ten thousand homeless trans and queer youth in New York City (Karp 1) and no shelter prepared to accommodate them, these youth have nowhere to go. Further, according to Angel Seda of FIERCE!, West Village residents are partially to blame for the increase in youth on "their streets" because it was intense pressure from community groups in 1995 that closed the West Village's only drop-in center catering to youth (qtd. in Lavers 2).

The increased presence of both displaced sex workers, who are mostly queer and trans people of color, and displaced queer and trans youth of color has resulted in counter-organizing efforts among some West Village residents and business owners who want to "clean the streets." One resident I interviewed, who identifies as a trans activist and advocate, told me: "I live near the river in the West Village and I call in a noise complaint almost every night because of the young kids, especially the prostitutes just hanging out in front of my building, just shrieking and calling out to the cars and everything. Most of them are transgender." This resident refuted the claim made by groups including FIERCE!, that "this is a racist, anti-trans thing to get our mostly black transgender teens out of this white neighborhood." Instead, she characterized the conflict as one about transgender "prostitutes that are loud [. . .] they urinate on the buildings and in the hallways, [and] leave condoms and needles, and you know, it is just not a pleasant environment." She told me: the "people who live in this neighborhood" do so because of the "mix of sexual orientations," their concerns are about safety and noise, nothing else.

Contrary to this claim, West Village residents have framed their concerns about increased prostitution in the neighborhood with racist language for years. Benjamin Shepard quotes a member of a local street association saying: "These are not our regular Greenwich Village queers that we've enjoyed and appreciated. These are low-class, vulgar transvestites that come from other areas of the city" ("Amanda" 160). He also quotes an angry West Village resident at a forum on prostitution shouting: "Most of these hookers are not white. They are black or Hispanic" (160). Elsewhere Shepard recounts the events of a February 2002 Community Board meeting where "self-proclaimed 'community members' argued with 'interlopers.' Code terms with racial overtones such as 'those people' were used [. . .]. One resident even stood up to proclaim that the neighborhood was becoming like, 'the Crips vs. the Bloods' a reference to the LA street gang wars charged with the symbolism of racial violence." Shepard stated: "calls to 'clean their streets' read as calls for class cleansing to the outsiders" ("Class War").

Further, some residents are now circulating a petition to "rid the West Village of transgender prostitutes" that includes language such as "the menace of transgender street workers who are slithering onto our streets" and characterizes queer and trans sex workers and youth as "he-shes," "scurge," "filth," "sub-human," and "scum." In this petition residents also accuse transgender sex workers of ruining the neighborhood. A resident of Horatio Street wrote, "they disturb the beautiful village reputation" and another petitioner commented: "we are not living here only for the glamorous nightlife and proximity to the river, but more importantly for the rich and unique history of our community." Such claims about the reputation and the history of the West Village are ironic in a neighborhood well known for being queer and trans friendly, the home of the Stonewall Rebellion where trans women of color were instrumental in fighting back against police brutality (Carter, Duberman).

Most angry residents and business owners are framing their concerns around issues of "safety." They have formed groups such as the Christopher Street Patrol, a vigilante group that patrols the streets with help from the Guardian Angels, and Residents in Distress (RID), an organization "aimed at combating crime" that was named by its founder, Jessica Berk, after a chemical product used to kill lice (Goldstein 2). These residents have also appealed to the local community board and other politicians, calling the neighborhood "a cesspool" and complaining that they cannot sleep and do not feel safe walking down the streets. They have successfully lobbied for increased police presence in the West Village, including twenty-three new officers dedicated to this neighborhood and a police initiative, Operation West Side, aimed at "cleaning-up" the streets. Although city crime statistics do not support residents' concerns about safety, with crime rates in this neighborhood steadily *decreasing* in recent years (Goldstein 2), this contradiction has not affected the way politicians and police treat the youth.

The Quality of Life Policies, put in place by Mayor Giuliani and continued under Bloomberg, have given the New York Police Department increased authority to police public spaces, allowing them to give court summons or make arrests for petty offenses such as public urination, panhandling, blocking a sidewalk, loitering with the intent to prostitute, spitting in public, riding a bicycle on the sidewalk, and homelessness itself, among others. FIERCE! organizers say that "the youth who make use of the pier as a public space have reported sharp increases in police harassment, false arrest, and racial and gender profiling—usually for just being in the neighborhood." For example, speakers at the Sheridan Square protest reported being harassed and arrested for "intent to prostitute" while doing safe-sex outreach. Further, at a community board 2 meeting in June of 2005 with FIERCE! and the 6th Precinct, several youth spoke about being screamed at, hit, kicked, and called "faggot" by police who gave them no reason for being stopped, detained, or ticketed. New York's quality of life policies seem not only to ignore the quality of the lives of trans and queer youth of color, but by criminalizing being poor and homeless they have ironically made the streets of the West Village more unsafe for youth who now find themselves repeatedly targeted by the police.

FIERCE! organizers argue that "through a mix of youth-led organizing and activist strategies [. . .] FIERCE! has been able to change the terms of the public debate about quality of life and public safety in the West Village so that the voices of merchants and residents, politicians and police, are not the only ones that are heard." While local politicians and police have been fairly receptive to the demands of residents and business owners, increasing patrols and initiating Operation West Side, they have been slower to hear what FIERCE! is asking for. Their demands are fairly simple: end the police harassment and arrests, develop a new drop-in center for queer and trans youth, and provide access to the pier without curfews (or make the curfew 4:00 A.M.) and fees (it would have cost $25,000 to rally on the pier instead of Sheridan Square). FIERCE! continues to "struggle to reclaim the West Village from the hands of wealthy residents, business owners, and the police that protect their interests"—the protest in Sheridan Square was one in a series of events aimed at reframing the public debate around quality of life and safety.

ASSIMILATION AND INCLUSION: CRITIQUING "MAINSTREAMED" GAY/LESBIAN ACTIVISM

During the last decade, nearly every national organization that previously fought for the rights of gay/lesbian people changed their missions to included bisexual and transgender people. While these moves toward inclusion are important in principle and supported by many trans activists, this principle has not translated into an organizational practice of dedicating resources and supporting work to ensure the rights of transgender people. Reflecting on this, one activist told me: "There are a lot of people who call themselves LGBT organizations who are really just lesbian and gay. They don't want to address transgender issues, or even the issues of women or people of color for that matter [. . .]. It is so problematic to have these groups who aren't doing the work to really understand what LGBT means in all its complexity." Another activist said trans activists need to "hold our so-called allies accountable to their work—the so-called 'LGBT organizations' [. . .]. Groups should not just add a T because it sounds good. Everyone is saying that they do T work but they aren't really." He asked, "What do you need to do in order to add the T to your list? I think you need to have a quarter of your staff, programming, and services dedicated to transgender. Then you are really an LGBT organization."

National organizations, even those transgender activists speak highly of, do not meet this level of inclusion (although the National Center for Lesbian Rights, with several trans-identified staff members and a history of working on trans issues, was cited as an exception). Another organization often praised, the National Gay and Lesbian Taskforce, has a transgender civil rights project with a full-time legislative lawyer on staff who, according to many activists I interviewed, is doing great work. Yet, while she was repeatedly described to me as "really dedicated" and "a great ally," the fact that she is non trans concerns many activists, especially when coupled with the absence of trans identified employees at The Taskforce. One person told me: "Even though she [is] tireless and great, it [isn't] right that our only advocate [is] a non-transperson [. . .] if you can't make your own decisions, you get eaten. Even if it is well-meaning allies making decisions for you, it just [isn't] appropriate."

The organization most frequently cited by trans activists for the damage they have done by not pushing an inclusive agenda is the Human Rights Campaign (HRC). In nearly every interview that I conducted, activists voiced concerns about the HRC, particularly their support of the Employment Non-Discrimination Act (ENDA) without protections for "gender identity and expression." An activist I interviewed early in my research commented, "HRC really needs to step up, they need to change and they need to start refusing non-inclusive legislation." Many similar comments were made during the first months of my fieldwork and then, in August 2004, the HRC board voted to only support ENDA if it included "gender identity and expression."

This was a victory for activists, and national transgender organizations all released statements applauding the HRC; however, many activists met this decision with limited enthusiasm. One told me, "I am highly critical of them and suspicious of their most recent move. We've been fighting with them for years." Many activists felt that in order to trust the HRC they would need to see them put their decision into action with demonstrable "proof of their intentions." This distrust was fueled in part by the fact that the HRC's August decision limited their support of trans inclusive legislation to ENDA. One activist described her feelings, saying: "The HRC, for the last decade it has been a process of pulling teeth to get them to accept transgender issues as a part of the whole and to advocate for trans issues [. . .]. There is still a lot of work to do with them. Their ruling last weekend was great but it is specific to ENDA and not to all their work."

Trans activists, already struggling to be included in the national agenda, found themselves with even less access to the movement in 2004 when the issue of gay marriage monopolized movement resources. To be fair, the gay marriage issue was largely forced onto these organizations when a Massachusetts court decision placed this debate center stage. A FIERCE! activist characterized this as the result of "focusing way too much on litigation and being in the courts and not talking to people on the ground." It was an issue of "thinking more about easy wins than long-term change." This lack of grassroots preparation, according to him, makes it "not a movement issue" and not "an accountable issue." He told me: "Clearly a lot of us maybe do support gay marriage or think it could be okay, but what are the impacts?" Similarly, a Washington DC based activist questioned the usefulness of LGBTQ resources being dedicated to the fight for same-sex marriage. She said: "It's like the issue with marriage. So many people are working on this and it is getting a lot of attention, but who does this help? There are more transgender women *murdered* than married in DC."

Not only did transgender activists critique same-sex marriage as an inappropriate priority, others were concerned about the specific ways LGBTQ organizations framed this issue. One activist said, "they want to sell the notion that 'we are just like you.' They exclude all sorts of people in their attempt to do this." In making gay marriage more palatable, gay and lesbian activists did not frame this issue in ways that necessarily include the marriage rights of transgender people, who are increasingly finding their marriages under attack. An activist told me: "There is no account of gender fluidity in the critiques most gay and lesbian organizations are creating. They aren't fighting for transgender marriage rights. All this fighting for 'same-sex marriage' should be framed as the right for any type of couple to marry." Trans activists argued that in framing it as same-sex marriage, mainstream activists failed to ask questions that could have framed the public discussion in vastly different ways. A non trans activist involved in ally work characterized the same-sex marriage issue as a "great example" of gay and lesbian activist organizations being "not particularly gender progressive." She said: "What is sex? What is gender? What if your sex or gender are not traditional? Where do you go? These questions don't seem to be asked. It is problematic because [. . .] same-sex marriage is getting a lot of airtime now. It is fighting for the rights of traditionally gendered people at the expense of non-traditionally gendered people." This activist's articulation of how some people's rights are prioritized at the expense of others aptly characterizes many of the critiques of the mainstreamed movement that I heard from transgender activists.

The painful results of the 2004 elections warned many LGBTQ activists of the shortfalls of their current assimilationist strategies and exclusionary tactics, and the need to refocus the national movement to help ensure more successful outcomes in the future. In his plenary speech at the Taskforce's 2004 Creating Change Conference, Matt Foreman, the executive director of that organization, spoke in tears about the results of the elections, telling the audience: "Let's not pretend that it does not hurt to have our second-class citizenship enshrined, because it does. At the same time, I am mad as hell [. . .]. Fundamental human rights should never be put up for a public vote." He went on to articulate a new vision for the movement and for his organization, stating: "It was a wake-up call. The number one priority of our movement has to be to build, nurture, and sustain our state and local movements. We will focus all of our resources and power on building a grassroots movement."

Matt Foreman's commitment to turning national resources back into local and state organizing through grassroots movement building marks a major change in the way national organizations in this movement have invested their time and money. If this departure from the Taskforce's previous strategies and goals and those of the other organizations they work closely with reflects a broader trend among national LGBTQ organizations, then this post-election organizational restruc-

turing and reprioritizing is a crucial moment for thinking about alternative organizing models. Thus, in the final section of this chapter I
present organizing models and principles from the activists involved in
FIERCE!, and allied organizations, to articulate possible solutions to
the challenges faced by the LGBTQ movement.

FIERCE! MODELS FOR SOCIAL JUSTICE ORGANIZING

The last question I asked trans activists during my interviews was:
"What would success look like?" Two activists that work with organizations allied with FIERCE! framed part of their answers in terms of
what success would *not* be. One told me that "it would not follow the
gay and lesbian, *Will & Grace*, cultural approach where more people are
comfortable with these words when they come in the package of white,
upper-class people." Similarly, the other stated: "Disaster would be
everyone becoming assimilationist: 'we are just like you except for this
one thing.' This is so problematic."

By "packaging" LGBTQ activists' work for sexual freedoms and
gender self-determination in the "most palatable" ways, trans activists
argue that the movement has prioritized issues that disproportionately
affect people who are more privileged at the expense of working with
the people with the greatest need. Activists involved with FIERCE!, and
other similar organizations, have argued instead for a "flood-up approach"
that very clearly sets movement priorities in a different way. A FIERCE!
activist told me that one of the important questions that needs to be
asked of other groups and activists doing work for trans and queer people
is: "Are you talking about middle-class trans people that are white or are
you talking about super marginalized sectors of our communities?"

Arguing that "the movement needs to be inverted" and "the focus
needs to be on the everyday needs of transgender people—having
enough to eat, a place to live, and not being in danger all the time";
the "flood-up," needs-based approach "prioritizes people who have the
greatest number of disadvantages as a result of experiencing multiple,
overlapping oppressions." In practice this means prioritizing the needs
and rights of queer and trans people who are low income and people
of color. It means framing new campaigns that would more directly
affect the people with the greatest need, such as fighting against police
brutality and finding alternatives to incarceration, and working to end
the discrimination and barriers low income people and people of color
face in accessing health care, housing, employment, and public benefits,

among others. An activist explained the logic of this approach, stating: "If we help the people on the bottom first, this guarantees to help the people at the top but the other way around might not." Rethinking movement priorities and reallocating resources in line with this flood-up approach might radically transform LGBTQ people's lives and create a more effective movement.

As part of this commitment to organizing by and for young people, FIERCE! has created innovative approaches for reaching out to and mentoring the next generation of youth organizers to sustain their organization and continue working to create social change for their communities with the Education for Liberation Project (ELP). An eighteen-month New York City Community Fellowship for FIERCE! staff member Bran Fenner in 2002 was used to begin the ELP, which is described as a paid political training for TLGBTSQQ youth of color, especially those who are low income in New York City. The program is aimed at increasing the organizing and leadership skills of current and future FIERCE! members through "comprehensive community organizing, political education, and anti-oppression trainings." Combining "interactive workshops and practical hands-on experience in organizing, [. . . this] unique program provides a systematic way for young people to gather the self-esteem, skills, and knowledge required to effectively advocate to transform the institutions that circumscribe their lives." The ELP provides a small stipend for youth activists to participate in several months of political education, ranging from the histories of people of color movements and theories of social justice organizing to skills training, such as facilitating a meeting or talking with the media. A trans activist not involved with FIERCE! commented on the importance of this program, stating: "To me, that level of community building, building that level of deep analysis within our community—nothing is going to replace that. When we look around at the heads of mainstream gay and lesbian organizations and we want to die with how stupid and useless and shortsighted they are, that is why. That work is so essential and hard and can only be done by people who are of and in and for those communities."

FIERCE! is committed to programs like the Education for Liberation Project because they see this work as critical for grassroots movement building. At the same conference where Matt Foreman tearfully spoke about the 2004 election and the "wake-up call" that experience had been, Rickke Manazala, FIERCE!'s campaign coordinator, presented the "Four Pillars of Transformative Social Justice Infrastructure": policy, consciousness, service, and power. In this model, adapted from the Miami Workers' Center, the pillar of policy is characterized by legislative and institutional changes. The pillar of consciousness involves media advocacy and public education campaigns to affect public opinions. The pillar of service addresses people's needs by providing critical services necessary to stabilize people's lives. And the pillar of power involves developing grassroots leadership and base building in oppressed communities. Using this model to frame trans activist's current work as essential parts of a social justice movement, Rickke highlighted the increasing disconnect between each of these pillars and the problematic absence of work being done to build the pillar of power.

Within the pillar of power, activists are working to build membership organizations that have scale and influence (a strategy centrally focused on quantity) and also on developing the depth and capacity of grassroots leadership (a focus on quality). The goal of work within this pillar is to achieve autonomous community power, a movement that is both by and for the people in the "base." Rickke characterized this as "the missing link" in social justice infrastructure and he stressed that while many people use the word "organizing" to talk about work within the other three pillars, for him, it is only work within this fourth pillar that is movement building and organizing. This is not to say that the work in the other three pillars is not necessary and important for stabilizing the lives of the base and for supporting a social justice movement. Rather, it is to say that there is no movement without grassroots, community-based leadership development and organizing. He argued that the best approach for 'truly winning liberation for all of our communities' is "long-term base building [. . .] where the people most affected by the issues we're working on are being developed as leaders in the struggle." FIERCE!'s attention to building grassroots power, to the underdeveloped pillar of power, offers examples that might usefully guide other activists and organizations within 'the LGBTQ movement' in building a more effective movement.

Building grassroots power and developing the base will require new, more accountable strategies and techniques for LGBTQ activists. One activist recounted an example of the need for more accountable methods of community building and grassroots organizing. In August 2004 transgender activists met outside the HRC offices in DC while the board met inside to decide on HRC's future support of a trans-inclusive ENDA. This activist showed up to watch the protest and was "disgusted." She told me: "there were all of these white people protesting [. . .] DC has a majority of people of color, so a white protest in DC is ridiculous." She continued: "I asked one of the organizers about this and he said that they had sent out emails and invitations to all the lists and groups but that they couldn't control who attended. 'If they didn't want to show up, that is their problem' he told me. That is crazy." Later, she went inside and talked to members of the HRC board, asking why there were no trans people on the HRC board of directors. She said: "they told me they had sent out invitations for a trans board member but had not found anyone yet. They couldn't control the fact that no one had volunteered to be a member. It was funny because they were both telling me the same lame thing." In this example, both the HRC and the white trans activists protesting them assumed their failures to mobilize targeted constituencies were "out of their control" rather than being accountable for their failures and seeking feedback to create more effective strategies and projects to bring new people into the struggle.

FIERCE! is committed to finding new ways to reach queer and trans youth of color and bringing them into the struggle, and this commitment is reflected in their diverse approaches. A FIERCE! activist told me: "Being really creative about how to get information out to people has been really important for us." After the demonstration in Sheridan Square and march down Christopher Street, FIERCE! activists brought people together again that night for a Mini-Ball. The ball scene, which became more widely known in the 1990s through Jennie Livingstone's documentary *Paris Is Burning*, began in the 1960s in Harlem for black and Latino gay men to compete for fun and status. Participants frequently affiliated with groups called houses (often named after a designer and headed by a Mother and/or Father), and David Valentine writes: "houses often serve as alternative families and support networks for their members or 'children' " (71). This scene, the ballroom scene, has traditionally been a place where trans and queer youth of color have gone for support and community and many youth displaced from the West Village and the piers had turned to the ball community. In an effort to bring these youth into the organization and their efforts, FIERCE! organized their mini-ball as an extension of this safe supportive space in order to draw in youth they may not have otherwise mobilized.

A FIERCE! activist commented on that event, stating: "The Mini Ball was really important for [getting information out to people] because so many people came who would never be at a conference or something like that. You can't just expect people to be at meetings so we have to be really creative." Instead of expecting people to come to their meetings, FIERCE! brought youth together in the Brecht Forum where they crowded around the edges of the dance floor as queer and trans youth of color danced in groups and alone, vogueing for the screaming audience. This Mini-Ball, and the rally and march that preceded it, were the result of the organizing efforts of the ten FIERCE! core members who graduated from the second level of the Education for Liberation Project three months after this action. Having been trained in social justice and anti-oppression theories, grassroots organizing techniques, and the histories of failures and successes in other social movements, these youth were prepared to not only organize a very successful rally and march but also to organize the more dynamic and creative Mini-Ball. Further, FIERCE! mixed the images of the "not so Mini-Ball" and the rally into a short video and posted it on their web page (www.fiercenyc.org) with the often-chanted Assata Shakur quote: "It is our duty to fight for our own freedom. It is our duty to win. We must love each other and protect each other. We have nothing to lose but our chains." FIERCE!'s creative, dynamic approaches to reaching youth and working to bring them into social justice activism, such as the Education for Liberation Project and the Mini-Ball, are useful examples for other activists to consider in their own work.

The final examples of FIERCE!'s organizing ethics and principles that I will offer involve a commitment to ally work, meaningful solidarity, and an effort to position queer and trans activism within a larger social justice context. A FIERCE! activist told me: "One way we are addressing accountability is to go to the events of other groups who are doing similar work. We are trying to do work with other people of color organizations who might not have a queer analysis yet and then they will get to know us and we can offer our services to do trainings with them." Similarly, another FIERCE activist explained that their commitment to solidarity work involved working with other organizations fighting gentrification, for example, even if those organizations currently do not address issues of transphobia and homophobia. A trans activist allied with FIERCE! questioned the lack of solidarity work of this type in the LGBTQ movement. He stated: "People in other social justice movements that are currently not aware of queer and trans issues are willing to become aware of them, why don't you stop trying to convince Republicans to vote gay and instead convince your natural allies to join with you? [. . .] You would have more friends to fight with."

FIERCE!'s solidarity work with social justice activists involved in other struggles is part of their broader vision of social change. When FIERCE! activists were asked what would success look like? their answers reflected a shared vision of this work as part of something larger than a LGBTQ movement in the United States. One activist commented: "what I see right now, particularly if we are going to call this a trans movement, is still very white, very middle-class, as far as who is visible, and I don't know if we will ever overcome that so I think what I want to put my resources into is pushing the movement that I feel like a part of." Similarly, another activist told me: "I feel like I am not a part of a trans movement. I am part of larger movements. My role is to be one of the people pushing for more inclusive politics—for trans and queer inclusion. I am part of a larger anti-imperialism movement and inside that I am fighting to have our rights and issues respected and not pushed aside." There was a consensus between both the FIERCE! activists that I spoke with and other allied activists who argued, "We are not building a trans movement necessarily but a viable place for trans and queer people in a larger movement" for social justice both in the United States and internationally.

CONCLUSION: RETHINKING THE MOVEMENT

When gentrification pushed trans and queer youth of color onto the streets of New York's West Village, a largely white, middle-class, and historically 'gay' neighborhood, instead of seeking ways to "rid their streets" of these youth, upset residents might more usefully have questioned the larger issues of racism, classism, homophobia, and transphobia, as well as the "privatization and commercialization of public space," that pushed these youth onto the streets in the first place (Shepard, "Class War"). Rather than calling the police and using their collective organizing efforts to further criminalize and dehumanize these youth, might these Village residents and business owners have been more successful in their efforts to have "safety" and quiet had they instead organized to increase services for these youth, such as shelters and drop-in centers? My point in asking what might have been different had residents allied with queer and trans youth, rather than fight against them, is to highlight the importance of taking new approaches in order to build a more inclusive and effective movement for social justice.

FIERCE!, and other allied trans activist organizations, are proposing an "inversion" of the movement, shifting priorities, resources, and allegiances in ways that would create what they see as a more accountable, inclusive, and effective social justice movement. As Matt Foreman suggested, national organizations could also turn more attention to local efforts, using their resources to support grassroots organizing. This would not be abandoning the national realm; rather, it is recognizing that the "base of any political movement is where people live, work, congregate, and make family" (qtd. in Vaid 387) and restructuring national organizations to support that work. The organizing principles of groups such as FIERCE! could guide them as they think about how to reallocate resources, reframe priorities, and reconsider projects and goals. FIERCE! activists are theorizing and actualizing multi-issue grassroots activism that is needs-based, by and for the people most affected, building power in multiply oppressed communities, and situating themselves in a larger movement for social change. I have presented these organizing principles and ethics being used by FIERCE! and allied trans groups as models that might usefully be incorporated into other areas of the LGBTQ movement. Rather than a standoff in the West Village, this conflict might be more successfully resolved by taking a different approach. Similarly, the LGBTQ movement could benefit from re-evaluating the strategies, priorities, and goals currently guiding much activism, and the examples offered here might usefully begin that re-thinking of the movement.

WORKS CITED

Burdick, John. *Blessed Anastácia: Women, Race, and Popular Christianity in Brazil.* New York: Routledge, 1998.

Carter, David. *Stonewall: The Riots That Sparked the Gay Revolution.* New York: St. Martin's Press, 2004.

Duberman, Martin. *Stonewall.* Rpt. ed. New York: Plume Books, 1994.

Goldstein, Richard. "Street Hassle: New Skool Versus Old School in Greenwich Village." *Village Voice* 24–30 April 2002. 2 March 2005. <http://villagevoice.com/news/0217,goldstein,34171.html>.

Highleyman, Liz. "Radical Queers or Queer Radicals? Queer Activism and the Global Justice Movement." In *From ACT-UP to the WTO: Urban Protest and Community Building in the Era of Globalization*, ed. Benjamin Shepard and Ronald Hayduk. New York: Verso, 2002.

Karp, Daria. "Fierce Gay Youth Confront Distressed West Village Residents." *Columbia University Journal* (2004). 6 January 2005. <http://www.jrn.columbia.edu/studentwork/ children/2002/hkarpgy.asp>.

Lavers, Mike. "Gay Youth Oppose Police in Village." *New York Blade* 22 October 2004. 23 October 2004 <http://www.newyorkblade.com/2004/10-22/news/localnews/village.cfm>.

Shepard, Benjamin. "Amanda Milan and the Rebirth of the Street Trans Action

Revolutionaries."In *From ACT-UP to the WTO: Urban Protest and Community Building in the Era of Globalization*, ed. Benjamin Shepard and Ronald Hayduk. New York: Verso, 2002.

———. "Class War in the West Village: FIERCE! Youth vs. 'Residents in Distress' and Other Gentrifiers." *Counter Punch* 5 October 2002 <http://www.counterpunch.org/ shepard1005.html>.

Vaid, Urvashi. *Virtual Equality: The Mainstreaming of the Gay and Lesbian Movement*. New York: Anchor Books, 1995.

Valentine, David. *"I know what I am": The Category Transgender in the Construction of Contemporary U.S. American Conceptions of Gender and Sexuality*. PhD Dissertation, New York University, 2000.

Warner, Michael. *The Trouble with Normal: Sex, Politics, and the Ethics of Queer Life*. Cambridge, MA: Harvard University Press, 1999.

CHAPTER 13

PRINCIPLES OF ENGAGEMENT

THE ANARCHIST INFLUENCE
ON QUEER YOUTH CULTURES

Neal Ritchie

There is a cop inside each of us. He must be killed.

—Wall graffiti, Paris, May 1968

Over the last decade, the word "queer" has become a label that thousands of youth all over the world identify with. Though it affects many if not all people belonging to **LGBT** communities, it is especially a youth phenomenon. "Queer" particularly resonates with young folks who are frustrated with the increasingly assimilationist politics, attitudes, and identities of many gay and lesbian organizations, as well as with those who generally see the proper project to be subverting boundaries and norms rather than reifying them. This conception of queer as a politically subversive project, so especially popular within youth cultures, to a large extent reflects the growing popularity of anarchist politics in other movements, most notably the "anti-globalization" movement, perhaps better labeled "the irresistible rise of global anticapitalism" (Notes from Nowhere 1). Much of contemporary queer youth's tactics, organizational structures, and overall goals have been heavily influenced by anarchism. Simultaneously, large anticapitalist demonstrations from Berlin to Quebec to Buenos Aires have borrowed from the aesthetics and carnivalesque qualities of many queer youth cultures, as well as directly learned from the experiences with direct action supplied historically by groups like the Gay Activist's Alliance and ACT UP.

The framework of this chapter focuses on activist strategies articulating relationships between radical queer youth cultures and a larger global anticapitalist movement. On the micro-scale this can be understood by the increasingly obvious adoption of anarchist philosophy and principles of direct political action by queer youth cultures in local communities. At the macro level, one can observe these same principles active in an international anticapitalist movement that links local communities to a global struggle against neoliberalism. By talking specifically about the queer scene in my town of Asheville, North Carolina, and then placing this community within a larger political context, it is my hope to highlight "new" strategies for queer political action, as well as the direction in which queer political action needs to be taken if we are to become serious about our own liberation. All of this discussion reaches back to a history of radical queer resistance that challenges not just legislation or discriminatory practices but the entire culture of heterosexism and all the social, political, and economic means by which our society reinforces this sexual and gendered domination.

The radical principles of political engagement that have (re)surfaced during the last ten years have developed in an environment many theorists refer to as "postmodernity." Postindustrial capitalism has not led to the "end of history," where turbulent social conflicts are subsumed by a peaceful democratic pluralism, but instead to a new series of radical and revolutionary movements that break free from many of the constraints of the modernist Right *and* Left. Queer activist and revolutionary groups like Gay Shame, Queer Fist, the Pollinators, Tranzmission, and the Gender Mutiny Collective[1] have found themselves taking up principles that replace much of the rigidity and hierarchy of leftist resistance movements with an emphasis on decentralism, networking, collective structures, and carnival.

To demonstrate these emerging principles and practices I want to provide a discussion of the queer youth culture in my hometown, Asheville, North Carolina. In particular I want to paint a picture of the communities in which queer youth like myself are involved: how decisions are made, how political action is taken, how the culture feels, smells, looks, and sounds. It is from these cultures that larger global movements draw their principles, and so it makes sense to start here and then look at the bigger picture of where queer politics are moving.

TENSIONS WITHIN THE CONTEMPORARY LGBT MOVEMENT

Many writers and social critics of contemporary LGBT politics recognize a drastically conservative and assimilationist trend in the last few years.[2] Exemplified by the writings of "gaycons" like Andrew Sullivan, who champion the cause of same-sex marriage and harshly criticize queer cultures for their "promiscuousness," their radical agendas, their gender-bending, and their campy (fabulous) style, this assimilationist trend has significantly weakened the gay and lesbian movement. The movement has gone from being a large, grassroots rebellion focused on challenging society's gender norms, heterosexist behaviors, and puritanical sexual moralism, with links to revolutionary groups like the Black Panthers, to a politically weak lobbying effort. In his book *The Trouble With Normal*, queer theorist and activist Michael Warner asks of this new trend in "liberal" LGBT politics, "Who's left? A potent constituency, to be sure. But with no politics, no public, no history of activism or resistance, no inclination to deviate from the norm, and no form of collective life distinct in any way from that of 'society'." (139). Along with many queer youth who are cynical or skeptical of the "movement" for same-sex marriage, Warner points out the depressing implications of LGBT communities, who previously understood the heterosexist state as an agent of sexual repression and harsh brutality, now embracing this state by dropping all other political priorities in favor of gay marriage.

Arguably, what is occurring with this conservative trend in LGBT politics is a split within the semantic manifestation of "queer." On the one hand are massive national LGBT groups like the Human Rights Campaign, which fund the Log Cabin Republicans, make legislative compromises that purposefully exclude trans people,[3] negotiate support for same-sex marriage by assisting President Bush's privatization of social security, and publicly endorse sweatshop-using corporations like Nike for their "gay-friendly" healthcare plans. Along with the HRC are the hundreds of more local LGBT groups that endorse voter registration and the Democratic Party, and thereby indirectly support the war in Iraq, institutionalized racism, the death penalty, gentrification, the Patriot Acts, police brutality, a lack of free healthcare, and the general class system firmly embraced by both political parties. All the while, the mainstream media and many of the members of these groups use the term "queer" as a self-referential umbrella term for anyone who is a member of such an LGBT community. In "Who Is That *Queer* Queer?" Ruth Goldman eludes to this trend:

> As "queer" gains currency, it is increasingly being appropriated and commodified, and thus increasingly risks collapsing into another term for white lesbians and gays, and ultimately white gay men. This is due to the fact that we live in a society in which the hegemonic discourses center around whites, men, and monosexuals, and so as "queer" becomes more popular amongst these "dominant" groups, it will increasingly come to *represent* these "dominant" groups. (171)

Juxtaposed with this limited version of "queer" is the New York-based Queer Fist's use of the term, whose mission statement reads:

> We are a group of radical queer and trans identifying people who oppose the gay mainstream's agenda of assimilation. The inclusion of gays in institutions such as marriage, the military, or a (mis)representative "democracy" will only further legitimize these systems of domination. The politics of "fitting in" serves those in positions of power and excludes people including, but not limited to, people of color, trans folks, immigrants, women, the working class, the poor, and sex workers. (Queer Fist)

This group's use of "queer" has a more directly political connotation. Here queer refers to that which is gender-bending, disruptive of power, carnivalesque, or sexually anti-normative. This connotation does not necessarily negate the self-referential and umbrella-like quality of the former, but deepens and broadens the word so that it doesn't just mean homo- or bisexual. Queer, in this context, is for many youth increasingly tied to principles which find their root in antiauthoritarian and anticapitalist struggle within the postmodern world. In this sense one can understand why Queer Fist chooses to focus on issues of "police brutality, public space, radical visibility, and trans identity," why they use the tactics of street theater, public visibility campaigns, and marches, and why their number one target for criticism, humiliation, and abolition has been the Human Rights Campaign. The creation of New York's FIERCE!, led mostly by youth of color, was "fueled by direct experiences of racial, economic, sexual, gender and age oppression," and their main projects have included turning gentrification, racist incarceration of youth of color, and police brutality against queer youth into public issues (www.fiercenyc.org). For many radical queer youth, there is absolutely nothing conceivably "queer" about electoral politics, corporate power, or marriage. Especially among service sector-class queer youth, we find ourselves consistently stuck between the alienation of our everyday lives and the complete irrelevance of reformist, national LGBT politics. In Asheville, North Carolina, specifically, the product of trying to resolve this precarious position is the creation of an intensely local, radical culture of resistance.

QUEER YOUTH CULTURE IN ASHEVILLE

If one of the many wealthy tourists that Asheville attracts were to walk down Carolina Lane during the night of a Tranzmission drag show, it would be a mistake. Their slight geographical error would pull them from the fancy restaurants and galleries of Pack Place into a dirty alley filled with drag queens, punks, traveling hobos, dogs, dumpsters, and the ever-present smell of malt liquor. Every available foot of wall space seems to be covered in graffiti; not just small tags and stencils in cracks and corners, but entire walls. Some space is dedicated to a member of our community who died of a heroin overdose last year; Carolina Lane is one of the few parts of Asheville where the do-it-yourself memorials to David have not been erased. In addition to political stencils, there are large and small stencils of ballerinas and of Charlie Chaplin littered throughout the street. This alley is now the home of the Asheville Community Resource Center (ACRC), a community space run by an anarchist collective that houses half a dozen other collectives, like the Prison Books Program, Earth First!, Food Not Bombs, and the transgender activist group Tranzmission. Carolina Lane is also the home of The Big Idea, a DIY art space that holds punk shows, skill shares, movie showings, and Tranzmission's somewhat regular DIY drag shows, all of which tend to benefit one cause or another.

Our wealthy tourist would find that Tranzmission's drag shows charge a donation of three to five dollars, with no one turned away for lack of funds (the tourist might get asked for more money. . .). At the front table there are usually dozens of stacks of zines on every topic available, ranging from DIY herbal gynecology to essays on transsexuality and capitalism. Copies are free thanks to our collective "ingenuity," so the zines are free as well. This free distribution of literature has proven to be an especially valuable way to spread helpful information about healthcare for trans people, who deal with numerous issues ignored by the mainstream healthcare industry. Zines like "Hot Pantz" that deal with DIY abortion techniques and homeopathic gynecology and zines that educate about free or cheap community healthcare providers are all quite common. In several instances, zines on sexual assault have been essential to exposing and confronting rapists within our communities, as well as providing a framework for rape victims to discuss their experiences in a public but anonymous forum. Zine "distro's" such as Tranzmission also serve as a way to share personal stories of triumph and tragedy, to communicate effective political strategies, to educate about other queer community organizing efforts going on around the country, and to connect the radical queer movement to other struggles around the world.

Our "punk rock drag" shows are always packed with a mix of people absent from the "normal" drag shows at gay bars on the other side of town. There are hippies, punks, goth kids, older and younger people, dirty traveling kids, well-dressed drag queens, bearded punks in strange combinations of dresses and skirts they found in a local house's free box, and college kids who look a little confused. The whole environment smells like a combination of alcohol and body odor, exaggerated by the fact that many people there are probably homeless, some can't afford to heat their water, others have squats in the woods with no running water at all, and the rest of Asheville's food-serving and dishwashing class really just doesn't give a damn. Tranzmission's decorum depends on the theme of the night—we've organized shows around the themes of abuse, the Scarlet Letter, a post-apocalypse show entitled Apoca-lipstic-a, and others—but there is always our tranarchy banner duct-taped to the wall behind the performers. The bar is run under the table in the back by Tranzmission folks or people who live in the basement of the Big Idea, and the money raised from the cheap dollar beers goes to benefit the local health collective, a domestic violence center, or the ACRC.

The performances at these shows reach out across a spectrum of light and playful to intensely serious, and often merge both elements. Sometimes a performer will take an older well-known song and adapt it to have new meaning within a "queer" context; at one show a drag king did a rendition of "Mr. Cellophane," from the musical Chicago, playing on the theme of the invisibility that queer people face in the mainstream world. At other times a performer will undergo physical changes during their act, starting in a "female" body and transitioning to a "male" body, while simultaneously incorporating body paint, costumes, and props to act out the drama of their changing gender identity. Using two life-size paintings of a man and woman, painted signs, costumes, and the Alanis Morrisette song "You Oughtta' Know," another Tranzmission organizer and I told the audience they ought to know there are more than two genders. Combined with a puppet show and literature at a local college campus, this performance prompted hours of discussion within the audience about gender and society, and ultimately helped a trans person on campus in their coming out process.

This is queer youth culture in Asheville. It is informal, inexpensive, and carries with it an aggressively antiauthoritarian social consciousness. At the last show we put on, cops tried to clear the alleyway halfway through the show. The responses were mixed; some began singing "Fuck tha Police" by NWA,[4] others began humming old Black Panther tunes,[5] one group just began mouthing off to the cops directly, while others began whispering the need for a Stonewall reenactment. The drag acts are performed both by experienced "kings, queens, and in-betweens" who also dance at local gay clubs, as well as by amateurs who've never before gotten on stage. Unlike other drag shows where only the performers come in drag, almost everyone at the Big Idea will be queering gender in some context. Effeminate and masculine behaviors get exaggerated or obscured, "straight" punk boys share make-up strategies, pronouns change, people who never before have done drag take the stage, and new sexual attractions rise to the surface.

The line between performer and audience thus gets blurred, so that at any point you might see *anyone* on stage. At any point a performer may pull someone on stage to share the spotlight, they improvise an interaction of some sort, and the performance changes. The musicians usually contribute to this process as well; the bands usually show up in drag as well, so the "performers' " acts blend with live music that follows them. There is a carnival atmosphere at these shows, a celebration that redefines what is and is not "political," that mocks the straight world outside its doors. "Straight" in this context doesn't necessarily mean heterosexual, but rather heterosexist, wealthy, powerful, or privileged. For example, it would not be uncommon for folks throughout Asheville's queer youth culture to refer to the Lesbian Business Owners' Association, which profits off of the tourist industry and actively assists in the racist and classist gentrification of downtown, or the local assimilationist LGBT paper, which criticized Tranzmission for holding yearly commemorations of the Stonewall riots, as straight. As a concept, then, "straight" is not separated from matters of gender and sexuality but is expanded to include more general power dynamics.

I've been with Tranzmission since its beginning as a small core of activists angered by the exclusion of trans issues from dominant liberal LGBT organizations. In the last three years, the group has grown in numbers, and now encompasses a large range of tactics to accomplish its stated goal of "the end of socially enforced, non-consensual gender tyranny." In addition to putting on these large punk/drag benefit shows, we also distribute large amounts of free literature, put on Trans101's, which are an educational mix of performance, puppetry, and discussion, organize trainings for nonprofit social service providers, do queer and trans prisoner support, and help put together Asheville's annual Stone-wall commemoration march. We also did a lot of work with the Women and Trans Health Clinic, which we are presently trying to resurrect. All decisions in our group are made collectively by consensus, without any formal positions or hierarchies. This mode of decision making is the norm in Asheville activism; majoritarian rule and hierarchical organizing tend to be seen as both ineffective and authoritarian by queer youth in Asheville. This is partly due to the inherently exclusive nature of majoritarian decision making, whereby a majority is able to dominate a minority with little recourse, thus leaving sizable minorities isolated and unaccountable for the group's decisions. Consensus also appeals to many queer youth because of their connection to anarchist philosophy and the international "anti-globalization" movement, which since its inception has relied mainly on decentralized affinity group models for organizing.

Largely due to this DIY educational work, there has emerged over the last three years in Asheville a sort of "transgender consciousness" within the different collectives and subcultures of our town. For all our problems we are in a very different place than three years ago. There is more gender play and drag, a general respect for peoples' pronoun choices, and a broad understanding that gender is about socialization and even choice, not genitalia. Though these things are basic, it is tremendous progress that demonstrates the possibility of a broad trans consciousness and politics outside of the relatively small group of trans folks in our town. For the trans community to become a trans move-ment capable of a serious challenge to the gender binary, this kind of broad consciousness is "essential." This kind of consciousness has been made possible by Tranzmission's willingness to reach across subcultural boundaries at events like our punk rock drag shows and the annual Stonewall Rally, its accessibility to the local service-sector class, and its refusal to be co-opted into a single-issue group.

In the last two years, a similar group called the Gender Mutiny Collective has established itself in Chapel Hill, North Carolina. A growing collective of trans folks, gender queers, and allies, its main focuses have been educating people about trans issues, supporting queer and trans prisoners with a pen pal service that has been coordinated with Tranzmission, and networking with other groups in the area to start North Carolina's first free trans-specific health clinic. Gender Mutiny Collective is also an advocate of direct action tactics and has been a part of two back-to-back "reclaim the streets" style demonstrations on a street where a queer-bashing and rape had occurred, as well as distributing literature during the mysterious disruption of a speech by Log Cabin Republican president Patrick Guerrero. Guerrero was sponsored and paid for in part by University of North Carolina's very own liberal GLBTSA and in return for this outright betrayal he was pied in the face, his speech was disrupted by a fire alarm, and the courtyard outside was made fabulous with a 200-square-foot banner-drop that read "Queers Bash Back!" with a circle-A.[6] While focusing on prison issues and using direct action tactics such as these tend to alienate those whose sexualities, genders, and incomes are already more assimilated, Tranzmission and Gender Mutiny Collective has grown with new people who were dissatisfied with the middle-class, single-issue focus of GLBTSA. We do not lobby politicians, and we do not commend corporations like Nike for their gay-friendly healthcare policies.

QUEERING ANARCHISM, RADICALIZING QUEER

Before discussing the relationship between anarchist politics and queer youth culture in Asheville, it may be necessary to provide a brief definition of anarchism. Anarchism is a both a philosophy of human relations as well as a social movement with a long history of struggle. As a philosophy it generally posits that both centralized government (the state) and authoritarian control over resources in the hands of the few (capitalism) are violent, unjust, and generally inhuman developments, and that human societies should be run in a decentralized, egalitarian setting with communities maintaining direct decision making power over how to run their lives. Over the last century especially, this philosophy has been expanded and has evolved to include critiques of patriarchy, racism, gendered behavior, the anti-ecological realities of industrialism, and other kinds of hierarchy.

On the movement side, anarchists are most distinguished from "other leftists" by their use of decentralization, the absence of an official "party-line," and especially their refusal to use the state as part of an overall strategy for social change. Anarchism has played an essential role in the American Industrial Workers of the World, the feminist writings of Emma Goldman, the hundreds upon hundreds of agricultural and industrial collectives and militias of the Spanish Revolution, the Ukrainian Mahknovist armed resistance to "Communist" Russia after the Russian Revolution, the syndicalist unions of South Africa, the massive worker and student rebellions in Paris of 1968, contemporary prison abolition and antiracist work of anarchist ex–Black Panthers like Lorenzo Komboa Irvin and Ashanti Allston, the past thirty years of eco-defense by groups like Earth First!, the Earth Liberation Front, and the Animal Liberation Front, the modern "anti-globalization" movement, the Zapatista villages of Chiapas, Mexico, the large European squatting movement, and hundreds of other contemporary settings throughout the world.

The development of a transgender consciousness in Asheville occurred at a point of intersection with these anarchist politics. This intersection is interpersonal, as "out" anarchists like myself flow easily from Earth First! meetings to Asheville Community Resource Center (ACRC) workdays, from Food Not Bombs to Tranzmission meetings. The politics of anarchism also make intuitive sense to many of the queer people in our town. There is a wonderful flexibility and anarchic character to the word "queer": it is a label imbued with paradox. Just as anarchism is a political movement of a fiercely antipolitical nature (in that it refuses to use the "political" system) so too is the label "queer" the ultimate anti-label. Just as anarchism is both about collectivism and autonomy simultaneously, so too does queer reflect an acknowledgment of social contexts like gender roles alongside a stubborn refusal to allow these contexts to tell us who we are.

The gendered fluidity of a transgender consciousness among Asheville's youth is inherently resistant to a rigid, bureaucratic way of viewing people, and so it follows that such a trans consciousness is opposed to the state, whose centralization necessitates rigid categories for the purpose of social control. This is not mere theory; it is evidenced historically by things like the U.S. oligarchy legislating Africans as three-fifths of a human being, the Dred Scott Decision, and the "one-drop" rules, which in the nineteenth century resulted in the acquisition (theft) of thousands of indigenous peoples' lands by private landowners, railroad companies, coal companies, and banks. One can also see this control-through-categorization process occur more recently through the formal and informal redlining of poor communities of color by banks.

And of course there is a similar trend with trans oppression, as trans people can be denied healthcare, jobs, housing, the ability to change their name, and adoption rights, as they have been beaten, raped, and murdered by police, all because they temporarily or permanently transcend the appropriate "m" and "f" boxes our society clings to. To be trans, it appears, is to be a thorn in the side of government. This is without even mentioning the daily reality of not being seen for who you are, the psychological wear-and-tear of complete invisibility.

In "Tracing This Body," Philadelphia AIDS activist Michelle O'Brien discusses the hidden relationship between the state and pharmaceutical companies, with regards to how the government facilitates these companies' denial of basic medical care to poor trans people. She writes:

> [. . .] the U.S. Federal Food and Drug Administration has not given approval for the use of any medications for transgender body modification. The Federal government does not supervise, regulate, approve or acknowledge the use of hormones to alter the gendered characteristics of one's body. The FDA has never acknowledged, I believe, that trans people even exist. (3)

The federal government thus provides a rationalization for these companies to continue excluding hormones from the "basic medical care" that is normally required to be covered by HMOs. The companies are then able to charge exorbitant prices for these hormones, knowing full well that they constitute essential medical care for thousands of poor people. Corporate interests and the state walk together, hand in hand.

In addition to this state-sponsored oppression faced by trans people, then, there is also good reason to expect anticapitalist principles to have a firm basis within the transpolitics of queer youth cultures such as Asheville. In the same article, O'Brien discusses poor trans peoples' invisibility to the pharmaceutical companies that produce the drugs that many need to survive:

> Already excluded from the wage economy, many poor trans women in Philadelphia turn to sex work to pay for their

hormones. Poverty, police abuse, and HIV have taken a severe toll on the lives of trans women in the city. As trans people modifying our bodies, we are using these corporations' drugs towards unapproved and unacknowledged ends: the gendered rebuilding of our bodies. We pay the bill, and we live with the consequences. (4)

O' Brien's article analyzes how trans people are "located within global flows of power" (14). Among other insights, her discussion of poor trans women in Philadelphia, and the massive power of pharmaceutical companies in shaping the lives of trans people generally, is her testament to the necessarily anticapitalist stance of queer theory and practice. Perhaps part of the reason many LGBT groups have successfully excluded anticapitalism from their groups is because they've so often avoided working with poor people. Poor trans people cannot reclaim their own lives without subverting capitalism in some way, because the profits of global pharmaceutical corporations are fundamentally dependent upon their exploitation.

The philosophical connection between queer, trans, and anarchist politics makes further sense when looking at the recent history of queer activism. In the 1980s and 1990s there was a surge in confrontational protest groups like ACT UP, Queer Nation, and the Lesbian Avengers, all of which would use direct action to push queer issues. At the World Trade Organization demonstrations in Seattle in 1999, the anarchists' tactics of street blockades and strategic property destruction, decision making through consensus, "de-arresting" protesters who have been picked up by the police, and especially the decentralized affinity group model of protest all became instantly more visible and accessible to the many queer groups that were involved in that demonstration. As Cleo Woelfle-Erskine and Andrea Danger of the Bay Area–based radical queer Pollinators group write:

Meanwhile, inspired by Gay Shame's fierce commitment to street actions, we got involved in [. . .] their struggles. We were frightened by their lack of security consciousness or tactical foresight, and we connected them to legal, tactical, communications, and facilitation workshops within the anarchist community. Through all of this we formed a greater affinity with Gay Shame. (269)

Over the last ten years these alliances have evolved and grown deeper. Tranzmission, for example, inspired by the tactics of New York–based Queer Fist, provided food and funding to the southern Anarchist People of Color conference, which held workshops on prison abolition in Philadelphia and issues facing queer people of color. As these networks grow deeper they also grow wider; one might find the Zapatista National Liberation Army linked to squatter movements in Barcelona through anarcho-queer community organizers in North Carolina, and simultaneously acting in solidarity with the occupied factories of Argentina. While I am personally a part of these networks, whether it be through organizing help to squat a factory in Barcelona for the global festival Queeruption, putting together a solidarity action and sending computers and money to the Zapatistas in Chiapas, or marching against the World Bank with Palestinian refugees, and have personally experienced the ways in which skills from different kinds of direct actions, street-fighting, and community organizing come to reinforce and strengthen supposedly different social movements, I think the best illustration of the truly global nature of the networks in which contemporary radical queer youth often find themselves is a quote from a participant in the first *encuentro*[7] held by the Zapatistas in 1996:

> On 27th of July 1996 over 3,000 grassroots activists from more than 40 countries spanning five continents gathered in five hand-built conference centers, beautifully carved out of the jungle, each hosted by a different autonomous indigenous community. Berlin squatters sporting green mohawks exchanged tactics with Mayan rebels in ski masks; the mothers of the disappeared in Argentina swapped stories with French strikers; Iranian exiles listened to Rage Against the Machine. It was a hallucinating mixture of cultures. (Notes from Nowhere 34)

In addition to these networks making their mark on queer youth in the forms of tactical, organizational, and philosophical inspiration, I've seen the anarchists in our community become more queer in their outlooks, their self-presentation, and even their own sexualities. This speaks to several points in queer theory. For one, it supports the notion that politics and identities are forever weaving, intersecting, and creating new outcomes. The revolutionary potential of many identities is their resistance to fixed definition (Rust 81). Secondly, the incorporation of "queer" into the politics and sexuality of many Asheville anarchists speaks to the social constructionism of queer theories, which posit the agency of people to change their own gender and sexuality in different contexts. What is perhaps unique in Asheville and challenging to much queer theory is the occurrence of these changes as a *social movement*; this transgender consciousness is not an individual but a collective transgression of normative gender politics.

CARNIVAL: QUEER YOUTH CULTURAL RESISTANCE IN A POSTMODERN CONTEXT

Referred to by one book as "the irresistible rise of global anti-capitalism," this "irresistible rise" reflects core values of decentralization, direct action, and radically direct "democracy" (Notes from Nowhere 1). As the editors of *We Are Everywhere* write, it is

> [. . .] a rebellion which is in constant flux, which swaps ideas and tactics across oceans, shares strategies between cultures and continents, gathers in swarms and dissolves, only to swarm again elsewhere [. . .]. Rather than one dominant political voice, one dogma, one party line, we present you with a collision of subjectivities. (Notes from Nowhere 14)

Often considered to have begun with the armed Zapatista uprising on January 1, 1994, this rebellion has spread to the successful riots against water privatization in Bolivia, the blockades and property destruction at free trade summits in Seattle and Washington, DC, the massive solidarity economy of Argentina, the international squatters' movement, the million-strong Landless Rural Workers' Movement (MST) of Brazil, the international indymedia movement, the direct action of Earth First! groups, the antiprivatization struggles of South Africa, the global network of Food Not Bombs, and hundreds of other struggles.

Particularly relevant to a discussion of queer youth culture is this global rebellion's use of carnival and aesthetics to subvert power structures, especially the appeal of consumerism. As Subcomandante Marcos of the Zapatistas said, "The revolution, in general, is no longer imagined according to socialist patterns of realism, that is, as men and women stoically marching behind a red, waving flag towards a luminous future. Rather it has become a sort of carnival" (Notes from Nowhere 176).

We can see this trend evidenced by the tactics of these struggles: Reclaim the Streets demonstrations, where streets might be occupied by partying protesters for an hour, a day, or a month, the "Tute Bianche," a tactic used at mass demonstrations for breaking police lines whereby a large group of extremely well-padded protesters push through police lines with sheer willpower and bravado, and Guerilla Street Theater, whereby activists converge for a minute or an hour in the street to put on an impromptu play about a relevant issue, are all examples of this new carnival. Even the imagery of contemporary popular struggle disrupts modernist and statist forms of dissent. Rather than long, formal lines of drab, bored-looking protesters, we see pink and silver blocs of fairies using hockey sticks to slap-shot tear gas canisters back at riot cops, while ten-foot-tall puppeteers on stilts meander among the crowd. At the demonstrations against the Free Trade Agreement of the Americas in Quebec in 2001, prior to destroying the security fence, militants used a giant catapult to launch teddy bears at their foe.

This carnival has tremendous relevance for queer cultures, which since their inception have always subverted power structures through a mocking kind of performance and exaggerated aesthetic. The dissolution of sharp divisions between spectator and participant in the carnivalesque demonstrations against global capital mirrors the fluid relationship between audience and spectator at Tranzmission's drag shows. (It also reflects the subversion of "the Spectacle" by Situationists in Paris '68, who were a large political influence on the contemporary anarchist movement.) Nor is the similarity between these demonstrations and Tranzmission's drag shows a mere coincidence. At almost every one of these anticapitalist gatherings there is a large queer presence that challenges the liberal, affluent gay and lesbian organizations that remain in their offices and government halls and also pokes fun at the seriousness and machismo of leftists who stagnantly remain in their permitted marches and ritualized "nonviolent" protester roles.

Tranzmission and Gender Mutiny Collective are in many ways a political product of these gatherings. When thousands of radicals converge to disrupt trade summits and government meetings, a culture of resistance is quickly created. Combined with the seminomadic lifestyle of some American anarchists, this culture can then be transported back to hometowns like Asheville, where spray-painted stencils, community centers, reclaim-the-streets demonstrations, and consensus decision making emerge as the background for collectives like Tranzmission.

These local collectives then contribute back to the larger movement through the production of zines, essays, ideas about political strategy, and a visible presence at regional gatherings and actions.

It is not enough for queers outside of academia to deal with racism and "classism" in their own groups. We need to be doing anticapitalist and antiracist organizing as visibly trans and queer people. We need to be working in HIV social services, challenging police brutality and working on community self-defense, organizing tenant unions, organizing our workplaces, expropriating abandoned buildings for the community, setting up free food programs, creating health collectives and DIY clinics that are truly trans inclusive, and making raucous, militant queer disruption any time wealthy leaders have the arrogance to meet in our towns to decide the fate of our life, our economy, our sexuality, and our Earth. Imagine, for instance, the potential intersection of DIY queer health clinics and the self-determination of poor people, or if, rather than using ineffective (and nonexistent) legislation, we fought heterosexist discrimination on the job *directly* through workplace actions.

I don't want to paint a picture where an emerging wave of radical queer youth activism overshadows the important contributions of past groups, nor do I want to pretend that groups like Gay Shame or FIERCE! have all the answers. But it is vital that we recognize that for any queer politics to be relevant to queer youth cultures, it must see itself as part of a global shift in the way we conceptualize "politics." This global shift is a part of the postmodern world; more and more it is the way resistance movements of all kinds are coming to see themselves. Due to its rejection of political parties and statist models, anarchism is a key component of this shift in our orientation toward the political. It is therefore no coincidence that anarchism is tactically and philosophically influencing queer youth organizations and cultures, nor should it be a surprise that to be an anarchist itself carries "queer" connotations in some youth cultures. For queer theorists and revolutionaries, it is less important to analyze whether anarchism as an abstract "ideology" has all the answers for queer people and more important to see the potential when queer youth begin to tap into global networks of resistance that can be characterized as "anarchistic."

Part of this potential is simply the reinvigoration of a LGBT "movement," which has become so stale and stagnant that it is almost nonexistent. Contemporary queer youth cultures may occasionally fall under the shadow of the Human Rights Campaign and the sexist, corporate beer sponsors of Pride marches, but our hearts lie in the riots of Stonewall and the direct action of ACT UP. It's time to get back to these roots, where the patriarch is not met with ballots and compromises, but blockades, bricks, and broken bottles. We need to remember that that first brick wasn't thrown by some fashionable white gay man in a suit, but by a pissed off Latina drag queen who turned tricks to get by. These are our roots.

NOTES

1. If you have more questions about some of these different queer and transgender groups, here is some basic contact information:

FIERCE (Fabulous Independent Educated Radicals for
  Community Empowerment)
www.fiercenyc.org
angel@fiercenyc.org
(646) 336-6789 x 103 with any questions

Tranzmission
(828) 254-0552
tranzmission@hotmail.com

Gender Mutiny Collective
gendermutiny@riseup.net
(828) 242-3841

Queer Fist
www.queerfist.org
info@queerfist.org

Gay Shame
www.gayshamesf.org
gayshamesf@yahoo.com

2. Some of these critics include Michael Warner, Sylvia Ray Rivera, Urvashi Vard, and Michelle O'Brien.
3. In the 1990s, HRC purposefully removed transgender people from a bill preventing job discrimination against gays and lesbians in order to make it more acceptable to Democrats. It didn't pass.
4. NWA was a well-known hip-hop group whose biggest hit, "Fuck tha Police," was an attack on police for their racist and classist harassment of black youth.

5. The Black Panther tune being sung was "The revolution has come. Off the pigs! Time to pick up the guns . . . Off the pigs!" It was sung both in meetings, at community programs, and in the streets.

6. The circle-A is a common symbol used by anarchists.

7. Encuentro literally means "encounter" but is commonly used to specify a large gathering or assembly.

WORKS CITED

Escoffier, Jeffrey. "Under the Sign of the Queer." *Found Object* (Fall 1994): 135.

Notes from Nowhere. "Carnival." In *We Are Everywhere: The Irresistible Rise of Global Anti-capitalism*. London: Verso, 2003. Anti-copyright.

O'Brien, Michelle. "Tracing This Body: Transexuality, Pharmaceuticals and Capitalism." 1–15. Published as a zine. Anti-copyright.

FIERCE <http://www.fiercenyc.org>.

Goldman, Ruth. "Who Is That *Queer* Queer? Exploring Norms around Sexuality, Race, and Class in Queer Theory." In *Queer Studies*, ed. Brett Beemyn and Mickey Eliason. New York: New York University Press, 1996.

Queer Fist <http://queerfist.blogspot.com/>.

Rust, Paula C. "Sexual Identity and Bisexual Identities: The Struggle for Self-Description in a Changing Sexual Landscape." In *Queer Studies*, ed. Brett Beemyn and Mickey Eliason. New York: New York University Press, 1996.

Warner, Michael. *The Trouble With Normal*. New York: The Free Press, 1999.

Woelfle-Erskine, Cleo, and Andrea Maybelline Danger. "The Pollinators' Toolbox." In *That's Revolting: Queer Strategies for Resisting Assimilation*, ed. Mattilda. Brooklyn: Soft Skull Press, 2004.

CHAPTER 14

DRAG IT OUT!

HOW QUEER YOUTH ARE TRANSFORMING CITIZENSHIP IN PETERBOROUGH

Ziysah D. Markson

In recent years, queer visibility has inarguably increased in both main-stream politics and entertainment media. Yet radical queer organizing seems more marginalized than ever. In painting our communities as mostly white, middle class, and able-bodied, mainstream gay rights campaigns fail to challenge racism and classism alongside homophobia. Rather than expose assumptions about love, monogamy, procreation, family, sex, and gender, the movement tends to focus on individual rights, ironically working to make queers normal. To illustrate this phenomenon, I use citizenship theory to explore a year of queer activism in the small city of Peterborough, Ontario.[1] I find that in challenging the binarisms of the mainstream, queer youth are blurring boundaries and illustrating the complexities of identities and experiences. Youth are at the heart of a movement that recognizes the need to redesign our communities. Through grassroots organizing, we are working to broaden politics away from mantras of equality and tolerance and toward true and holistic transformation. Through imagination, performance, and fresh articulation, we are asking, how do we re-radicalize 'queer'? Essentially, I am arguing that youth-led queer activism is contributing greatly to the reconceptualizing of citizenship.

279

I begin by exploring theories behind the transformation of citizenship (Faulks, Joseph). Using the concepts of "deep citizenship" (Clarke) and the "not yet citizen" (Wray), I apply these theories to a notion of queer citizenship. From within this context, I take a look at Peterborough's first Pride march and the newspaper feature it inspired, in order to examine the limitations inadvertently imposed upon queer organizing. It is clear that both the march and the feature succeed at heightening queer visibility and issues of homophobia in the community. However, when we apply transformative citizenship theory, we see that both events follow the pattern of seeking approval from the mainstream community. In failing to place the queer subject at the center of a discourse of citizenship, the march and the feature fall short of challenging the normative modes at the root of an exclusionary citizenship. With this in mind, I turn to the grassroots youth activism that spawned *Drag It Out!*, an annual drag show. I use theories of performativity to explore the unique qualities of *Drag It Out!* and its potential to challenge concepts of citizenship in Peterborough. Through a strategy of participation and queer performance, *Drag It Out!* endeavors to recenter queer politics, blurring the rigid lines of heteronormative standards and unfolding binaries of sex and gender into a spectrum of possibilities. Critiques of the event suggest that much more work must be done to foster truly radical queer space. Yet the youth activism that produced *Drag It Out!* is transformative in that it challenges its community to rethink citizenship outside of its heteronormative underpinnings, and to instead create its own basis for inclusion and justice.

DEEP CITIZENSHIP: THEORIES OF TRANSFORMATION

What does this radical queer activism look like? Throughout this chapter, I rely on Paul Clarke's concept of "deep citizenship" as a framework for analysis. Clarke uses this term to denote "the activity of the citizen self acting in a variety of places and spaces" (4). Through this process, politics becomes an act of communal participation, rather than a function dominated by the state. Theorist Keith Faulks echoes Clarke through his own emphasis on an "ethic of participation"—a framework that distinguishes a citizen from a "mere subject" by assigning the citizen an active rather than a passive role (4). In exploring performance as an expression of citizenship, May Joseph similarly asserts that citizenship emerges from "public and psychic participation" (3). Deep citizenship is not simply a package of rights that can be handed out; citizens call the process into being through their own involvement. A second key component of deep citizenship is its relevance within a local context. According to Faulks, citizenship can only be defined within a particular context, dependent upon the power structures at play; its definition is constantly interpreted and reshaped as it is expressed by members of the community. Joseph explains the same phenomenon: "The citizen and its vehicle, citizenship, are unstable sites that mutually interact to forge local, often changing (even transitory) notions of who the citizen is, and the kinds of citizenship possible at a given historical-political moment" (3). In short, the citizen is a subject with the rights, responsibilities, and political participation relevant to the context of a particular community.

Part of reworking citizenship studies is examining the potential of citizenship for those who have been historically excluded from full citizenship. An emerging queer scholarship is theorizing both the status of the queer subject in broader society and the nature of citizenship within queer community. Canadian scholar B. J. Wray has demonstrated how bringing queerness into a discussion of citizenship necessitates refocusing. As opposed to ethnic or nationalist notions of citizenship, queer culture is not defined by geographical boundaries (Patton and Sanchez-Eppler). Wray explains that "these conditions require that our paradigms of citizenship seriously account for the complicated and wonderfully playful operations of the imagination in queer community making" (33).

Yet our paradigms are often seriously curtailed by liberalist notions of citizenship. Wray problematizes a citizenship that entails "longing for one's rightful place within the national body" (30) and critiques the politics of rights movements as being "most frequently *additive* rather than transformative of the categories at hand" (32, original emphasis). In other words, we add groups or issues to those included within a problematic structure, rather than transform the structure itself. Wray illustrates what Peggy Phelan terms the "visibility trap" (qtd. in Wray 28), by explaining how a liberal rights effort requires a constitution and articulation of a marginalized, essential gay identity. In requiring proof of marginalization, such a movement demands that queers present themselves as "other," indeed as "unnatural" (30) in order to secure naturalization as citizens. Wray clearly exposes this irony: "The 'not yet' status of these subjects must be reiterated over and over again in order to stabilize and delineate the domain of subjectivity" (31). Adding to Faulks's assertion that citizenship must be dissociated from the nation-state, Wray further complicates this conundrum, stating that "organizations seeking recognition of difference and diversity are unable and unwilling to critique the operations of national discourse, precisely because those operations hold the promise of sameness and equality for a community in need of validation" (31–32).

Wray contends that we must creatively explore the relationship of sexuality to citizenship in order to forge a "transformative cultural politics" (30). Imagination and performance are key to Wray's conception of citizenship; they are seen as prerequisites in transcending the boundaries of individual rights and egalitarian politics. Performance has the ability to critically engage with key binaries that Wray identifies as "center/margin; homosexual/heterosexual; and normal/deviant" (34). In terms of *Drag It Out!*, we may add to this list of binaries: male/female. As we will see in this paper, queer youth in Peterborough are moving from a heterosexist and normative understanding of citizenship to one that always already involves a broad spectrum of identities, working to evolve the generally accepted views around inclusion, participation, and subjecthood.

"NOT YET" CITIZENS AND THE VISIBILITY TRAP: PETERBOROUGH'S FIRST PRIDE

In order to set the scene for an examination of *Drag It Out!* I first explore Wray's concept of "not yet" citizens by looking at Peterborough's first Pride march, and the newspaper feature it inspired. Students at the Sir Sandford Fleming College initiated the Peterborough Pride Commission (PPC) in the summer of 2003, pulling together a community group to organize Gay, Lesbian, Bisexual, Transgender, Transsexual, and Two-Spirited Pride Day. An event clearly aimed at contesting heteronormativity and homophobia in the public sphere, the Pride march, and the ensuing media reaction, is a useful site for examining the production of Peterborough's queer residents as "not yet citizens" (Wray). Based in careful tactics to present an image of queer community that would be acceptable to the public, the event nonetheless incited passionate antigay reactions and revealed a deeper struggle around questions of citizenship.

The struggle over defining citizenship became publicly visible in all its colors at the march on September 13th. Perhaps in reaction to public antigay sentiment, an estimated four hundred marchers arrived on the steps of City Hall—a significantly greater queer presence than the PPC had anticipated (Newman para. 3; Kim A1, A5). Meanwhile, across the street, several protestors, armed with signs displaying phrases such as "Peterborough Supports Family Values," and "Adam and Eve, not Adam and Steve," told reporters that they were against a public display of homosexuality (Newman). Members of the rehabilitative group New Direction for Life Ministries were also present at the march, politely handing out pamphlets about how Christianity can help in the recovery from a homosexual lifestyle.[2]

The march earned a color center-spread in *Peterborough This Week*, the city's most widely distributed newspaper. While taking a positive stance on the march, even the short captions on the photo spread betrayed the queerphobic assumptions of the editors. The caption accompanying a photo of a young girl with her father stated that there was no nudity at the march. Another caption dubbed leather boots "outlandish" ("Happy Pride Day" B9). Rather than describe the goals and statements of the queer organizers, the editors seemed to be reporting on their own queerphobic expectations, conflating queer identity with illegal acts and modes of dress. Eager to further capitalize on the controversy generated by the local Pride march and the national gay marriage debate, *This Week* launched an ongoing feature on gay community. Published every Wednesday for three weeks, the series included a profile of a "normal" gay male couple (Rellinger A1, A9–A10), a focus on local queer groups (emphasizing queerphobia experienced by students and youth) (Kim A1, A5), and a story on trans issues (Tuffin A1, A8).

Like the Pride march, the "gay feature" succeeded in bringing queer issues to the forefront of the media and community debate, and opened a space for queer voices. At the same time, however, its overall heteronormative editorial framing maintained a clear distinction between the queer "other" and the citizen "normal." In various ways, as will be described in more detail, this unselfconscious editorial positioning presented queer residents as "not yet" citizens, awaiting the approval of their heterosexual counterparts. From the reactions to Pride, one might expect some homophobic responses to these articles, and indeed, the passionate antigay voices were plenty (see de Waard, Doherty, Fox, Hawkins, and King). Yet what is most notable to our discussion is the heteronormativity pervading pro-queer statements and initiatives.

To begin with, the series title itself, "The Gay Community: Proudly Emerging from the Shadows," exemplifies a problematic framing. In addition to denying the longer history of queer activism in Peterborough,[3] this headline is a symptom of the visibility problem highlighted previously (Wray). That is, in order to make a case for their rights, gays must first be understood as helpless victims, cast out in the "shadows." In this narrow articulation of queer community, disempowerment is a necessary prerequisite for a right to space. Not surprisingly then, many who wrote in to support the feature gained legitimacy by speaking of the ways their gay friends faced discrimination (Duffett A6; Wyatt A6). The fact that the several-page article on transsexuality was presented under the label "Gay Community" also points to a narrow understanding of sexual and gender diversity.

This Week's attempt to include queer issues in a community paper is subtly undermined by its heteronormative tendencies, especially its inability to adequately integrate the queer subject. For example, in a post-feature piece, the editors react to queerphobic outrage by defending their choice to run the feature. They do so by highlighting the paper's otherwise heterosexual content and playing up the "isolation and confusion over the people in our community who do not fit in the heterosexual mold" ("Series Opened Our Eyes" A6). Their statements address the most homophobic of their readers and leave queers and even their allies to be perpetual "others." While exposing heterocentrism, the editorial simultaneously perpetuates it by discussing queers as "they" and assuming the heterosexuality of the reader, as in the following statement: "If you don't want to read their [queers'] stories, you always have the option of turning the page. But if you were curious enough to take a peek into their world from their perspective, we hope you gained a new understanding of their views" ("Series Opened Our Eyes" A6). Ultimately, though the authors of queerphobic rants are rebuffed, they nonetheless effectively maintain their citizen status as the "normal" readers of *Peterborough This Week*.

I argue that both the Pride march and the feature operate within a limited concept of citizenship, sustaining a polarity of groups based in essentialized identities. Specifically, each prioritizes increasing visibility by presenting an acceptable queer citizen that can be contrasted with deviance, maintaining an idea of "normal." In the instance of *This Week*, the first issue showcases an exemplary "normal" local couple, who happen to both be men. As one of the pair himself states, "We're no different than any other couple [. . .]" (A9). The paper downplays their sexual lives and defends them from deviant stereotypes, stating that they "go about their life in an unsensational manner" (A1), that leather and bondage supplies are nowhere to be found in their home, and that they are not attending the Pride march because "we don't need a special day to say we're gay" (A10). This approach may succeed as an additive method, opening up citizenship to gay-identified people, but it simultaneously reinforces the strict boundaries of such a citizenship. By catering to sexual and familial norms, we fall into the visibility trap.

Peggy Phelan warns us of this problem: "visibility is a trap; it summons surveillance and the law; it provokes voyeurism, fetishism, the colonialist/imperialist appetite for possession" (qtd. in Wray 28). It is important to recognize that this trap is set by the dominance of heteronormativity, ensuring that antigay rhetoric shapes the planning process. As Ash Phipps, student and Pride organizer, notes, "We knew that we were going to be under a microscope if anything went slightly wrong on Pride Day—that was extra stress" (qtd. in piKe, "2003" 10). Ultimately, this context conditioned the organizers to gain legitimacy by distancing events from any practice that could be deemed deviant. As a queer community event organized in large part around visibility, the Pride march was also ambiguous in its liberatory potential. Phipps articulates that the goal of Pride was to "celebrate [queer community] but also dissuade people from thinking negatively about queers in Peterborough" (qtd. in piKe, "2003" 10).

On these terms, queer residents and allies marched down the street with rainbow banners, while "normal" citizens (i.e., those who did not need to march to proclaim their citizenship) acted as spectators. In this case, the "normal" citizens could enjoy a sort of parade, consuming queer performance, while assuming no risk. Indeed, according to municipal candidate Joe Baptista, "Drag queens in high heels is hardly an issue worth considering. It's nothing more than a show [. . .] there are more serious concerns [in Peterborough] than gay flesh on parade" (para. 6–7). While Baptista may be ignorant of the liberatory potential of drag for gender expression (a potential that is discussed rigorously in the section exploring *Drag It Out!*), he nonetheless points to a notable risk inherent in PPC's organizing—"normal" citizens have the ability to consume queer culture, and spit it right back out. A show of queerness can serve to reinforce the audience's normalcy. While the two sides battle each other over rights, we are not moved to challenge strict categories, to recognize the multiple facets of our identities, or to acknowledge our interconnectedness within community.

TRANSFORMATIVE PERFORMANCE: THE *DRAG IT OUT!* SHOW

Critiquing the visibility tactic, Wray asks, "Is there no other viable means through which a more diverse cultural imaginary may be fostered?" (29). If public demonstrations and media coverage cannot transform

citizenship, then what can? Only weeks after the newspaper feature, one
evening of creativity suggested that transformation was indeed possible.
Peterborough's first *Drag It Out!* event took place on March 11. Undertaken by Trent University's queer collective (TQC), the event took
place at the Trasheteria dance club. Participants used their own interpretations of drag to perform a full evening of entertainment. Whereas
the Pride march and the gay feature came hard up against structural
walls that reinforced heteronormativity and the victimized status of
queers, *Drag It Out!* signified a substantially distinct approach. Rather
than make a literal statement of inclusion, or seek approval from the
broader community, *Drag It Out!* relied on its use of performance to
communicate queer possibilities, and to engage its community through
full participation and self-reflection.

Performance as a vehicle for deconstructing gender is not a new
concept. Feminists, particularly, have looked to theater as a mode of
challenging norms. Jill Dolan talks about theater as a "laboratory" in
which the concept of gender can be explored: "If we stop considering
the stage as a mirror of reality, we can use it as a laboratory in which
to reconstruct new, nongenderized identities" (9). In the past ten years,
drag has taken on different ideas for the queer movement. As the
umbrella of queer has broadened to encompass drag kings and queens,
cross-dressers, intersexed, trans and gender queer, the concept of queer
has evolved to embody the tenets of Clarke's deep citizenship—it is
participatory, contextual, and works to recenter a politics of belonging.
If drag performers can be seen as more than imitators, the possibilities
are endless. Marjorie Garber imagines this potential when she describes
the cross-dresser as "both terrifying and seductive precisely because
s/he incarnates and emblematizes the disruptive element that inter-
venes, signaling not just another category crisis but—much more dis-
quietingly—a crisis of 'category' itself" (177–178). This is precisely the
type of activity Faulks, Wray, and Joseph call for to transform citizenship: breaking down boundaries, exposing entrenched binaries, and
realizing a fluid sense of identity.

One of Faulks's main critiques of contemporary citizenship is that,
while it may profess to be egalitarian, the structures that are in place
do not make its provisions equally accessible to all citizens. *Drag It Out!*
provides a concrete example of how performative cultural projects can
undermine oppressive systems. While working most overtly to challenge a binary notion of gender, *Drag It Out!* also undertook to organize in innovative ways as an anti-oppressive project. In challenging

notions of citizenship, the organizers envisioned more than a safe space for homosexual couples—they strove to model a place of validation and belonging for all community members. Several initiatives demonstrated this goal: the event was advertised months in advance with posters that encouraged people to try out drag for the first time; a drag workshop provided participants with the tools and information needed to perform; the location was wheelchair accessible and opened to all ages; and efforts were made to provide sign language interpretation.

Feedback expressed that, despite these efforts, accessibility issues persisted. The stage setup prevented wheelchair users from easily navigating the space; the prevalent use of alcohol may have limited participation of nondrinkers; interpreters could not be secured; and most participants were university aged (Trent Queer Collective, "Feedback"). The age issue was attributed to the loud and late nature of the dance club. The following year, a couple in their sixties accepted an invitation to perform. One of them felt her participation surprised the younger crowd, and she asked me: "Where are the grandmothers?" Participants were also discouraged by a notion of drag that solely imitates white American popular culture. One woman recounted that she chose not to participate because her idea of drag—donning the traditional clothing of a Mohawk man—would be culturally inappropriate when taken out of context. Here, the factors of racism, colonization, and the gaze on the exotic intersect with *Drag It Out!* in complex ways.

Anti-oppression has remained on the agenda as the drag show has continued as an annual event. In an interview in Trent's student paper, Amelia Patterson, organizer of the third *Drag It Out!*, explains that the organic structure of the event, whereby new organizers revamp it each year, allows for flux (Orr). The third *Drag It Out!* was held in a different venue—a theater as opposed to a club, in an effort to create "more space for [the] audience and performers" (Patterson qtd. in Orr para. 4). The event thus became easier to navigate for participants of varying ages and abilities. Indeed, more people in their forties and fifties seemed to participate. Another new initiative in the third year responded to safety concerns by seeking volunteers to walk participants home after the show (Patterson qtd. in Orr para. 7). Space has also been carved out for culturally diverse expressions of drag. The second year of *Drag It Out!* featured a Latin dance piece, including international students, political refugees, Euro-Canadians, and Spanish dialogue. The third year of *Drag It Out!* featured a Bollywood drag performance featuring popular clothing and dance, and a comical sketch in which a young Indian

man and his white boyfriend tell his parents (all in drag) that they are
in love.

The Bollywood dance piece was so well received that the audience
demanded an encore at the end of the show, and the group has already
performed upon request at other events. For Zahra Murad, one of the
choreographers, the piece allowed her to explore gender identity in a way
she never could from within her Pakistani community. The group hoped
that the process would be about "problematizing parts of our own culture
in our minds, as well as enjoying it within the [Peterborough] community" (Murad). In an e-mail, Murad explains that far from feeling torn
between two cultures, she experienced the performance as "a way of
beginning to bridge the gap between 'western' me and 'eastern' me, and
seeing where they meet." Murad relates, however, that one woman of
color who was contacted to be part of the process declined in apprehension that the piece would turn into a spectacle. Murad is now reassessing
the so-called success of the piece, and wondering how much of a part
cultural objectification played in audience appreciation.

As microcosms of the drag show itself, each of these pieces recenter
politics so that the culture they are representing is at the center. Rather
than explain or exoticize for its mostly white audience, these performers explore their own "normal" as just that, forcing other participants
to open up their ideas of drag. Yet, this type of participation is complex.
In my own experience, my rap about attending a bar mitzvah in drag
raised many concerns. Would I alienate the predominantly non-Jewish
audience, and offend Jewish participants through my appropriation of
male religious symbols? Certainly, factors such as the popularity of
Bollywood and Latin dance in mainstream media, the fact that Judaism
has become somewhat conflated with Euro-Christianity, and the involvement of the various choreographers in queer organizing con-
verged to make these aforementioned pieces palatable to a predominantly
Euro-Canadian audience. Demonstrating the local and contextual key
to deep citizenship, these pieces suggest that our community has the
potential to culturally expand our images of drag, even as we continue
to problematize the process. These are the issues Wray explains can be
best investigated through the "interstices between imaginary and real."
Rather than wax academic, we are exploring cultural possibilities through
tactile, sentient experience.

Ultimately, *Drag It Out!* honors theorist Judith Butler's conviction
that "true transformation requires that we are highly cognizant of the
exclusions by which we proceed" (53). While it does not begin with

a perfect citizenship of complete participation, it marks a vital and dynamic process of learning how to create a truly participatory space in a normative world. One of the greatest features of *Drag It Out!*'s expression of participatory citizenship is its treatment of the audience. Rather than oppose spectators to performers, audience members are organically integrated into the event, mingling, dancing, interacting with the staged show, and admiring each other's costumes as much as those on stage. This approach means that everyone present is, in a sense, performing. Because drag is expected, even your usual presentation could be perceived as drag.

The Trasheteria does not usually host queer events. As a result, regular patrons were surprised by the evening's theme. At one point, two students walked into the club, and, upon hearing about the event, began to spout homophobic comments under their breath. One of the audience members yelled after them, "Hey, are you boys or girls?" (Trent Queer Collective, "Feedback"). This dynamic speaks to Butler's appraisal of "aggressive re-territorialization" (86) as the drag organizers transformed a conventionally heterosexual space into a queer-centered one. There were no bystanders at this event; all present were implicitly involved, reflecting a key tenet of deep citizenship: participation.

One participant and performer, who does not identify within the queer community, remarked that at a previous drag show she had felt like a guest, whereas at *Drag It Out!*, she was invited to "share the celebration inside" (Castro). An important quality of *Drag It Out!* is that it makes queer priorities accessible to all participants regardless of gender identity or sexual orientation. In promoting the first *Drag It Out!*, organizer piKe Wright made it very clear that while drag "creates a place of safety for those who don't necessarily identify with the feminine or masculine genders," the organizers are inviting everyone—"not just queer people"—to attend in drag. "It's really fun to play with gender," she promised (qtd. in Christopher, "Kings, Queens, and Inbetweens" para. 6, 9). In this way, the possible outcomes are much more profound. The activity of participation threatens to destabilize heteronormative foundations within each member of the community.

Not only did *Drag It Out!* include a wide variety of people, it carried the potential of drag further than most theorists have prophesized. Men dressed as women who lip-synched to women pop stars were popular at the show. In contrast to many other drag shows, however, these men shared the stage with a wide variety of interpretations of drag. Observers commented that what they appreciated most about the show was that it challenged the idea that drag was only about men impersonating women (Trent Queer Collective, "Feedback"). There were people dressed ambiguously. For one piece, I was split down the middle, one half man, one half woman. The next day, the student newspaper's cover featured an androgynous-looking audience member with a T-shirt reading: "Fuck Gender!" (*Arthur* 1). One performer dressed in high femme drag and lip-synched to a song written by a trans guy about his strap-on (Bitch and Animal), thereby denying easy categorization as a King or a Queen.

Drag It Out! was advertised as a trans-inclusive event, and promised to donate all funds raised at the door to trans organizing in Peterborough. The organizers were interested in connecting drag to the queer and specifically trans communities, disallowing the invisiblization of trans people that occurs when drag is associated solely with homosexuality. Organizer Jonah Marcovitz explains, "drag performers and trans people together challenge the concept of a binary gender system and I find that beautiful!" (qtd. in Christopher, "Kings, Queens, and Inbetweens" para. 8). While honoring this relationship, it was simultaneously important to distinguish trans identity from drag performance. In promoting the third *Drag It Out!*, Patterson made a public appeal to participants to think deeply about the politics of drag:

> [F]or many people who are "otherly" gendered, transgender or transsexual, we have to deal with the social stigma around gender and expression daily; this show is a time for us to celebrate who we are as well as reflect on what it means to be who we are [at all times] outside of this night. (Qtd. in Orr para. 8)

While drag may expose the ridiculousness of gender regulation, it often allows spectators to understand performers within a binary gender framework: drag kings are "really" women dressed as men. Conversely, the diverse performances at *Drag It Out!* make understandings difficult. Through broadening the concept of drag, no gender or sexual orientation can be assumed, and any behavior or thought process that hinges on these categories is thereby destabilized. No one can be judged by their "real" identity, and everyone flirts with everyone else.

Drag It Out! approaches "deep citizenship" in that it is participatory, it is defined by its local context, and it keeps queer subjecthood at the center. Further, it allows citizens autonomy and self-action. As a grassroots initiative, it evades Wray's problem of establishing "not yet" status to gain legitimacy. With no overarching mandate to fulfill, participants themselves forge the event. There is no need to present the historical marginalization of queers to justify funding,[4] no need to exploit queers to sell tickets. As Clarke hopes, politics becomes a communal activity involving individually empowered agents.

Through autonomy and self-determination, participants express themselves freely without thought to a political agenda. As Susan Driver explains in her introduction to this volume, liberal models support youth as long as they do not look or act "too queer." Conceptions of queer youth desexualize and depoliticize us, casting us as victims. At an event such as *Drag It Out!*, youth are able to explore their sexual and gendered identities without fear of delegitimizing a movement or of being "outed" in the media. In contrast to the march and the feature, *Drag It Out!* is focused inward—it is a place for an ever-expanding community to explore its own identities and broaden its ideas and boundaries around sexuality and gender—for the sake of all participants, not for the viewing (dis)pleasure of outside observers.

QUEERING CITIZENSHIP: REFLECTIONS

The year 2003–2004 was a banner one for queer activism in Peterborough as organizers presented the city's first Pride march and the local paper featured a series on queer identities. While these initiatives carved out much-needed spaces for queer citizens and their allies to express their needs for rights and recognition, they hinged on a heteronormative center. With Peterborough's queerphobia laid bare, and queer communities mobilizing, *Drag It Out!* stepped in with a dose of creative energy to push the envelope of citizenship further. As a youth-initiated and run event, this drag show emerged from a transient and dynamic culture, a distinct entry point into the realm of queering citizenship. By explicit, broad, and actively sought participation, this queer drag show challenged the boundaries that separate sexual and gender communities. It added the main ingredient in Faulks's recipe for citizenship: participation. Performers were actively engaged in self-expression, suggesting the images and languages of their identities. Audience members were obligated to accept their own responsibility as performers and community members. The show was not initiated by, or in reaction to, an oppressor, a mainstream, or an idea of "normal." It was created on its own terms to reflect all participants, exemplifying a citizenship whereby queer is always already at the center, demanding broad understandings of gender, sexuality, and relationships.

Drag It Out! highlights the role of youth in reimagining community. Where adult organizations are steeped in societal norms and institutional loyalties, youth, still involved in the dynamic process of self-discovery, organizing in organic, creative, and impulsive ways, demonstrate the most potential to challenge the roots of heteronormativity, and to forge new concepts of citizenship. While initiatives such as *Drag It Out!* may not result in federal policy changes, they have the potential to affect change at an intimate and local level, without compromising the goals of an anti-oppressive participatory vision. The questions our efforts raise, in our successes and in our shortcomings, are a call to all communities to develop further initiatives that recenter politics, reimagine the public, and challenge a historically exclusive and rigid notion of citizenship.

NOTES

1. Like queer citizenship, Peterborough (a city of 74,000, located 140 kilometers northeast of Toronto) is often a contradictory space. It is comprised of its original Aanishinaabe (Ojibwe) inhabitants, growing communities of recent immigrants from over forty countries (New Canadians Centre Peterborough), diverse post-secondary student bodies, and the descendants of the city's Christian Western European founders. The latter are the majority and currently dominate the overall conservative politics of the municipality. Queer organizations include the campus groups at Sir Sanford Fleming College (FAQS²—Fleming Association of Queer Students, Faculty, Alumni, and Queer Supporters) and Trent University (TQC—Trent Queer Collective); the Rainbow Service Organization (RSO), who serves the broader Peterborough area; the Rainbow Youth Coalition (RYC), run through the Community AIDS Resource Network (PARN); gay straight alliances within at least three local high schools; a transgender support group ("Transgender Support Group"); and a sporadically active ad hoc group that organizes queer town hall meetings to discuss queerphobia, experiences of harassment, and institutional heterosexism (Trent Queer Collective, "Human Rights Advisor"; Barton 3; Christopher, "Nathaniel Declares War"). Other than some semi-regular dances, there are no officially queer spaces in the city.

2. New Direction "offers Christian support to men and women choosing to leave homosexuality, and equips the church to minister effectively and compassionately" ("Services Offered" para. 1).

3. Queer organizing has been active in Peterborough since at least the 1970s when the Trent Homophile Association, purportedly Canada's first gay campus group, was initiated (piKe, "Is Trent Still Bent?").

4. Funding for *Drag It Out!* came solely from the student groups Theatre Trent and the Trent Queer Collective (Trent Queer Collective, 18 January and 14 March 2004).

WORKS CITED

Arthur. 15 Mar. 2004, 1.

Baptista, Joe. "Peterborough and the Gay Pride Insanity." Online posting. 14 August 2003. *Dot-God.* 10 April 2004. <http://www.dot-god.com/bod/jb/ptbo.elections2003/perth/archives/ptbo-all.current/mst00023.html>.

Barton, Tucker. "Sticks & Stones . . ." *Queer Lines* 3 March 2004, 3.

Bitch and Animal. "Best Cock on the Block." *Eternally Hard.* Bitch and Animal, 2001.

Butler, Judith. *Bodies That Matter: On the Discursive Limits of "Sex."* New York: Routledge, 1993.

Castro, Renée. "Remembering Drag . . ." E-mail to the author. 21 May 2006.

Christopher, Nathaniel. "Kings, Queens, and Inbetweens." *Arthur.* 9 March 2004.

———. "Nathaniel Declares War on Homophobia." *Nathaniel Christopher.* 11 February 2005. 1 April 2005. <http://www.nathaniel.ca/News/Homophobia.html>.

Clarke, Paul Barry. *Deep Citizenship.* London: Pluto Press, 1996.

de Waard, Cathy. "Gay Community Stories Don't Belong on Page 1." *Peterborough This Week.* 25 February 2004, A6.

Doherty, Theresa. "Don't Plead Freedom of Speech in this Case." *Peterborough This Week.* 11 February 2004, A6.

Dolan, Jill. "Gender Impersonation Onstage: Destroying or Maintaining the Mirror of Gender Roles?" In Senelick.

Duffett, Pauline. "Courage Is to Be Admired." *Peterborough This Week.* 20 February 2004, A6.

Faulks, Keith. *Citizenship.* London: Routledge, 2000.

Fox, C. "Reader 'Sick' of Gay Lifestyle." *Peterborough This Week.* 20 February 2004, A6.

Garber, Marjorie. "Dress Codes or the Theatricality of Difference." *Vested Interests: Cross-Dressing and Cultural Anxiety.* New York: Routledge, 1992.

"Happy Pride Day." *Peterborough This Week.* 17 September 2003, B9.

Hawkins, Bev, and David Hawkins. "How About Featuring Christian Families, Ways?" *Peterborough This Week.* 18 February 2004, A6.

Joseph, May. *Nomadic Identities: The Performance of Citizenship.* Minneapolis: Public Worlds, 1999.

Kim, Clark. " 'Queer-Positive Spaces.' " *Peterborough This Week.* 11 February 2004, A1, A5.

King, Russell. "Decency Is What's Needed." *Peterborough This Week.* 20 February 2004, A6.

Mroz, Brendon, Jonah Marcovitz, and piKe Wright. "Drag It Out!" Poster. Peterborough: Trent Queer Collective, 2004.

Murad, Zahra. "Bollywood at *Drag It Out!*" E-mail to the author. 19 May 2006.

New Canadians Centre Peterborough. "Annual General Report, 2004–2005." Peterborough: New Canadians Centre Peterborough, June 2005.

Newman, Brad. "First Pride: 300 Strong." *Arthur.* 22 September 2003.

Orr, William. "How to Drag It Out." *Arthur.* 5 April 2006.

Patton, Cindy, and Benigno Sanchez-Eppler, eds. *Queer Diasporas.* Durham: Duke University Press, 2000.

piKe. "2003: The Year of Peterborough's First (but not Last) Pride Day." *Queer Lines.* March 2004, 10, 15.

———. "Is Trent Still Bent?" *Arthur.* 16 September 2002.

Rellinger, Paul. "Just Living their Life." *Peterborough This Week.* 4 February 2004, A1, A9–A10.

"Series Opened Our Eyes—How About You?" *Peterborough This Week.* 18 February 2004, A6.

"Services Offered." *New Direction.* 2003. New Direction for Life Ministries—Toronto, Inc. 19 May 2006. <http://www.newdirection.ca/services.htm>.

"The Gay Community: Proudly Emerging from the Shadows." *Peterborough This Week.* 4, 11, and 18 February 2004.

"Transgender Support Group." *Canadian Mental Health Association—Peterborough Branch.* Pamphlet and Online resource. 8 March 2002. 5 April 2004. <http://www.peterborough.cmha.on.ca/transgender>.

Trent Queer Collective. "Drag Shows." Hub Meeting minutes. Peterborough: 18 January 2004.

———. "Feedback from *Drag It Out!*" Hub Meeting minutes. Peterborough: 14 March 2004.

———. "Human Rights Advisor." Hub Meeting minutes. Peterborough: 12 October, 2002.

Tuffin, Lois. "It's a Whole Different Life." *Peterborough This Week.* 18 February 2004, A1, A8.

Wray, B. J. "Imagining Lesbian Citizenship: A Kiss & Tell Affair." *Torquere: Journal of the Canadian Lesbian and Gay Studies Association* 1 (1999): 25–46.

Wyatt, Jane. " 'Judge not and ye shall not be judged.' " *Peterborough This Week.* 18 February 2004: A6.

LIST OF CONTRIBUTORS

CASS BIRD is a photographer based in New York City who exhibited a series "J.D.'s Lesbian Utopia" at Deitch Projects (NY) and has shown work at Palazzo Cavour in Turin, Italy. Bird's pictures are featured regularly in *The New Yorker, Fader Magazine* and *The New York Times Magazine.*

MEGAN DAVIDSON received her PhD from Binghamton University/ SUNY in the Department of Cultural Anthropology. Her thesis is based on 18 months of participant-observation fieldwork with trans activists in the US, including interviews with over 100 activists. She lives in Brooklyn, New York with her partner and children.

CRISTYN DAVIES is completing her doctorate "NEA vs Finley, Or, Performing America in an Era of Moral Panic" at the University of Sydney, Australia. She also works as a research officer for the Narrative, Discourse and Pedagogy research concentration at the University of Western Sydney. Her research focuses on discourses of gender and sexuality.

ANDIL GOSINE is Assistant Professor in the Department of Sociology at York University.

JUDITH HALBERSTAM is Professor of English and Director of the Center for Feminist Research at USC. Halberstam is the author of *Skin Shows: Gothic Horror and the Technology of Monsters* (Duke UP, 1995); *Female Masculinity* (Duke UP, 1998); *In a Queer Time and Place: Transgender Bodies, Subcultural Lives* (NYU Press. 2005); co-author with Del LaGrace Volcano of *The Drag King Book* (Serpent's Tail, 1999). She is currently finishing a book titled *Dude, Where's My Theory? On the Politics of Knowledge* and has published journalism in BITCH Magazine and The NATION.

VALERIE HARWOOD is a Senior Lecturer in the Faculty of Education, University of Wollongong, New South Wales, Australia. She has recently published a book in 2006 titled *Diagnosing 'Disorderly' Children*, which critically examines the growing phenomenon of the diagnosis of behaviour disorders in children and young people.

ANNA HICKEY-MOODY is Lecturer in Creative Arts Education at Monash University, Victoria, Australia. Her first sole authored monograph, *Unimaginable Bodies*, will be published by Sense in 2007. She is co-author of 'Masculinity Beyond the Metropolis' (Palgrave, 2006) and co-editor of *Deleuzian Encounters: Studies in Contemporary Social Issues* (Palgrave, 2007).

MARK LIPTON is an Assistant Professor in the School of English and Theatre Studies at the University of Guelph.

ZIYSAH DANIELLE MARKSON is a writer, performance poet, and activist working with immigrants and refugees in Peterborough, Ontario. She began this paper as part of a degree in Equity Studies at Trent University.

DAVID MCINNES teaches in the literature and cultural studies programs at the University of Western Sydney. His research interests include gender non-conformity, melancholia and masculinity and gay men's sexual cultures.

MARY LOU RASMUSSEN is a Senior Lecturer in the Faculty of Education, Monash University, Australia. In 2004 she co-edited (Rofes and Talburt) *Youth and Sexualities: Pleasure, Subversion and Insubordination,* and in 2006 authored a monograph *Becoming Subjects: Sexualities and Secondary Schooling.* She is currently researching sex education curriculum in Australia.

JACKIE REGALES holds two degrees in American Studies and teaches classes on popular culture at Anne Arundel Community College, Arnold, MD. Her work has appeared in "Clamor," "Bitch," "hip Mama," "off our backs," and "The Encyclopedia of Third Wave Feminism," and is forthcoming in "LGBTQ America Today," Greenwood Press, 2007.

NEAL RITCHIE is now a 23-year old skinny, revolutionary anarchist queer white boy from North Carolina. He resides in Carrboro, NC, where he is very busy with mutual aid projects like the prison books collective, supporting immigrants in his neighborhood with an anti-border, free grocery and food program called Comida No Migra!, and organizing monthly really really free markets.

MELISSA RIGNEY has a PhD in Queer Literature and Film from the University of Nebraska. Her work has appeared in Film Criticism, The Quarterly Review of Film and Video and Senses of Cinema. She is an independent scholar and live in Omaha, Nebraska.

JAMA SHELTON is a social worker whose focus is community-based work with queer young people. She is currently the Director of Housing for the Ali Forney Center, a program serving street involved LGBTQ youth in NYC. She received a B.A. in Theatre from the University of the South, Sewanee and an MSW from the NYU School of Social Work.

ZEB J. TORTORICI is a Ph.D. candidate in History at UCLA. His dissertation examines sexuality in colonial Mexico through criminal and Inquisition cases. He has published in the journal of *Ethnohistory*, will contribute to the forthcoming *Ethnopornography*, and is co-editing a collection on animals and colonialism in the Atlantic world.

ANGELA WILSON is a Communication Studies doctoral student at Montréal's Concordia University. She studies gender, sexual identity and cultural production, and the political potential of music communities and youth subcultures. Angela hosts a radio program showcasing independent female musicians, and she is a punk rock and soul DJ and amateur music journalist.

INDEX